People who begin to study a particular aspect of ritual magic often have a very poor understanding of how their own practices fit into the general scheme of Western occultism. They lack a historical context that would provide a perspective on their beliefs and techniques. They also lack a theoretical understanding that would allow them a firm sense of why they are doing a given ritual action. They tend to believe that their chosen occult tradition is the only real or significant tradition. Generally they lack any notion of the way their magic has descended from other paths, and still retains the influence of those paths. This is true even of occultists that have been working within a particular magical tradition for years.

This book is designed to remove the psychological blinders from the eyes of those who are seriously interested in magic yet cannot see beyond the horizon of their own beliefs and experience. It integrates practical Western occultism, shows its evolution through history from its ancient roots, and reveals the crosscurrents of influence that flow between the major modern systems.

Occultists need to know the influences, similarities and differences between Golden Dawn magic and the magic of Aleister Crowley, between druidism and witchcraft, between the Satanism of Anton LaVey and the cult of Thelema, between the spirit possession of Voudoun and Shamanism. They need to know where Enochian began and how it came to pervade so much of modern ritual magic. They need a clear understanding of the true origins of the Golden Dawn, Thelema, Satanism, druidism, witchcraft, and rune magic. They need a straightforward explanation about the nature and beginnings of the Enochian calls, the Tarot, the magic squares, the four elemental instruments, the ritual of the pentagram, and other aspects of modern Western occultism so widely used and discussed but so little understood.

Whatever your own particular occult interest, *Ritual Magic* is designed to help you learn what it is all about, where it comes from, and how to do it correctly. There is an enormous amount of practical information in this book. By using it as a road map of Western occultism the reader will be enabled to make sense out of confusion and separate historical truths from the many modern myths and outright lies presently circulating in the occult literature.

About the Author

Donald Tyson is a Canadian from Halifax, Nova Scotia. Early in life he was drawn to science by an intense fascination with astronomy, building a telescope by hand when he was eight. He began the university seeking a science degree, but became disillusioned with the aridity and futility of a mechanistic view of the universe and shifted his major to English. After graduating with honors he has pursued a writing career.

Now he devotes his life to the attainment of a complete gnosis of the art of magic in theory and practice. His purpose is to formulate an accessible system of personal training composed of East and West, past and present, that will help the individual discover the reason for one's existence and a way to fulfill it.

To Write to the Author

If you wish to contact the author or would like more information about this book, please write to the author in care of Llewellyn Worldwide and we will forward your request. Both the author and publisher appreciate hearing from you and learning of your enjoyment of this book and how it has helped you. Llewellyn Worldwide cannot guarantee that every letter written to the author can be answered, but all will be forwarded. Please write to:

Donald Tyson
c/o Llewellyn Worldwide
P.O. Box 64383-835, St. Paul, MN 55164-0383, U.S.A.

Please enclose a self-addressed, stamped envelope for reply, or $1.00 to cover costs.
If outside U.S.A., enclose international postal reply coupon.

Free Catalog from Llewellyn

For more than 90 years Llewellyn has brought its readers knowledge in the fields of metaphysics and human potential. Learn about the newest books in spiritual guidance, natural healing, astrology, occult philosophy and more. Enjoy book reviews, new age articles, a calendar of events, plus current advertised products and services. To get your free copy of the *New Times*, send your name and address to:

The Llewellyn New Times
P.O. Box 64383-835, St. Paul, MN 55164-0383, U.S.A.

Llewellyn's Practical Magick Series

RITUAL MAGIC

WHAT IT IS & HOW TO DO IT

DONALD TYSON

1992
Llewellyn Publications, Inc.
St. Paul, Minnesota 55164-0383, U.S.A.

FIRST EDITION

Cover painting by Randy Asplund-Faith
Illustrations on pages 110, 111, 113, 120, 121, 129, 149, 155, 167, 179, 201, 203, and 221 by Donald Tyson

Library of Congress Cataloging in Publication Data
Tyson, Donald, 1954-
    Ritual magic : what it is and how to do it / Donald Tyson.
        p. cm. — (Llewellyn's practical magick series)
    ISBN 0-87542-835-5 : $12.95
        1. Magic.   2. Ritual.   I. Title.   II. Series.
    BF1623.R6.T96   1992
    133.4'3—dc20   92 13332
                                                                  CIP

Llewellyn Publications
A Division of Llewellyn Worldwide, Ltd.
P.O. Box 64383, St. Paul, MN 55164-0383

ABOUT LLEWELLYN'S PRACTICAL MAGICK SERIES

To some people, the idea that "Magick" is *practical* comes as a surprise.

It shouldn't. The entire basis for Magick is to exercise influence over one's environment. While Magick is also, and properly so, concerned with spiritual growth and psychological transformation, even the spiritual life must rest firmly on material foundations.

The material world and the psychic are intertwined, and it is this very fact that establishes the Magickal Link: that the psychic can as easily influence the material as vice versa.

Magick can, and should, be used in one's daily life for better living! Each of us has been given Mind and Body, and surely we are under Spiritual obligation to make full usage of these wonderful gifts. Mind and Body work together, and Magick is simply the extension of this interaction into dimensions beyond the limits normally conceived. That's why we commonly talk of the "supernormal" in connection with domain of Magick.

The Body is alive, and all Life is an expression of the Divine. There is God-power in the Body and in the Earth, just as there is in Mind and Spirit. With Love and Will, we use Mind to link these aspects of Divinity together to bring about change.

With Magick we increase the flow of Divinity in our lives and in the world around us. We add to the beauty of it all—for to work Magick we must work in harmony with the Laws of Nature and of the Psyche. *Magick is the flowering of the Human Potential.*

Practical Magick is concerned with the Craft of Living well and in harmony with Nature, and with the Magick of the Earth, in the things of the Earth, in the seasons and cycles and in the things we make with hand and Mind.

OTHER BOOKS BY DONALD TYSON

The New Magus, 1988
Rune Magic, 1988
The Truth About Ritual Magic, 1989
The Truth About Runes, 1989
How to Make and Use a Magic Mirror, 1990

CARDS AND KITS

Rune Magic Deck, 1988
Power of the Runes, 1989

FORTHCOMING

Three Books of Occult Philosophy
    Written by Henry Cornelius Agrippa of Nettesheim,
    edited and annotated English edition of 1651

CONTENTS

MAGIC IS ALIVE

Magic is a living force that moves beneath the surface of the modern world, transforming and improving the lives of those who have discovered its power. More ancient and unchanging than the pyramids, it is forever new, adapting effortlessly to any need or circumstance. For unbroken thousands of years, men and women have never ceased to practice it despite the most severe repression by sovereigns and priests.

Those who dared to work magic were persecuted because magic takes responsibility away from the collective institutions of church and state and places it into the hands of the individual. Magic is the art of empowerment. Through magic, it becomes possible to control your fate and attain your destiny. Magicians do not need a priest to tell them what to believe or a legal court to show them how to live. They have their own older, more profound wisdom beside which the conventions of religion and social ethics appear childishly simplistic. Little wonder magic was viewed as dangerous.

In the past, the church and other social institutions were the domain of men, but magic was open to everyone, man and woman, rich and poor, young and old, educated and ignorant, each according to his or her abilities. It gave the peasant in his hovel access to more personal power and wisdom than the lord in his castle. It allowed the outcast and the disenfranchised to seize control of their lives. As it was then, so it remains today. Magic is liberation and independence.

The magical view is in harmony with the modern ecological

Dissident traveling magicians

movement. Magic has always recognized the Earth as the Great
Mother, a living, sentient being that nourishes with infinite love
the least of her trillions upon trillions of children—human, animal,
and plant. Magic allows no division between man and the world.
Human clay and the soil in the furrow are one flesh. You and the
beasts of the field are a single family. You cannot hide your eyes
from the consequences of your actions, or inactions, because you
are the world, and you can never escape from yourself.

Today there is growing disenchantment with the official structures that are supposed to provide direction in life. People are turning away in increasing numbers from the larger established
churches, which are little more than lifeless, hollow shells, and
renouncing psychiatry, psychology, and social counseling in favor of
alternate approaches to personal transformation such as channeling,
past life regression, acupuncture, color therapy, creative visualization, hypnosis, and so on. These are only passing fads, here today
and gone tomorrow, but magic lies at the heart of all of them. It is
magic that gives these techniques whatever efficacy they possess.

An equally strong attraction for those seeking meaning in their
lives is the philosophical and religious techniques of the East.
Yoga, Buddhism, Tantra, Zen, Tao, all contain esoteric practices
that rely on magic to give them their effectiveness. They have been
preserved in sacred texts and passed from *guru* to *chela* down
through the centuries because they *work*. Yet there is no need for
Westerners to turn to oriental philosophy. The occult tradition of
the West stretches back for unbroken millenia through the Tarot
and Kabbalah of the Middle Ages to the magic of Rome and
Greece even to that of Egypt and Babylonia. It is a subtle and profound system of practical occult philosophy no less effective than
that of India and Tibet.

Magic is suited to the West and to the modern industrial age
because it concerns itself with the here and now in an active, con-
structive manner. There is very little navel gazing in ritual magic.
Through ritual the power of the art is applied directly to problems
in life. The purpose is to attain benefits in the present material
world, not in some hypothetical afterlife.

What is this ancient power? Where does it come from? How
does it work? Is it mere myth and delusion, or can it truly move
mountains and make the dead speak, bring rains from a clear sky

and calm the seas, turn the outcome of great battles and call down the moon from heaven? Which part of the claims made for magic are strictly true in the most literal sense and which are poetic exaggerations that must be interpreted symbolically? How can magic be used to improve your life?

This book answers these and many other questions in a clear and direct manner. Its purpose is to separate the wheat from the chaff and make sense of nonsense. It evolved from a pamphlet I wrote several years ago called *The Truth About Ritual Magic,* which was designed as a basic introduction to some of the ideas and techniques of modern occultism. In the course of enlarging the original, I have been able to expand its purpose. In addition to explaining what the occult revival is about, the present work shows how modern occultism grew from a single root into a number of clearly defined branches. Ninety per cent of the text is new material.

Section One deals with the basic questions in the mind of any intelligent person approaching magic for the first time. It not only explains what is possible in ritual magic and what is absurd, but tells exactly how magic works, where it comes from, and how it is used today by individuals and groups to improve human life.

Section Two sorts out the similarities and differences between some of the better known occult currents presently pursued in the Western world, such as Witchcraft, Druidism, Voudoun, shamanism, Satanism, and so on. Key features that distinguish each system and make it unique are highlighted.

Section Three involves the actual practice of magic. The preparations and tools of ritual are described in precise detail. Two complete rituals are given to show how these magical elements fit together and act in harmony to bring about desired ends. A three-level reading program of further study is suggested for those who wish to deepen their knowledge of ritual magic. It is composed of a selection from the fundamental source works that have given the modern occult tradition its present shape.

You will not find here the sacred-mysteries-that-cannot-be-revealed approach, which is invariably a cloak for the ignorance of the writer. This book describes what magic is and how it can be used. It will be gratefully received by experienced students of the occult who find themselves awash and drifting on a sea of irreconcilable techniques and conflicting assertions. It reveals the underlying foundation of practical ritual magic presently employed by almost all of the esoteric schools and pagan sects, cutting through the superficial and trivial idiosyncracies.

Magic is alive. Scientists and clerics can abuse it as much as they like. They can scorn it, hold it up to ridicule, nail it to a cross and water it with vinegar, but it will not die. It endures because it had no beginning and therefore can have no end. Magic is coeval with the universe, the creation of which was a magical act. No matter how often it is dressed in a new suit and given a mask to disguise its face, it remains the same, eternally present and all-pervading. It is the very lifeblood that sustains the world. Those who mock it exist only by virtue of its power.

This book is your guide into the heart of the entrancing, astonishing, and at times frightening, secret garden of magic. Use it to separate the real from the illusory, the face from the mask, to discover what is possible, and to learn how to become the being you are already in your unspoken dreams. Then set forth boldly on the path of life and take the treasures that have always been there waiting for you.

SECTION ONE

BASICS

Faust seeks occult wisdom in a magic mirror.
—from an engraving by Rembrandt, 1652

CHAPTER ONE

WHAT IS MAGIC?

Three beggars blind from birth were walking down the road when they encountered an elephant for the first time. When told the name of the animal, they touched it wonderingly. Later, they began to argue. The first man, who had felt the leg of the beast, said an elephant was like a thick tree. The second man, who had spread his hands across its broad side, maintained than an elephant was like a mountain. The third, who had examined its trunk, vigorously asserted that both were fools. An elephant, he said, was like a great serpent. Arguing in this manner among themselves, they wandered off the road and fell into a ravine, where all were killed.

The moral of this parable is that we each define our world within the limits of our own comprehension. Only if we widen our perception and deepen our understanding can we bring our definitions a step nearer to the underlying hidden reality. As it is with elephants, so it is with magic. There are as many definitions as there are personal responses to this difficult subject. It is pointless to spend much time arguing over them because each attempts to describe magic from a different limited perspective. They are all correct to some extent from their own points of view, and all are incomplete.

Definers of magic may be divided into two groups: those who are convinced that magic has no validity or efficacy beyond what may be produced by the superstitious credulity of the ignorant and those who believe that magic works. Members of these groups do not always come right out and admit their bias, but it is usually obvious from their statements and writings.

3

Behemoth, demon of animal strength—one view of the elephant.

One of the earliest skeptics was the Roman naturalist Pliny the Elder, who wrote in the first century of this era: "Therefore let us be convinced . . . that magic is detestable, vain, and idle; and though it has what I might call shadows of truth, their power comes from the art of the poisoner, not of the Magi" *(Natural History*, bk. XXX, ch. V).

This very well expresses the modern scientific opinion of magic, and it may be codified in three statements: 1) Magic is a completely worthless, futile pursuit incapable of bringing about any of the results it claims; 2) despite its ineffectuality, it is somehow also a wicked and dangerous practice; 3) any apparent efficacy of magic is attributable to unknown natural effects that have either been deliberately concealed by the magician or are not yet known to science.

Pliny was not the first or the last to confuse magic with poisoning. Over the centuries, it has been tumbled together with a wide variety of human activities, among them astrology, alchemy, medicine, religion, philosophy, hypnosis, dreaming, superstition, abortion, sexual perversion, divination, and insanity. The confusion arose because magic is a very basic function that underlies many other actions and is bound up with them. Before the experimental method began to establish natural laws and order the phenomena of the world, it was impossible for anyone to clearly separate the underlying essence that is magic from physical effects that are completely predictable but were not at that time understood.

In the Middle Ages, it was reasonable to suspect a Witch of magically poisoning a stream by scattering dust over it. No one knew then what caused such diseases as cholera or typhus or where they came from. Had the priests of the Inquisition been told that plague results from a host of organisms too small to see that invade the body and destroy it from within, they would naturally suppose these malignant entities to be the legion of possessing spirits described in the New Testament in Mark 5:9. They could never have conceived of an invisible entity that has the awesome power to enter the flesh of a human being and cause death as other than an evil demon sent by Satan.

As the proximate causes of more and more natural effects became known, magic was pushed back into the shadows by the expanding sphere of science. An attempt was made by the English anthropologist James G. Frazer, in his monumental work *The Golden Bough* (1890-1915), to define magic in scientific terms, on the presumption that it could then be analyzed and dissected like any other human pursuit. Although his definition is too narrow to describe all magical phenomena and practices, it remains highly influential to the present day:

> If we analyse the principles of thought on which magic is based, they will probably be found to resolve themselves into two: first, that like produces like, or that an effect resembles its cause; and, second, that things which have once been in contact with each other continue to act on each other at a distance after the physical contact has been severed. . . . Both branches of magic, the homeopathic and the contagious, may conveniently be compre-

Demon of the plague.
—*from* Feldtbuch der Wundarzney *by H. von Gersdorf, Strassburg, 1540*

hended under the general name of Sympathetic Magic, since both assume that things act on each other at a distance through a secret sympathy, the impulse being transmitted from one to the other by means of what we may conceive as a kind of invisible ether, not unlike that which is postulated by modern science for a precisely similar purpose, namely, to explain how things can physically affect each other through a space which appears to be empty (Frazer 1951, 12, 14).

Frazer at least tried to describe the mechanism of magic, even though he was convinced that magic was a primitive delusion destined to be supplanted by religion, just as religion was only a stage in the orderly evolution of human thinking toward science. He went out of his way to distance himself from any suggestion that he actually had empathy for the subject he had devoted his life to investigate and ascribed the type of thinking that allowed a belief in magic to "the crude intelligence not only of the savage, but of ignorant and dull-witted people everywhere" (Frazer 1951, 14). Frazer was horrified that anyone might suppose that he believed in magic or saw any value in myth beyond its cautionary instruction in the primitive workings of the human mind.

The same magiphobia, to coin a word, is evident in dictionary definitions. *The Oxford English Dictionary* defines magic as "The *pretended* art of influencing the course of events, and of producing marvellous physical phenomena, by processes *supposed* to owe their efficacy to their power of compelling the intervention of spiritual beings, or of bringing into operation some occult controlling principle of nature" (my italics). Webster also begins its definition "The pretended art . . ." Curiously, these same dictionaries do not describe psychotherapy as the "pretended art" of curing the mentally ill, yet the evidence for the efficacy of magic is just as strong as that for psychoanalysis.

How different is the tone of those who have actually used magic in their own lives! The great German occultist of the Renaissance, Henry Cornelius Agrippa, wrote:

Magick is a faculty of wonderful virtue, full of most high mysteries, containing the most profound contemplation of most secret things, together with the nature, power,

> quality, substance, and virtues thereof, as also the
> knowledge of whole nature, and it doth instruct us con-
> cerning the differing, and agreement of things amongst
> themselves, whence it produceth its wonderful effects,
> by uniting the virtues of things through the application
> of them one to the other, and to their inferior suitable
> subjects, joining and knitting them together thoroughly
> by the powers and virtues of the superior bodies. This is
> the most perfect, the chief science, that sacred, and sub-
> limer kind of philosophy, and lastly the most absolute
> perfection of all most excellent philosophy.
> —*Three Books Of Occult Philosophy*, Book I, Chapter 2

Some three centuries later, the father of the modern occult revival, Eliphas Levi, echoed this veneration:

> Magic, therefore, combines in a single science that which
> is most certain in philosophy, which is eternal and infal-
> lible in religion. It reconciles perfectly and incontestably
> those two terms, so opposed on the first view—faith and
> reason, science and belief, authority and liberty. It fur-
> nishes the human mind with an instrument of philo-
> sophical and religious certitude as exact as mathematics,
> and even accounting for the infallibility of mathematics
> themselves (Levi 1986, 29).

The most audacious, if not the greatest, magician of the 20th century, Aleister Crowley, had little patience for airy platitudes. His approach to magic was completely practical. His definition has the greatest currency among ritual occultists of the present day. It is breathtaking in its daring and scope:

> Magick is the Science and Art of causing Change to occur
> in conformity with Will (Crowley 1976, xii).

At first sight Crowley appears to be saying that every deliber-ate act is magical, but this is not so. He understood the true will to be the intention that is in harmony with the essential nature of the individual. Since the individual is a microcosm of the universe, true will is also in harmony with natural law. No man at war with himself can effectively undertake magical acts regardless of his

"Learn about the egg and cut it with a flaming sword. In our world there is a bird more sublime than all others. To search for his egg be thy only concern." The egg of alchemy is a symbol for magical realization.
—*from Michael Maier's alchemical work,* Scrutinium chymicum, *Frankfurt, 1687*

desire, because his intention is not supported by his true will. Crowley believed that most persons are in perpetual strife with their essential natures and that this internal division limits their ability to work magic.

In all these definitions, there is little attempt to get at the root of magical potency. They merely describe the action of magic, not how the force of magic originates. Agrippa comes closest to postulating a mechanism of magic, which he perceived to be the empowerment of mundane things by uniting them through occult similarity with their transcendent correspondences. For example, onions have the virtue of Mars because they are hot on the tongue, and Mars is the fiery god of war. This is shrewd observation based on experience, but it fails to reach the ultimate source of magical efficacy.

Hints of the truth are scattered here and there among the writings of anthropologists and mystics and occultists. One of the first men to examine magic analytically, Edward Burnett Tylor, observed in his *Primitive Culture* (1871) that the distinguishing feature of magic was its unreality, its unity consisting precisely in the absence from its beliefs and practices of the natural laws of cause and effect. Magic was the strange and unpredictable—if it could be explained in ordinary terms, it was not magic.

Claude Levi-Strauss, searching for the essence of magic in the concept of *mana*—a kind of nebulous, pervasive, occult potency—reduced *mana* to the level of a pure symbol; that is, a symbol lacking any form or quality. Magic was whatever defied classification and analysis, the unattainable mystery that can be observed to act but not predicted or understood. "Always and everywhere notions of this type intervene, somewhat as algebraic symbols, to represent a value of indeterminate meaning, which being itself empty of meaning is therefore susceptible to the reception of any meaning whatsoever" (Mauss 1950, xliv).

The anthropologist Marcel Mauss stumbled over the ultimate source of magic, but since he himself believed magic to be only a delusion he did not realize the significance of his casual observation. Speaking about the projection of the soul, he writes:

> In India we also have the case of the Yogins, although their mystical theology is really more philosophical than religious, and more religious than magical. In applying themselves to a task (verb *yuj*), they are joining (verb *yuj*) with the primary transcendental principle of the world, a union which produces (verb *sidh*) magical power *(siddhi)*. The *sutras* of Patanjali are explicit on this point and even attribute the capacity to other magicians beside the Yogins (Mauss 1972, 34).

Buddhist writers frequently warn against too deep an involvement with magical manifestations that occur during meditation, such as spirit communications, clairvoyance, clairaudience, and telekinesis, which they regard as illusory. This is the religious view, analogous to the assertions by Christian mystics that pursuit of worldly goals is valueless in comparison with spiritual perfection. Nonetheless, Buddhists perceive these *siddhis* as preliminary signs of union between the mind of the individual and the universal mind that pervades all things, before that union has become pure and formless.

This understanding has been lost in the West, where too often the attempt is made to reduce magic to the predictable and therefore safe level of a natural phenomenon as yet not fully understood. Magic is called a science, or characterized by quasi-scientific jargon. This wrong-headed effort to materialize magic is doomed to failure and plays into the hands of those who wish to discredit magic, because magic is precisely that thing which cannot be explained or predicted in ordinary physical terms. Although the desires of the magician are necessarily expressed in the material forms of symbols and rituals, and the effects of such rituals frequently reveal themselves in concrete ways, the actual circuit between wish and fulfillment is not bound by the laws of time and space.

This would seem very different from Isaac Bonewits's definition of magic as "folk parapsychology, an art and science designed to enable people to make effective use of their psychic talents" (Adler 1979, 8), but the conflict may only be apparent. I might as easily define parapsychology as an aspect of magic formalized in scientific terminology. No one knows how *psi* works; no one can even predict its action with reliability. Psychic events are often examples of magic. Merely calling magic parapsychology does not mean that we understand it or that we can predict its workings. Neither does it permit us to relegate it into the category of natural phenomena soon to be exposed and harnessed by the experimental method. It may be comforting to diminish the mystery of magic by equating it with an as yet unexplained but perfectly ordinary and predictable function of the human brain; unfortunately, magic will not stay in this box.

It must be emphasized that my transcendent view of magic is not the common view of those who practice its diverse forms. Most modern magicians seem driven by an unarticulated impulse to take the magic out of magic and define it in mundane terms. Perhaps this impulse arises from the desire to comprehend magic and thereby conquer and command it, as if it were just another form of physical energy such as steam or electricity. But in my opinion the essence of magic lies in the fact that it can never, by its inherent nature, be completely controlled or predicted. This is a more dangerous view, and a more difficult one to live with for those who demand an orderly predictable world, but I believe it is a more useful understanding. I do not offer it as absolute truth—the resplendent grandeur of the elephant is scarcely less dim to my eyes than it was to the three wandering beggars.

After examining and criticizing the definitions of others at such length, it is only fair that I give my own definition of magic, upon which my personal magical philosophy is based:

DEFINITION
Magic is the art of affecting the manifest
through the Unmanifest.

In common with other arts, it draws its power from the deep well of potential in the center of the human soul. Within this well are the waters of the unconscious, and below the surface dwell all possibilities awaiting their turn to be pulled up into the light and made real. So long as they remain under the surface, they do not exist, but the moment they are captured and brought forth, they come to be. The act of pulling a possibility from the well of potential into being is an act of creation, which brings me to the first corollary of the preceding definition:

FIRST COROLLARY
Every creative act is magical;
and every magical act is creative.

The manifest is all that can be seen, touched, manipulated, imagined, or understood. The Unmanifest is none of these things. It is the place, or rather the non-place, from which everything issues. All that comes into being comes from the Unmanifest, the highest deity and source of creation. All that passes away goes back to the Unmanifest. This includes human souls. The passage between manifest and Unmanifest is completed by ideal forms, not material substances. The soul comes forth into being and passes away—the body is built up from clay and clay it remains. Physical substance is only the cloak or garment for spiritual forms. These forms are the basic reality, not the clothing of earth that reflects their identities.

It follows that every magical act is a direct communion with the divine essence regardless of how this essence may be conceived by the individual. The yogis of India knew this vital truth. It is not necessary to talk much about God in connection with magic, which is an art for causing real change in the world that has little to do with common religious sensibility, but it must be stated that magic taps this ultimate source of creative power. Magic has been trivialized and maligned precisely because this fundamental connection has not been grasped.

Many common events that are not considered to be occult are magical. As has been pointed out, all artistic creation draws upon the hidden well of potential that is the Unmanifest, but even more everyday occurrences, such as the sudden, unexpected awareness of the beauty of a sunrise, or a completely unpremeditated loving action, or a sense of absolute inner peace and rightness, are magical happenings in the true sense.

Once the true root of magic is understood, several important insights follow. Since magic reaches beyond the limits of the natural world, it transcends cause and effect. Magic can never be predicted with certainty. The same magical ritual does not always produce the same result, or a result at the same time and place. The uncertainty of magic makes it impossible to verify by the scientific method. Aleister Crowley was incorrect in describing magic as a "Science and Art." Magic is not and cannot be a science so long as science is limited by cause and effect. Attempts to pin down magic with experiments and measure it with machines are doomed from the start. This brings me to my second corollary:

SECOND COROLLARY
What can be predicted is not magic;
what is magic cannot be predicted.

This principle of uncertainty was intuited by Edward Burnett Tylor in his *Primitive Culture*. He saw that magic was that indefinable something that could never quite be pinned down. It was further developed by Claude Levi-Strauss in his exposition of *mana* as the absolute symbol capable of taking on any uncertain identity.

Deity transcends the universal laws of cause and effect that govern the universe. Magic is able to circumvent these laws through its communion with deity. No other way of transcending cause and effect is possible.

THIRD COROLLARY
Magic in action looks like luck.

Those who practice ritual magic know that it works but cannot always say where or in what manner the working will take effect. This is very frustrating to scientists, who are inclined to dismiss the entire subject. The psychiatrist Carl Jung came close to understanding the mechanism of magic with his examination of the phenomenon he called synchronicity—the seemingly chance co-occurrence of significantly related events. Such fortuitous coincidences, for better or for worse, indicate the working of magic, which is usually unconscious on the part of the worker.

FOURTH COROLLARY
Magic, like water, always seeks the easiest course.

Just as a river will not flow through an obstacle when it can flow around it, magic is seldom spectacular because it seldom needs to be. Once a desire has been formulated and a ritual conducted to bring it about, magic acts in the simplest and most mundane way possible to allow the fulfillment of that desire. It is up to the ritual magician to take advantage of the chance for fulfillment that magic has opened, or it will be lost. If you desire to eat an apple, magic will make it possible for you to get the apple. It may even put it into your hand. But you must bite into the apple yourself—magic will not chew for you.

As a river will cut through the hardest rock when there is nowhere else for it to flow, so magic will pierce and shatter barriers when there is no way around them. If spectacular results are absolutely necessary, magic is spectacular. The focus of the art is on the fulfillment of the ritual desire, not on the method of its attainment. If there is an obstacle in your way, one that you cannot surmount by ordinary physical means, magic will enable you to bypass it in some manner or other, even if the obstacle seems impassable.

FIFTH COROLLARY
*Magic is unbounded by time
and space.*

It is possible to realize the purpose of a ritual immediately anywhere on the surface of the Earth, no matter where the ritual is
worked, and indeed anywhere in the entire universe. In practice
the fulfillment of magic is usu-
ally confined to the Earth,
because humans have little
knowledge of places beyond the
surface of this planet.

It is equally possible for a
magical effect to take place before
a ritual is worked to bring it
about. Nevertheless the working
of the ritual is a necessary part of
the fulfillment of the ritual desire.
Aleister Crowley observed this
curious phenomenon and com-
mented upon it:

> I have noticed that the effect of
> a Magical Work has followed
> it so closely that it must have
> been started before the time of
> the Work. E. g. I work to night
> to make X in Paris write to me.
> I get the letter the next morn-
> ing, so that it must have been
> written before the Work. Does
> this deny that the Work
> caused the effect? (Crowley
> 1976, 74-5).

This may sound fantastic to
those who have not personally
experienced the effects of magic,
but I can testify to its accuracy.
The identical experience occurred

Aleister Crowley as a young man

in my own ritual work. I once performed a ritual to receive a letter
of response from a person I had been waiting to hear from for many
months. The letter came, not the next morning as in Crowley's case,
but later that same day. I have also after intense ritual work found
myself thinking forward in time. An idea will come into my mind,
often a new and subtle philosophical concept, and I will have no
notion of its origin; then, a few days later, I will be reading, and there
is the idea which I had several days before plucked out of the future
of my mind stream. This has occurred quite often.

If these ideas seem too strange and esoteric to comprehend,
take heart. It is not necessary to know what magic is in order to
work magic. Magic has been successfully practiced for thousands
of years by people who have no idea what they are doing or how
they are doing it. Most primitive magicians are not philosophical
in the least. They use magic to help them overcome the practical,
everyday problems that arise in their lives, or to help others solve
similar problems.

Magic is an art that can be employed for both exalted and crass
purposes. Each magical act is a communication of the higher self
with deity. This does not mean that magic is always used for
refined and noble purposes. To resort to magic to charm away
warts, for example, is like playing *Chopsticks* on a Steinway con-
cert-grand piano. But the warts will vanish. The work done within
any art depends on the ability and intention of the artist. A great
painter will produce a masterpiece with the same materials that an
untalented beginner uses for his clumsy sketches. How you use
this most sacred and exalted of human arts is ultimately in your
own hands.

CHAPTER TWO

WHAT IS RITUAL?

R itual is the medium through which the art of magic is practiced. It consists of an action or series of actions, which may be entirely mental or mental and physical, whereby the power of magic is released and directed towards the fulfillment of a specific desire.

The bare physical actions of ritual have no force in themselves. Someone who buys a book on magic and stumbles through a ritual found in its pages will be unlikely to produce any result without the necessary mental training and conditioning. Rituals become effective to the degree they are able to alter the mind and create a channel through the unconscious to the well of potential in the Unmanifest. The purpose of ritual is to bring about a heightened or exalted state of awareness that enables the focus of will upon the magical fulfillment, whatever it may happen to be. Ritual is only an instrument to direct the mind.

In theory, ritual would be unnecessary for the working of magic were it possible to exalt the mind at will to instantly bring about a communion with the Unmanifest. In practice, it is doubtful if magic can be worked without the supportive framework of ritual. There would be nothing for the mind to grasp and manipulate. Often the ritual is very brief and completely mental—the inner utterance of a single word of power with specific intention, for example. But, for the energy of magic to be released and directed, some structure is required, however simple.

To work magic without ritual would be like trying to draw water out of a well without a bucket. Ritual is the bucket. The water itself is the raw magical potency that can assume any shape.

17

The act of drawing it forth is the practice of the art of magic. It can then be carried in the bucket, and this is the focusing of the ritual upon the object of desire, the purpose for which the ritual is worked.

In the modern world, formal rituals are most commonly practiced in the services of the major religions such as Judaism, Christianity, Islam, and Buddhism. Although the priests of these faiths might vigorously maintain that their rituals are not magical by nature or intent, there is little ground for distinguishing religious rites from magical rites, as Margaret A. Murray observes:

> In all studies of witches and magic, one point must be kept in mind, that when anything regarded as out of the ordinary course of nature is brought about by human means it is called a miracle if the magician belongs to the beholder's own religion, but it is magic—often black magic—if the wizard belongs to another religion (Murray 1970, 129).

Or, in the words of the great German antiquarian scholar Jacob Grimm, who along with his brother Wilhelm was responsible for the collection of folk tales known as *Grimm's Fairy Tales:* "Miracle is divine, Magic is devilish."

Many rites of the churches seek to bring about miracles of transformation for specific practical ends. What is the changing of wafers into flesh and wine into blood in Roman Catholic communion if it is not a magic ritual? When a Catholic prays before a plaster image of a saint for a specific favor, and as payment offers sacrifices of money or goods, or performs certain observances, how is it essentially different from a magician who evokes a demon and asks for favors in return for certain specified conduct or sacrifices? Surely the feeding of the statues of gods in Hindu temple worship with milk and other nourishing substances is similar in kind to the feeding of the drums with blood in Voudoun rituals.

James G. Frazer attempted to divide ritual into propitiatory rites and presumptive rites. The latter only he referred to as magical:

> The [primitive] rites are magical rather than propitiatory.
> In other words, the desired objects are attained, not by propitiating the favour of divine beings through sacri-

fice, prayer, and praise, but by ceremonies which, as I have already explained, are believed to influence the course of nature directly through a physical sympathy or resemblance between the rite and the effect which it is the intention of the rite to produce (Frazer 1951, 477).

This type of primitive magical religion is shamanism, where the roles of priest and magician are inextricably bound together, as indeed are the roles of magician and physician. Shamanism dates back to the stone age, yet it is still practiced today in parts of the world that have been insulated from technology, or turned away from its influence. The magic of the shaman is the root of all human studies. In earliest times, religion, science, medicine, philosophy, and art were all mingled together, all supported by the vital lifeblood of magic. Only in later ages did specialization occur.

Frazer was expressing the idea that, when rituals ask for favors instead of demanding results, they have ceased to be magical and have become religious in the modern sense. He believed religion is evolving into a purely propitiatory state when it will no longer be tainted by the primitive vestiges of magical thinking. There is no evidence that this is so among the general population of worshipers, where all religions are actually practiced. Attempts to purge religious rituals of the miraculous and magical have resulted in a draining away of faith, because the heart of religion is essentially magical. When magic is driven from a religion, that religion ceases to live.

Magic is more fundamental than religion and underlies its practice. A religious ritual becomes magical when it succeeds in forming a bridge between the worshiper and the deity, regardless of what the link may be used to accomplish. In religious rites, the purpose is usually to adore deity or exalt the emotions or plead for favors. Religious magic tends to be less focused on practical material results than secular magic. Often it seeks union with the Unmanifest for the sake of union, not for some ulterior motive.

Magical potency only flows forth when the magician, for an instant at least, becomes united with the divine and takes on the cloak of omnipotence. In theory the magician can accomplish any willed purpose. In practice he or she is limited by a lack of expectation—what in religion is called faith. The only limits in magic are self-imposed, but knowing this does not make these barriers any easier to surmount. In the same way a compulsive personality can consciously know an act to be unproductive yet still be unable to stop doing it, or the victim of a phobia can realize that a fear is foolish yet be unable to cast off the fear, so the magician can know that he or she is potentially able to do everything yet still achieve dismal results from rituals.

You are united with the Unmanifest at all times and can never be separated from this limitless well of potential, but you do not realize this truth. Ritual is a makeshift way of allowing you to perceive this union, if only partially and briefly, so that magical potency can manifest itself in your life. In a sense, by ritual you are able to trick your mind into forgetting for a moment its delusion of ignorance. You forget that you have forgotten your power, and for that brief moment of insight you are able to recognize your true identity. This communion with the higher self is so brief it is usually not even perceived, but it is this oneness that releases magical force and makes ritual effective.

A ritual is a kind of drama that takes you out of the limited awareness you mistake in your ignorance for your true self. While exalted by ritual, you catch a glimpse of the higher reality and are able to act upon that perception to realize specific desires. The same sort of thing happens when you watch an engrossing film or stage play. The drama lifts you out of yourself and you become the characters, at least by sympathy. Stage drama is a degenerate form of magical ritual. As with so many magical things, such as dice, cards, letters of the alphabet, and draughts (checkers), what was in its beginning used for a serious occult purpose has come to be used as a source of entertainment.

Drama was at first wholly magical and was enacted by the shamans before an audience of either men or gods to achieve a magical result. Later, it came to be a support for religion, as in the Greek mysteries at Eleusis, where the higher cult secrets of Ceres were mimicked before initiates. Still later, drama appeared in the medieval mystery and miracle plays, where biblical stories and moral parables were enacted on the steps of the great cathedrals of Europe. In modern times drama is almost wholly a secular amusement without a deliberate magical content, yet even today it has the power to profoundly move the heart and mind and shape the actions of human beings.

*A magician evokes an angel to visible appearance from within his protective cir-
cle, which prevents the watching demons from harming him. His occult books
and magic wand are upon the altar.*
——*from* The Astrologer of the Nineteenth Century, *London, 1825*

In rituals of magic the desired purpose is dramatically represented as already achieved, or the process of fulfillment is enacted. For example, if a magician wished to magically cause the death of another person, he or she might name a doll after that person and give it a funeral service and burial. Alternately the magician might stab a nail through the heart of the christened doll, ritually enacting in this way the murder of the person. If both actions were combined, the ritual would be even more effective.

In one of Stephen King's lesser novels, a Gypsy speaks the single word "thinner" at a man he wishes to kill magically. The man immediately begins to lose weight and continues to become thinner no matter how much he eats. The single word might be regarded as a ritual representation in the form of a verbal symbol of the realization of the magical desire of the Gypsy. Here the dramatic content of the ritual consists of the meaning inherent in a single word, enacted by its utterance. Rituals need not be long or complex to be effective. It is the way they work on the mind of the magician, not their content, that gives them force.

Rituals are living things. They begin as a seed of desire and grow into a shape that is determined by the circumstances surrounding them. Eventually they reach a mature form that expresses their greatest efficacy. Some rituals retain their vitality for many years, even centuries, but eventually they begin to lose their relevance to the world in which they are worked and at last, like all other living things, they die.

The grimoires of medieval magic began life as the workbooks of individual magicians, who merely recorded their experiments and practices so they would not forget them. Generation to generation, they were passed from master to apprentice and copied by hand, each copyist refining their contents according to personal experience and adding new material, until they attained a stable form that could not be radically altered without destroying their essential identity. Most grimoires have been debased and have lost their vitality over time. The rituals contained in their pages are regarded by the majority of modern occultists as quaint relics of the past. This is perhaps too intolerant a view. The grimoires still repay careful study with many fascinating insights into the art of magic.

Formal rituals written by others are only a starting place in magic. In the beginning, it is useful to learn a dozen rituals or so and practice them regularly and often, keeping as close to the letter of the instructions as possible. Public, received rituals are similar to the musical scales and other exercises in the study of the piano. They instill needed knowledge and build up the proper skills. Eventually the pianist will seek personal expression through improvisation and likely will want to compose original scores. The same is true in magic. The magician begins by adhering strictly to rituals found in books or passed down from teachers. Then, as confidence grows, these rituals are modified or amplified to suit specific needs. Finally, a level of skill is reached that allows the creation of completely unique, original rituals soundly based upon the timeless principles of magic.

To be effective, a ritual often must be worked over and over. Even though most magical texts imply that success will follow immediately after the conclusion of a rite, in my own experience I have found it the exception rather than the rule to obtain a useful result from a single performance. When a ritual is devised to attain a specific desire and then repeated night after night, it will subtly alter with each repetition. New elements will arise that seamlessly incorporate themselves into its body. This is a process of natural growth and must not be frustrated. If these new aspects are suppressed and ignored, the ritual will lose its force and die.

I am often amazed in my own work how effortlessly the evolution of a new ritual takes place. It is exactly as though some higher intelligence is rewriting and editing the ritual drama as it is being enacted. Prayers and invocations spring fully formed into the conscious mind. The body naturally conforms itself to changing actions and gestures as if moved by an outside will. It is always possible to frustrate these innovations, but to do so is to lose all value in the working.

Eventually, after many nights, the ritual will, seemingly of itself, assume its mature form and the innovations will become much less frequent or cease altogether. At this point it is useful to record the ritual so that it will not be forgotten. This is the same procedure that gave rise to the grimoires centuries ago. Indeed, each magician's journal is a grimoire.

There is a danger in becoming too casual about the content of rituals. Merely because a ritual lives and evolves does not mean it can arbitrarily be altered to suit the whim of the moment. When does a composition cease to be music and become mere noise? This can only be determined by the effect that playing the composition has on the mind of the person who hears it. Similarly, the proof of ritual is in the working.

Some modern occultists mistakenly believe that, because the source of ritual power does not lie in a slavish adherence to the exact written form of the ritual, they are free to do anything that strikes their fancy. Unfortunately they lack the inherent sensibility to distinguish viable ritual from theatrical nonsense. They are like would-be painters with no talent who slap colors on canvas and declare the result as good as the work of the masters, because they cannot themselves see any difference between their paintings and those of Van Gogh.

These anarchistic magicians end up being cynical and bitter about magic. Since magic has not worked for them, they jump to the mistaken conclusion that all magic is fraud and cunning deceit and must be understood with a nod and a wink, metaphorically, not as a practical tool for material change but as an exercise in imagination. They cannot understand that their rituals remain impotent because they are producing only magical noise, not magical music.

It is far better to choose a few solid, widely accepted rituals from the traditional schools of magic and work them without modification. Not every artist is born to be creative. Some are interpretive. By making a well-constructed and potent ritual your own, you can make it work for you. Later, when you are perfectly sure you have understood the principles on which your adopted rituals are based, you may experiment in a conservative way with original rituals. The rapidity with which you pass from received to original rituals will depend on your inherent magical talent. Your own inner sense of rightness must be your ultimate guide.

Modern rituals of ceremonial or high magic, as it is often called, tend to be complex and exhibit a well-defined structure, perhaps because the modern occult revival began in formal and rather stuffy Victorian England. This formality may also in part be traced to the magic of the Middle Ages and the Renaissance, which was strongly patterned after Church rituals. It is possible to analyze the general structure of a modern magical ritual and examine its parts.

All formal occult rituals begin with a period of preparation.

This may involve fasting, prayers, meditation, the collection of ritual substances, and the manufacture of instruments. The more important the ritual, the more extensive this period. Major rituals require weeks or months of preparation. Where the ritual is repeated many times, this preparation of mind and body becomes a sustained state of readiness. Practicing ritualists may maintain a personal conditioning that allows them to conduct effective rituals on any day they choose.

If attention is paid to astrological times, as is usually the case, it will be necessary to consult an ephemeris and table of houses to determine the most favorable position of the Sun, Moon, and planets. Some degree of astrological knowledge is more or less expected in magic, although it is not absolutely essential.

If the ritual is new or a significant modification of an existing ritual, it is best to write it out and rehearse it until it is memorized and can be presented without hesitation or error. Real magicians seldom read from a printed text when they work magic, anymore than professional actors hold scripts in their hands when performing a play. The popular image of the bearded wizard who stands in his circle reading an invocation from a great book stems from a superstitious belief that the efficacy of a spell lies in the words that compose it, when in reality it is the condition of mind these words can, with proper preparation, encourage in those who speak or hear them that gives a ritual its power. Without preparation, the words themselves will probably yield no result, although there are modern practitioners who hold that certain words of power and some arcane symbols are so potent that they can produce transformation even in the uninitiated.

It is important to distinguish the grimoire, a kind of recipe book composed of rituals, prayers, invocations, bindings, and other techniques for working magic, from the Book of Spirits, which contains the personal symbols, occult names, likenesses, and signatures of spiritual beings that serve the magician. Traditionally, spirits swear obedience and even sign their own names or make their marks on the pages of the Book of Spirits, which then becomes an empowered instrument for their summoning and commanding. The spirits might almost be said to reside within the book. The making of this book is seldom clearly set forth. One of the best descriptions appears in the *Book of the Sacred Magic of Abra-*

Sample pages from a Book of Spirits. Not to be confused with a grimoire, the Book of Spirits acts as a talisman that embodies and controls the spirits depicted within its pages. Its presence during evocations of these spirits was considered essential.
—*from* The Magus *by Francis Barrett, London, 1801*

Melin the Mage (reprinted by Dover, 1975) on pages 132-5, but even here many of the necessary instructions are implied rather than explicitly set forth.

Shortly before the appointed time, the magician undertakes a purification of the body, usually a bath, and dons the magical robes which are only worn for ritual work. This marks a transition from the everyday personality to the magical persona. By the bath and prayer of cleansing, the detritus of ordinary life is sloughed off the soul, making it a clean slate ready to receive the ritual purpose. The purification should not be thought of as removing sins in the religious sense, but rather as a way of eliminating discordance and focusing the will in a single-minded way on the ritual. The robes to some extent represent the magical identity of the ritualist. They both empower and protect, forming a shield against the pessimism and doubt of the mundane world.

Faust conjures a demon by reading the text of a grimoire. Notice that he stands inside a magic circle with his wand in his right hand.
—*from* The Tragical Historie of the Life and Death of Doctor Faustus
by Christopher Marlowe, London, 1631

Entering the place of ritual, the magician unwraps the instruments of the art such as the wand, the cup, the lamen, and so on and places them upon the altar. The nature of these instruments varies widely among the different styles of magic, but always they are treated with reverence. They are sacred because they possess *mana*, magical potency. It is best not to touch them directly with unpurified hands, but to wrap them in silk or linen when not in use. The flame at the center of the altar is lit. Consecrated water, salt, or other materials for purifying and banishing the ritual place are set out. Appropriate incense is ignited. Music, if employed to help focus the will, is turned on. The lights are dimmed—it is always best to use natural light or the light of flame for ritual.

The magician proceeds to divide the sacred space from the ordinary world and purify it, just as was done with the temple of the body. There are various ways to exalt the place of ritual, but the most common is to draw a magic circle around it. The function of the circle is similar to that of the robe or other ritual garment—it separates inside, where magic will be wrought that transcends cause and effect, from outside, which remains bound by natural law. When the circle is cleansed by prayer with water, salt, and fire, it becomes a *tabula rasa* upon which to write the will. The circle acts both as a barrier against the intrusion of discordant spirits and other influences and as a retaining wall to concentrate magical power.

The ritual proper is then performed within the circle. It takes many forms, but always consists of a dramatic enactment of the fulfillment of ritual desire. The instruments and substances already selected and gathered together are employed in this drama, presented on the stage of the altar. Usually rituals contain both propitiatory aspects, such as prayers seeking the cooperation of gods and other emanations of the Unmanifest, and also presumptive aspects intended to yield their result as surely as night follows day. Modern magicians, like the ancient shamans, see no inherent conflict between the two—both approaches are combined in the ritual to make doubly sure of its outcome.

At the moment of dramatic climax, there is a catharsis when the pent-up occult energy gathered by all the ritual actions leaves the circle through its central point and sets the fulfillment of the ritual desire in motion. This may be likened to a battery that is slowly charged over time, then discharged in a moment with a flash of arcing electricity. This lightning bolt marks the moment of union with the Unmanifest when the frustration of the ritual desire is at last released. The stronger it is, the more effective the ritual.

Union occurs and the ritual desire is realized at the same moment outside of ordinary time and space, but it often requires days or weeks for the magical potency to overcome the inert clay of matter and set it into motion. Even though the ritual has been completely successful, the magician may not have this confirmed until much later. Alternately, the desire may be fulfilled almost at once, despite the fact that it involves events set in motion long before the actual working of the ritual. Magic transcends ordinary cause and effect.

After the catharsis, it is useful to summarize verbally the purpose and expected fulfillment of the ritual. This is usually a brief prayer addressed to the god or spirit under whose auspices the ritual in worked, thanking the god for its part in the fulfillment. Or it may be a simple statement addressed to the unconscious mind that the ritual desire has been realized. It is important that the magician maintain a calm inward assurance of the success of the ritual during this prayer or statement.

The ritual is concluded by following in reverse order the same steps that opened it. Whatever was done to divide and exalt the sacred space from its ordinary surroundings must now be carefully undone and the place of ritual reintegrated with the rest of the natural world. I prefer to unmake the magic circle just as carefully as it was made at the commencement of the ritual, in this way emphasizing its reality, but most magicians simply let the circle fade from their awareness. The instruments are carefully wrapped and put away, the flame on the altar is extinguished, and the magical robe or other garments are removed. It is customary for a period of rest to follow, perhaps an hour, when the mind is relaxed and turned toward casual matters.

Not all magical rituals fully express all these steps. For a magician who is already mentally and physically trained and has an established place of working and a full set of ritual instruments, little preparation may be required. Prayers are often dispensed with—magic does not require supplication to the gods, even though it does involve a communion below the conscious level with the highest deity, the Unmanifest. Neither is the circle absolutely necessary, nor specifically any one of the magical instruments. However, this general pattern will be found in most formal rituals of modern magic. It descends from the theurgic practices of the Egyptians and Greeks and has survived for so many centuries because it is effective.

The structure of ritual may be easier to understand by comparing this general account with the two actual rituals that are presented in Chapters Eighteen and Nineteen.

*Thoth, Egyptian god of wisdom and magic, who has
the head of the ibis. Thoth is closely related to Hermes Trismegistus.*
—*from* The Gods of the Egyptians *by E. A. Wallis Budge, London, 1904*

CHAPTER THREE

THE ROOTS OF MAGIC

For purposes of comparison, I shall arbitrarily divide magic into four rough categories according to the geography of its origin: 1) Western, 2) Eastern, 3) African, 4) Aboriginal. All four of these groups have an ancient history and a modern expression.

Western magic as we recognize it today began to assume its form in Egypt and Persia, spread throughout the Greek and Roman empires, survived the Dark Ages in Europe, and was carried abroad to America and the other European colonies by Christian emigrants.

Eastern magic began in India and East Asia and extended its influence throughout China, Tibet, Japan, and Southeast Asia, aided in its spread by the expansion of Buddhism into these regions.

African magic is the synthesis of African tribal occultism carried to the melting pots of the Caribbean and Brazil by the slave trade. It finds its expression as Voudoun, spiritism, Umbanda, and related cults.

Aboriginal magic is the taproot from which the three previous classes have arisen. It is a broad category embracing the native occult practices of the aboriginal peoples of the world and expresses itself in such diverse forms as the modern shamanic revival, traditional Native American magic, the magic of the Australian aborigines, and the *tahunas* (native priests) of Hawaii.

These categories have frequently overlapped and mingled both in ancient and modern times. The ritual magic worked in the industrialized Western nations is mainly in the Western tradition, although there have been strong incursions of Eastern methods in the last 150 years, and more recently still a growing fascination with shamanism. It is the course of the Western tradition that concerns us.

When ancient Greece first began to rise as a world power, the reputation of Egyptian magic was already legendary. Egypt was the land of living magic, looked upon in much the same way we regard Tibet, but on a much grander scale. How much of its magic was indigenous and how much was borrowed from outside sources would form the basis for an extensive study, but by the time Menes united the two kingdoms of Upper and Lower Egypt around 3000 BC, it had achieved its own unique identity.

The magic of Egypt was bound up with the religion of Egypt. This was a theological system of great complexity containing many subtle concepts. High magic was the domain of the hierophants who ministered to the innumerable temples of the gods. Magic was a sacred art. Many of the greatest Greek philosophers undertook the extended and often dangerous voyage to Egypt to study the occult wisdom of the Egyptian priests. Pliny the Elder mentions Pythagoras, Empedocles, Democritus, and Plato (*Natural History*, bk. XXX, ch. I). There were many others.

The reason for the universal veneration of Egyptian magic was probably its power to command the gods. E. A. Wallis Budge writes:

> But whereas the magic of every other nation of the ancient East was directed entirely against the powers of darkness, and was invented in order to frustrate their fell designs by invoking a class of benevolent beings to their aid, the Egyptians aimed at being able to command their gods to work for them, and to compel them to appear at their desire (Budge 1971, 3–4).

This Egyptian assurance of humanity's superiority over the gods is expressed in the *Poimandres* of Hermes Trismegistus: "Nay, if we are to speak the truth without fear, he who is indeed a man is even above the gods of heaven, or at any rate he equals them in power" (Scott 1985, I:205). Elsewhere Hermes says:

> Willing then that man should be at once a thing of earth and capable of immortality, God compacted him of these two substances, the one divine, the other mortal; and in

that he is thus compacted, it is ordained by God's will that man is not only better than all mortal beings, but also better than the gods, who are made wholly of immortal substance (ibid., I:337).

The Egyptian hierophants exerted their power by means of words. "These great results were to be obtained by the use of certain words which, to be efficacious, must be uttered in a proper tone of voice by a duly qualified man" (Budge 1971, 4). About these words of power, Hermes says: "when the Egyptian words are spoken, the force of the things signified works in them" (Scott 1985, I:65) The use of words of power was adopted by the Greeks and continues to be a significant part of magic down to the present.

Other features of Egyptian magic include a strong belief in soul travel, astrology, ritual purification, protective symbolic amulets, and a complex hierarchy of spiritual beings. The Egyptians perfected a technique, described by Hermes in the *Asclepius*, for causing gods to indwell their statues of stone and wood. The empowered statues were then used to serve human will in any number of ways: "statues which have foreknowledge, and predict future events by the drawing of lots, and by prophetic inspiration, and by dreams, and in many other ways; statues which inflict diseases and heal them, dispensing sorrow and joy according to men's deserts" (Scott 1985, I:341). This technique is probably the most precious secret of practical magic sought after by the visiting Greek philosophers.

The power of Egyptian magic was legendary throughout the ancient world, and the greatest magician of all was Nectanebus, the last native king of Egypt, who reigned about 358 BC. According to his Greek biographer, pseudo-Callisthenes, the king knew what lay hidden in the depths of the Nile and in the highest spheres of heaven. He was unsurpassed in his skill of reading the aspects of the planets and interpreting natural omens. He could foretell the future of the unborn child and predict the fortunes of men. His was the power to project prophetic dreams into any sleeping person anywhere in the world by means of wax images or through animal messengers.

Whenever an invading fleet threatened Egyptian shores, Nectanebus would create wax figures of the enemy ships and troops and his own naval forces and place them both on the surface of a great, water-filled bowl. With a black ebony wand and muttered words of power, he would invoke the gods and demons. Suddenly the wax images would spring to life and enact the coming battle, and those representing the Egyptian ships would overcome the ships of the foe and sink them. At that same moment, the real enemy ships sank to the bottom of the sea.

At the birth of Alexander the Great, the Egyptian magician is supposed to have caused Olympias, mother of Alexander, to withhold the delivery of the child until the alignment of the heavens was at its most auspicious. This same story, by the way, is told about the English court magician John Dee in connection with the birth of Queen Elizabeth I. Its truth must be doubted when we consider than Dee was born in 1527 and Elizabeth in 1533. The fabled relationship between Nectanebus and Alexander is similar in many respects to that of the Druid Merlin with King Arthur.

Alexander the Great conquered Egypt in 332 BC, taking it out of the hands of the Persian occupiers and placing it under the domain of the Greeks for the next three centuries. During this period, there was a complete fusion between Greek and Egyptian magic. The Greeks eagerly absorbed Egyptian concepts of the gods and the nature of the soul. The exoteric religion and philosophy of the Greeks resisted this mingling, but more and more the esoteric doctrines showed an Egyptian influence. Greek theurgy, or god-magic, is primarily Egyptian in origin. It is the root of modern Western high magic.

The attraction the Egyptian hierophants held for the Greek philosophers was not wholly their wonderworking reputation. Egyptian occult philosophy contained the most profound and subtle wisdom about the nature of the gods and humanity, the structure of the universe, the hierarchy of spiritual realms, the workings of the human mind, advanced medical techniques both physical and psychological, chemistry, botany, ancient history, astronomy, and a host of other matters. Egyptian learning held the same fascination for the Greeks that classical learning exerted over Europeans during the Renaissance—it opened a whole unexplored vista of knowledge. The esoteric doctrines of Egypt came to form the heart of the Greek school of philosophy known as Neoplatonism, which is based on a magical view of the world.

Greece did possess its own indigenous magic. This was prac-

An amulet for vanquishing the malice of foes, from the Graeco-Egyptian period.
—from Egyptian Magic *by E. A. Wallis Budge, London, 1901*

ticed by the Witches of Thessaly, a region in northern Greece, who were reputed to possess incredible powers such as the ability to draw down the Moon from heaven, to move standing corn from field to field, to uproot trees, to make the stars all fall together, to stop the course of the Sun and turn day into night, and other prodigal feats recorded by the poets.

It is interesting that the division of Greek magic into Egyptian theurgy, practiced by a philosopher class made up largely of men, and native Witchcraft, practiced mainly by rural women, is reproduced in later European history when magic was divided into a ceremonial branch called theurgy, which was usually worked by literate males, and an indigenous folk branch called Witchcraft, which did not require book learning and which was usually worked, or perceived to be worked, by females. The perception, false though it is, of theurgy as the magic of the noble and Witchcraft as the magic of the peasant persists even today.

Greek Witches descended from female religious cults such as that devoted to Dionysus, or Bacchus. These bacchantes worshiped Bacchus with frenzied abandon and are credited in fable with tearing gentle Orpheus into pieces in their religious madness. Entertaining accounts of Thessalian Witches and Witchcraft occur in *The Golden Ass* of Lucius Apuleius and the *Pharsalia* of Lucan.

It is not to be expected that a seafaring, trading society like that of the Greeks could resist foreign influences on its culture and beliefs. The magic of Greek Witches was not purely native but was influenced indirectly by religious practices imported from Syria and other Eastern cultures. For example, Dionysus took on many of the attributes of the Phrygian god Sabazius and the Lydian god Bassareus. But the magic of the Witches is certainly more indigenous than Egyptian theurgy. In tracing sources, it is sometimes difficult to know where to call a halt. Ultimately all magic is shamanic.

In 30 BC, the Emperor Augustus took control of Egypt out of the hands of the Ptolemies and placed it under the authority of Rome. By this time, Greek ideas in philosophy, art, and religion had completely permeated Roman culture. The Romans were great organizers, warriors, and builders but possessed little creative originality. They drank in Greek and Egyptian mysticism like a thirsty sponge and made it their own, just as they adopted wholesale the Greek art of drama and the Greek gods. The magic described by the Roman poets such as Virgil and Ovid is really Greek magic.

Along with the overwhelming influence of Greek and Egyptian culture, strong occult currents flowed from farther east. The gods and goddesses of Persia, Syria, and other Eastern nations began to appear in Roman temples. Attempts were made by Augustus to ban these foreign gods, but these attempts proved unsuccessful. Rome became a great bubbling cauldron of magical influences. The Roman Empire extended across the world and came into intimate contact with many strange ideas and practices. Some the Romans were able to suppress. Others proved too vigorous and were simply tolerated and absorbed into the body of the empire.

Under Roman peace, it was possible to travel and exchange ideas through written correspondence to an extent never before known. A Roman might visit the Druidic priesthood in Britain, receive initiation into the mysteries of Egypt under the hierophants of Isis, consult the oracle of Apollo at Delphi, and learn the art of astrology in Chaldea. Or he could remain in his native city and do the same things. Rome drew magicians, teachers, astrologers, and priests like a magnet. It was the city of wealth and power.

A priestess of Bacchus.
—*from a painting by John Collier*

Two influences were especially important in the subsequent development of Western magic. The first was the magical tradition of Zoroaster that came out of Persia. This comprises all the techniques attributed to the magi, the priesthood of Persia that gave magic its name. Pliny the Elder, who wrote at this time, says: "Without doubt magic arose in Persia with Zoroaster" (*Natural History*, bk. XXX, ch. II). This view was almost universal among ancient writers. Pliny mentions a Greek magician named Hermippus who had preserved two million verses supposedly composed by Zoroaster. In his own work, Pliny records hundreds of fragments attributed to the magi, most on the subject of magical cures for disease. The *Chaldean Oracles*, attributed to Zoroaster, play an important part in some modern rituals.

The second significant Eastern incursion into Roman magic came from Judea. Pliny says: "There is yet another branch of magic, derived from Moses, Jannes, Lotapes, and the Jews, but living many thousand years after Zoroaster" (ibid.). Jewish magic was not at that time the Kabbalah, which grew up centuries later, but undoubtedly it focused on amulets, which contained names of God and spirits written in words of power in the sacred Hebrew characters, and involved number magic.

There is a cross-current here—remember, the Jews were supposed to have been captives in Egypt, where Moses studied the esoteric techniques of uttering the words of power correctly. In the New Testament, it is written: "And Moses was learned in all the wisdom of the Egyptians, and was mighty in words and in deeds" (Acts 7:22). The true formative influence on Jewish magic was probably Babylonian rather than Egyptian. The Babylonians were obsessed with complex demonic hierarchies, and this is reflected in Jewish occultism.

The Romans were perhaps the most superstitious race that ever lived on earth. They eagerly embraced the Chaldean art of astrology, and numerous astrology textbooks circulated throughout the Empire, the most famous of which in the present day is the *Matheseos* of Firmicus Maternus, a late work of the 4th century that integrates all the teachings of older texts in a logical, compact format.

The Roman techniques of divination and of reading omens, without which no state or important private business could be conducted, came largely from the Etruscans, an older culture that flour-

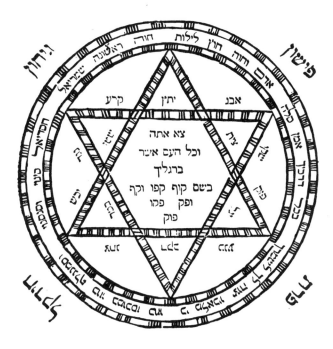

Hebrew amulet in the form of a hexagram containing holy names and sacred verses.
from The Book of Raziel

ished on the northern Italian peninsula centuries before the rise of
Rome. The arts of reading the entrails of sacrificed animals (and in
early times of men), of interpreting the fall of lightning bolts and
the flight of birds, or analyzing the movements and sounds of animals were pure Etruscan. The Etruscans by their own account came
from Lydia in Asia Minor. Roman diviners were trained in Etruria
to insure a uniformly high standard of competence.

Although the Romans were aware of the indigenous magic of
Northern and Western Europe, they do not appear to have been
greatly influenced by it. Northern Europe was at that period a
trackless forest filled with warring barbarian tribes. Celtic magic
may have found its highest expression in the practices of the
Druids. Julius Caesar had communications with Druids during his
northern wars, and Cicero was personally acquainted with a Druid
named Divitiacus. The headquarters of the Druidic brotherhood
was in Britain, but each year they held a great convocation in Gaul.

They communicated their secret teachings only by the spoken word, but were highly educated and used Greek in ordinary written communications. Druids believed in reincarnation. The Emperor Augustus forbad Roman citizens to practice Druidic rites, so some attraction must have existed for them among the Romans. The Druids were further suppressed by Tiberius and Claudius.

German magic was embodied in the runes, 24 occult symbols that also served as letters of writing, supposed to have been received by the god Woden during a mystical trial of endurance. The god allowed himself to be bound to the trunk of the great ash tree Yggdrasill, which is the axis of the world, for nine days and nights without food and water. He peered into the very heart of the earth and snatched up the fiery runes with a cry of mingled pain and triumph, and at that moment his bonds burst asunder.

The use of runes was common throughout northern Europe. At the time of the Caesars, they had yet to undergo the evolution that would in later centuries result in different rune alphabets in Scandinavia and England. Then, there was only the 24-rune elder *futhark*. The Roman historian Tacitus mentions them in his short work *Germany* (sec. 10) without actually naming them, but runes do not seem to have been widely adopted by the Romans for magic. The German magicians were probably shamans. Little solid information is possessed about their religious practices.

After the downfall of Rome during the Dark Ages of Europe, this rich magical broth might have been lost had it not been preserved in the libraries of the great monasteries and practiced within the rising empire of Islam. Greek and Roman magical texts were translated into Arabic in Spain and other Moslem strongholds of learning. The art of astrology was especially esteemed by the Arabs, perhaps because it is a mathematical art and they were great mathematicians.

Under the threatening but often benign yoke of Islam, the Jews developed the doctrines of the Kabbalah. The *Zohar* was written in Spain in the obscure Aramaic tongue by Moses de Leon between 1280 and 1286. Although other seminal works are centuries older, they received their greatest scrutiny by the Jewish mystics of Spain in this same period, which was a flourishing time in Jewish esoteric thought. Some of the works existed in both Herbrew and Arabic versions, but the lack of Latin texts kept the ideas of the

Kabbalah from being readily assimilated into Christian Europe. Hebrew was not a common language among non-Jews.

All this changed with the writings of two men. The first is Giovanni Pico della Mirandola (1463–94), an Italian who began to study the Kabbalah under the tutelage of a Jew named Flavius Mithradates who had converted to Christianity and so felt free to convey the sacred teachings. Mithradates translated some Kabbalistic texts and helped Pico unravel their meaning. It was the aim of both men to use Kabbalism to explain and exalt the mysteries of Christianity and to synthesize Christian and Jewish occultism.

In 1486, Pico carried a collection of his own *Conclusions* based upon his study of the Kabbalah to Rome, where he hoped to publicly debate them. They were never debated, but they were published. Included among them are such assertions as "no science can better convince us of the divinity of Jesus Christ than magic and the Kabbalah." The *Conclusions* were not solely Kabbalistic but also concerned Hermetic philosophy, the Orphic hymns, the *Chaldean Oracles,* and Platonic and Neoplatonic esoteric doctrines.

The second man responsible for the integration of the Kabbalah into European occultism was the German Johannes Reuchlin (1455–1522), who under the inspiration of Pico's ideas made a thorough study of Hebrew and the texts of the Kabbalah and wrote the immensely influential *De Verbo Mirifico* (1494) and *De Arte Cabalistica* (1517). Reuchlin was committed to making the Kabbalah a Christian magic, thereby absorbing its occult potency into Christianity, through the use of the name of Jesus as a word of power.

During the Renaissance the great books of Greece and Rome were being rediscovered and debated in the universities. The very different disciplines of classical and Jewish magic, both newly opened to European thinkers, were merged and Christianized to purge them of their pagan taint. The whole subject received a popular impetus with the publication in 1531–3 of *De Occulta Philosophia Liber Tres (Three Books of Occult Philosophy)* by the German magician Henry Cornelius Agrippa (1486–1535).

Agrippa was firmly committed to magic as a path to knowledge and salvation. He had not only studied the works of Reuchlin, Pico and other contemporary writers on classical magic such as Marsilio Ficino, but had also read many of the grimoires on practi-

Johannes Reuchlin, father of the Western Kabbalah.
    —from a 19th-century German engraving

cal magic that circulated in manuscript form. He had himself experimented extensively with ritual magic as a young man under the guidance of his magical master, Johannes Trithemius (1462–1516), abbot of the Benedictine monastery at Spannheim and later of the one at Wurzburg. Agrippa had travelled all over Europe talking with astrologers, alchemists and magicians and corresponded with those he could not reach personally. His *Occult Philosophy* was the first encyclopedia of magic and proved immensely popular as a source book to scholars, artists, and priests seeking to understand the new occult ideas.

At the same time Agrippa was writing his *Occult Philosophy,*

Renaissance magician Cornelius Agrippa.

—from Scheible's Das Kloster, *Stuttgart, 1846*

Witches were being burned or hung in wholesale lots all over Europe. In fact Agrippa himself, in the course of his duties as magistrate of the German town of Metz, was able, at great personal risk, to save the life of one such unfortunate woman accused of Witchcraft. Part of his defense was that she knew nothing about magic—something he could easily prove, since he was widely recognized as an expert on the subject.

The magical practices of European Witches are not well known but must have consisted largely of folk remedies and local superstitions, since those accused of Witchcraft were primarily uneducated peasant women. The few nobles who dabbled in magic and were accused of Witchcraft were more likely to have access to the grimoires and the books being written in that period on Greek and Jewish magic, but usually they were concerned with straightforward crimes of abortion and poisoning. Often the nobles were guided in these black arts by their servants, but this sort of superstitious criminal activity can scarcely be called magic.

Whatever ritual and magical practices were performed by legitimate Witches, if indeed there were any Witches as we understand the term, have been lost. Perhaps some shadow of their nature can be gained by studying the records of the Witch trials, but these are so filled with lies and fantasies as to be almost worthless as historical documents. Modern Witches work mainly in the classical Greek tradition as it has descended through Ficino and Agrippa. Their magic has more in common with the Witchcraft of ancient Greece than with medieval Europe.

Agrippa's influence on practicing magicians has been immense. John Dee, the magician and court advisor to Elizabeth I of England, relied on methods described by Agrippa in his early communications with spirits, communications that would later yield the Enochian language and spirit hierarchy so influential in modern ritual magic. All the subsequent European pretenders to the magical art such as Cagliostro and the Comte de Saint Germain were undoubtedly very familiar with Agrippa's work.

In 1801, the English occultist Francis Barrett plagiarized a large portion of the *Occult Philosophy*, adding to it bits and pieces from other works, and brought it out in a handsome volume with hand-colored plates and steel engravings titled *The Magus*. It was his purpose to establish a magical society based upon this work, but nothing is known about his success or failure. It seems probable that his students became disillusioned when they realized how little of the wisdom he claimed actually belonged to him. Nonetheless, *The Magus* exerted an important shaping influence on the magical system developed by the Hermetic Order of the Golden Dawn.

This brings us to the 19th century, when the modern occult movement that continues in the present really began. In the cen-

*Francis Barrett, who plagiarized much of an earlier English
edition of Agrippa's Occult Philosophy in his work,* The Magus *(1801).*

turies between the Renaissance and the Industrial Revolution
magic did not altogether die, but it languished in obscurity and
was seriously pursued by only a few solitary scholars, small
groups of university students, and of course the cunning men and
wise women of local villages who had their own hereditary tradition. In the 19th century, magic once again flowered forth and
became a daring, fashionable diversion for artists and intellectuals.
This modern rebirth will be the subject of the next chapter.

Eliphas Levi
—*frontispiece to* Transcendental Magic, *London, 1896*

CHAPTER FOUR

MAGIC IN THE MODERN AGE

The impetus for the modern revival of ritual magic in English- and French-speaking nations came from the writings of Alphonse Louis Constant (1810-75), better known by his pen name of Eliphas Levi.

The son of a cobbler, Levi escaped a life of poverty by showing a scholastic aptitude at an early age and declaring a desire to serve the Catholic Church. He obtained in this way a free education. He ascended to the rank of deacon but balked at becoming a celibate priest. In 1836 he left the seminary of Saint-Sulpice and quickly became entangled with a group of mystics and occultists while barely supporting himself by private tutoring and whatever hack writing jobs he was able to find. In 1841, he wrote a tract called *La Bible de la Liberte (The Bible of Liberty),* extolling the virtues of mystical socialism, and was placed into prison for six (or eight) months on the charges of blasphemy and subversion.

While his interest in socialism faded with his youth, his fascination for occultism grew. In 1854, he published the first half of his great work, *Dogme et Ritual de la Haute Magie (The Dogma and Ritual of High Magic).* The second half came out two years later. His other significant works are the *Histoire de la Magie (History of Magic),* published in 1860, and *La Clef des Grands Mysteres (The Key of Great Mysteres)* in 1861. He produced other writings on occultism, but they are much inferior to these three.

Reading these books today, it is difficult to understand why they aroused any excitement. They are verbose, diffuse, and shallow. Much of what Levi says is mere bombast, and a large portion

Stanislas de Guaita, 19th-century French occultist.

of his statements is historically incorrect. Levi was talking through his hat, pretending to a much greater knowledge than he actually possessed, but he wrote in such a winning style that his readers were entranced. The French occultist Stanislas de Guaita remarked that Levi's books were like *"le coup de foudre occultiste"* (the occult clap of thunder). From then on, his destiny was clear. De Guaita was not the only one to have this reaction. The English magician Aleister Crowley thought highly enough of Levi to declare himself Levi's reincarnation.

The most important feature of the *Dogma and Ritual* from a practical standpoint is its emphasis on the Tarot, a set of 78 playing cards of uncertain origin. Levi was not the first to regard the images of the 22 Tarot trumps as occult glyphs, but he was instrumental in relating them to the Hebrew alphabet and fusing them into the frame of the Western tradition of magic. Also significant is Levi's inclusion of the numerical magic squares of the seven ancient planets, emphasized by Agrippa and prominently used in many modern magical operations.

The royalties from his books were not enough to support Levi.

He gave private lessons in occultism to those who could afford them to supplement his income, often charging outrageous sums for very brief talks—the aunt of Madame Blavatsky once complained that she paid 40 francs for one minute of conversation with the great man (King and Sutherland 1982, 57). Levi himself declared that he demanded nothing in payment from his students, and also refused nothing. Presumably they did not remain his students long if their "gifts" were meager.

His influence was even greater in England than in France. By his own account, he visited London in 1854. At the instigation of a friend of the famous novelist Edward Bulwer-Lytton (1803-73), Levi conducted an extended evocation of the ghost of Apollonius of Tyana. Bulwer-Lytton was the writer of such influential works as *Zanoni* (1842), an occult novel about an immortal magician, and *The Coming Race* (1871), an early science-fiction novel that set forth the notion of *vril*, the potent, all-pervading occult energy responsible for the destruction of Atlantis. Apollonius was one of the greatest magicians of the ancient world, an almost Christlike figure who lived during the reign of the Roman emperor Nero. If there is any truth at all in this story, it suggests that Levi's fame rests not solely on his books but also on his personal charm and persuasiveness.

While Levi was evoking Apollonius in a London flat, a young Russian woman named Helena Petrovna Blavatsky (1831–91) was, again by her own account, studying esoteric Buddhism and learning the secrets of the Tibetan *bon* religion in the Himalayas. This knowledge, along with countless other scraps and pieces of occult lore, she would later stitch together into the bewildering fabric of her two mammoth works, *Isis Unveiled* (1877) and *The Secret Doctrine* (1888). In 1858 she returned from Tibet to Russia and gained renown as a spirit medium, a talent she found very useful in her later years. She traveled to the United States around 1870 and became an American citizen, achieving equal fame as a medium on this side of the water. With the aid of Henry Olcott, she founded the Theosophical Society in New York in 1875.

Blavatsky had immense personal energy and charm. She convinced her followers that she possessed magical powers, which she occasionally demonstrated using the tricks she had picked up during her years as a medium. Despite her exposure as a fraud on several occasions, her disciples continued to regard her as little less

H. P. Blavatsky, founder of the Theosophical Society.
—from the frontispiece to Isis Unveiled, *New York, 1877*

than divine and hailed her turbid writings as sacred writ.

Theosophy is not truly in the mainstream of the Western tradition, but it exerted a powerful influence over the minds of those who were weary of the austerities of Protestantism and were eager to embrace a magical view of the world. It owes its importance to the openness with which it received new members and the early date of its establishment as an organized society. Although the Hindu and Tibetan doctrines it taught were far from orthodox, there was at that time nothing readily available in English translation to dispute their accuracy. Many students who would later graduate to the Golden Dawn cut their teeth on Theosophy.

Indeed, in the early years, the founders of the Golden Dawn tried to keep up cordial relations with the Theosophists but were snubbed by Blavatsky, who perhaps rightly decided she had no need of their good opinion.

It is to the Hermetic Order of the Golden Dawn that modern ritual magic owes its form and content. The story of the founding of this Victorian magical society is romantic, mysterious, and completely bogus. In 1887 a London coroner, Freemason, and Theosophist, Dr. William Wynn Westcott (1848–1925), acquired a manuscript containing five rituals written in the form of a cipher. There are various conflicting accounts of just where he got it. In it was the name and address of a Fraulein Anna Sprengel. He wrote to her expressing interest in the rituals, and she authorized him to establish an English branch of the German occult order *Die Goldene Dämmerung* (The Golden Dawn). Westcott got together with two fellow members of the Societas Rosicruciana in Anglia, an occult Masonic fraternity, and with their help set up the Isis-Urania Temple of the Hermetic Order of the Golden Dawn in London in 1888.

One of Westcott's friends, Samuel Liddell Mathers (1854–1918), expanded the skeletal rituals in the cipher into a practical working form. He was the son of a London clerk. As a youth he had been deeply influenced by Bulwer-Lytton's novel *Zanoni*. Heavily involved in Masonic activities, he spent his time studying the occult manuscripts in the British Museum Library. He had already translated a portion of the Latin *Kabbalah Denudata* of Knorr von Rosenroth, and in fact had given Madame Blavatsky a copy of his manuscript in 1886. Mathers was the most skilled in practical magic of the three chiefs of the Order.

The other chief, Dr. William Robert Woodman (1828–91), played little part in the Order due to his death early in its history. He was a scholar of Hebrew and the Kabbalah and probably had the most solid education of the three. Ithell Colquhoun asserts that Woodman was Westcott's guru for seven years (Colquhoun 1975, 172).

Although it matters little from a practical standpoint, it seems probable that Westcott concocted the cipher manuscript, along with his subsequent correspondence with the nonexistent Anna Sprengel, merely to provide authority for the Order rituals. He may have done this in collusion with either or both of his Masonic brothers. As the Golden Dawn evolved, it became expedient to break off this apocryphal German connection and establish direct communication with the Secret Chiefs, spiritual beings of immense power and wisdom who began to convey their occult teachings directly through Mathers and his wife, Moina, the sister of the famous French philosopher Henri Bergson.

If Westcott was the organizational genius behind the Golden Dawn, Mathers was its magical heart. He was completely dedicated to the practice of magic, and it was his influence that saved the Golden Dawn from becoming just another vapid Masonic lodge or quasi-religious society. In 1892 he formed his own psychic link with the Secret Chiefs and, at great physical cost to his health, received from them the purely magical teachings that constitute the inner or Second Order, the Ordo Rosae Rubeae et Aureae Crucis.

Mathers was completely sincere in his belief that he was supernaturally inspired. He lived in a perpetual waking dream, one foot in the material world and one foot in the astral at all times. The victim of persistent delusions of grandeur, he believed himself to be a Scottish lord and took to wearing a kilt and signing his name "MacGregor Mathers." He confessed that he was not really certain himself if the Secret Chiefs were living men or spirits, but he tended to believe they were humans possessed of superhuman powers. He and his wife communicated with them in direct face-to- face meetings, by clairaudience, through rapping tables and the movements of a pendulum, and by copying the writings in books that mysteriously appeared and then vanished.

The time must have been ripe for magic in England. There is no other way to explain the fashionable attraction the Golden Dawn held for young intellectuals and artists. Among its more prominent members were the famous actress Florence Farr, who was the lover of George Bernard Shaw; the poet William Butler Yeats; his lover, the Irish political activist, Maud Gonne; Allan Bennett, who would later found the *Buddhist Review* and the Buddhist Society in Britain; the writers Arthur Machen, Algernon Blackwood, and Arthur Edward Waite; Constance Wilde, the wife of Oscar Wilde; Dion Fortune; and of course Aleister Crowley.

Waite, Fortune, and Crowley all went on to form their own occult orders when the Golden Dawn gradually began to collapse into chaos. Waite's group, which continued to meet in the old Isis-Urania Temple, relied on Christianized Golden Dawn rituals and

MacGregor Mathers, one of the founders of the Golden Dawn.

had as little to do with magic as possible. In 1907 there was a formal concordat signed with another offshoot, the Stella Matutina. In 1914 Waite, according to his own account, closed down the Isis-Urania Temple and thus abolished his personal mutation of the Golden Dawn. It was probably a great relief to him since he had not the least talent or sympathy for magic.

Dion Fortune, a determined woman born with the unlovely name Violet Mary Firth (1891–1948), founded the Fraternity of the Inner Light in 1922 with the blessing of Mathers' widow, Moina, ostensibly as a public outer order that would attract suitable candidates into the still-very-secret Golden Dawn. Fortune declared her independence in 1928 and then went her own way, building up a small but dedicated following at her London temple. After her death, the renamed Society of the Inner Light followed the pattern of other occult orders and moved away from magic toward religion.

Aleister Crowley (1875–1947) was the most successful of the three writers who went on from the original Golden Dawn to found their own occult movements. He was utterly dedicated to the practice of magic in the way that Mathers had been, pursuing it to the exclusion of all lesser concerns such as physical health, monetary prosperity, a stable family life, social respectability, and his own sanity. Fortunately his mind was founded on the bedrock of English middle-class reality. He succeeded in driving many of those around him insane but preserved his own peculiar view of life intact.

Crowley's system of magick (spelled with a "k") draws upon the Golden Dawn teachings, higher yoga, the sex techniques of the German occult society known as the Ordo Templi Orientis, and the teachings Crowley himself received from his spirit master, Aiwass, in Cairo in 1904, which are recorded in his *Book of the Law*. The great value of Crowley's writings is that there is nothing theoretical about them. Crowley spent his whole life testing these magical methods to the limit of his intellectual and physical stamina. He wrote from personal experience.

Born Edward Alexander Crowley, he was the only child of a wealthy brewer. At an early age he reacted strongly against his puritanical upbringing. His father died when he was a boy. As soon as Crowley came into his inheritance he spent it on extravagant and decadent amusements. Gifted with a fine natural intellect, he failed to get a degree at Cambridge due to his indifference toward his required studies. Robust of body, he entertained himself by climbing mountains but was troubled throughout his adult life by asthma, for which he began to take opium.

He received initiation into the Golden Dawn in 1898 under the tutoring of Allan Bennett. Crowley was never well liked by the rank and file of the Order. His wildness offended their Victorian sensibilities. In 1909 he established his own occult order, the Argenteum Astrum. The name was borrowed from one of the

A young Aleister Crowley as he looked during his days in the Golden Dawn.

already existing offshoots of the Golden Dawn. In 1912 he was received into the German Ordo Templi Orientis and made head of the British branch of the O.T.O. the following year. Crowley enthusiastically embraced the Tantric-based sex magic of the O.T.O. It perfectly suited his own sensual, anarchistic temperament.

At Cefalu on the island of Sicily, Crowley established his

Tantra utilizes sexual energies generated by prolonged arousal to bring about alterations in consciousness. This energy can be used for magic.
—from a 19th-century Indian manuscript

Abbey of Thelema, named after a reference in the writings of Rabelais, in 1920. Serious occultists and others merely seeking cheap thrills beat a path to his door to receive his magical wisdom. This was the high point of his life. After Cefalu things turned sour. Try as he would, he could not shake off his heroin addiction—it seemed the will of the poppy was stronger than the will of the Beast. His personal fortune long since exhausted on foolish extravagancies, he was forced to subsist on the charity of his followers. The thought of working for a living never even entered his mind. Fortunately for him, he was able to gull several quite wealthy patrons, but he wasted their money as fast as they sent it to him. He died in poverty a hopeless heroin addict, his magical powers long since lost, generally neglected by those who had lionized him during his prime.

All three of these former Golden Dawn members promulgated its system of magic in ever-widening circles, both through their copious writings and directly by means of their occult societies. Crowley had the most enduring success of the three, largely on the strength of his many books. His disciples such as Frater Achad carried the magic of Thelema to America, where it is now firmly rooted. Among his followers he has achieved the status of demigod, and he has certainly lived up to his magical motto, "I will endure."

Crowley was the first to publish the until then secret documents of the Golden Dawn. They appeared in his periodical, *The Equinox*, beginning in 1909, very much against the wishes of Mathers, who failed in a court action to have them suppressed. Crowley did not credit Mathers as their author, and indeed there is uncertainty about who actually wrote what of the Golden Dawn rituals and teachings. They would seem to be beyond Mathers' talents, to judge by his other published works, which are mostly translations. Perhaps the Secret Chiefs actually did dictate them psychically to Mathers and his wife.

After an extensive examination of their works, I find in both Mathers and Crowley a surprising lack of creativity. Crowley was especially barren, although he possessed great ability to reshape and manipulate the works of others. He was a user, not a maker. The felicity and wit of his many excellent writings often obscures this essential lack of originality. If Mathers did consciously write all the Golden Dawn rituals and invent the occult correspondences used by the Order, he was a creative genius, but there is no sign of genius in his other works.

Israel Regardie (1907-85) read *The Equinox* in America, wrote to Crowley, and was given permission to come to Europe to serve as his personal secretary in 1928. In 1934 he was admitted to the Hermes lodge of the Stella Matutina, where he obtained the Golden Dawn documents he would edit and publish in four volumes between 1938-40 through Aries Press of Chicago. This was the first time the true Golden Dawn system of magic had been fully revealed and accurately represented. The books sold slowly at first but had, and continue to have, an enormous influence on occult groups and individuals seeking a legitimate structure for their ritual practices.

There have been few truly gifted solitary magicians in this century, but in passing it is worth mentioning Austin Osman Spare (1886-1956), a graphic artist who created his own unique brand of symbol magic. He was drawn to Crowley and became a member of the Argenteum Astrum in 1910, contributing two drawings to *The Equinox* (I:2, 140 & 161). Spare's magic, described in his works

Gerald Brosseau Gardner, father of modern witchcraft.

The Book of Pleasure (1913), *The Focus of Life* (1921), and the *Anathema of Zos* (1924), used sigils created by combining letters in significant phrases into a single visual symbol. These were then activated by sexual energy.

His writings are obscure and deliberately difficult, but his drawings that depict the spirits he actually observed moving in the space around him are of immense magical potency. In fact, they can be quite dangerous to the unwary, as they are apt to come alive if looked upon for any length of time. Spare was following in the footsteps of William Blake, who also saw spirits with his waking eyes and sometimes made drawings of them. It is difficult to imagine how so great an artist as Spare can have contrived to die in poverty and obscurity, but this was his fate, a fate he shared with Mathers, Crowley, and many other magicians of earlier ages. Magic is not the short path to riches.

In 1954 an ex-customs official named Gerald Brosseau Gardner (1884-1964) published *Witchcraft Today*, in which he claimed that Witchcraft existed in the modern world, that it had descended in an unbroken hereditary line from the Middle Ages and beyond, and that moreover he had personally been initiated into a coven of Witches in England just prior to the outbreak of the Second World War. The book caused a minor sensation. Curious people wrote to the author asking how they could themselves be initiated into the benign nature religion he described so eloquently. Some of these Gardner began to initiate, and before long covens of Gardnerian Witches were springing up all over Europe and North America.

Gardner was familiar with the theory of the anthropologist Margaret A. Murray that the Witchcraft of the Middle Ages was the survival of an ancient Goddess religion. She had caused a stir in scientific circles with her two provocative works, *The Witch-Cult in Western Europe* (1921) and *The God of the Witches* (1931). Murray wrote a brief and vapid preface to *Witchcraft Today* that said very little but that lent the authority of her scholarship to his book. Gardner also knew Aleister Crowley, who in return for a large fee made Gardner the head of an O.T.O. lodge in England.

It seems fairly clear that Gardner's story about a surviving hereditary Witch coven at Christchurch near the New Forest was false. It is possible he was initiated into some sort of occult group. At the time, he was associating with the daughter of the Theosophist Annie Besant. But the group was not composed of hereditary Witches. Gardner concocted his Book of Shadows, a collection of rituals supposedly received from the coven, from the book *Aradia* by Charles Godfrey Leland, which treats of Witchcraft in Italy; from the writings of Aleister Crowley; from the poetry of Rudyard Kipling; and from a scattering of other sources that struck his fertile fancy.

The other prominent influence on the rise of modern Witchcraft is the Englishman Alex Sanders, who according to his biographer June Johns (*King of the Witches*, 1969), was initiated into the craft in 1933 at age seven by his grandmother, a hereditary Witch. Johns further says that Sanders was elected "king of the Witches" in 1965 by a group of his own followers.

Sanders' Book of Shadows is said by Leo Martello to be "a direct replica of Gardner's." Nonetheless, Sanders' flamboyant personal style attracted a large number of acolytes who were initiated for money by Alex and his wife, Maxine. One of these initiations is charmingly described in all its sordidness by Margot Adler in *Drawing Down the Moon* (pt. II, ch. 5). Sanders' followers are called Alexandrian Witches to distinguish them from Gardnerian Witches and other later mutations of the craft. A strong aspect of Alexandrian Witchcraft is ritual magic, and this is firmly in the Golden Dawn system via Aleister Crowley.

Modern Witches had the writings of Margaret A. Murray and Gerald Gardner and Charles Leland to draw upon for the religious aspects of Witchcraft, or Wicca as it is also known, but these sources were insufficient when it came to the practical details of ritual magic. Some covens got around this by denying the importance of magic and excluding it as much as possible from their worship, but most drew upon the Golden Dawn system indirectly through a network of derivative writings. Many of the authors of these writings had themselves no clear idea where their magical techniques actually originated. By and large, Witch magic is a simplified form of high ceremonial magic in the Western tradition— simplified, not because Witches are simple-minded, but because the focus in Wicca is more on celebration and worship than it is on magic.

Although the Golden Dawn claimed a German authority through Fräulein Sprengel, it is likely this woman never existed. German occultism has always been a bit distant from that practiced in the rest of Europe and in English- and French-speaking nations around the world. The German magicians relied for many of their practices on the Faust books, a loose collection of grimoires attributed to Johannes Faust, a wandering juggler and mountebank mentioned with contempt by the Abbot Trithemius in a letter written in 1507. The legend of how Faust sold his soul to the devil is entertainingly presented in plays by Christopher Marlowe and

The Germanic god Thor.

Johann Wolfgang von Goethe. For some reason, the Faust grimoires never achieved widespread currency in England, even though the magic they present is in the Western tradition and very much in the style of other grimoires.

Even more of a divisive factor in separating German occultism from that worked in the rest of Europe is the early incorporation of the Germanic runes, 24 symbols of magical potency that were also used as letters in writing. About the time the Golden Dawn was gaining strength in England, a German visionary named Guido von List was trying to revive interest in the ancient runes among occultists in Germany seeking a practical basis for a purely Aryan magic that had been purged of Jewish mysticism, which they regarded as a weakening and corrupting influence. In 1908 List published *The Secret of the Runes*, setting forth his crack-brained theory that all runes came from a primal 18-rune alphabet that lay concealed in the 28 stanzas of the "Havamal" poem in the Norse *Poetic Edda*.

It is strange that Mathers never incorporated runes into any of the Golden Dawn teachings, and equally strange that Crowley did not use them, since he must have had some knowledge of their existence. but very little was known about the runes until quite recently, and, as I have said, neither Mathers nor Crowley were original thinkers. Perhaps they simply could not imagine how to incorporate runes into their magical systems.

There is another possibility. Both Mathers and Crowley fondly claimed to be descended from noble Celtic families in Scotland. Both claims were equally without foundation. Runes are part of the Saxon tradition in England, not the Celtic tradition. Mathers and Crowley may have harbored a secret distaste for such blatantly Teutonic magic, which had no part at all in the great current of Western occultism that flowed from Egypt and Greece, and no part in the indigenous tradition of Celtic magic.

Runes really belong to the aboriginal or shamanic branch of magic. Only in the last decade have they begun to integrate themselves with Western occultism. This reception of the runes into ritual magic is as important in the present century as the embracing of the Tarot that occurred in the previous century. Cornelius Agrippa knew nothing about the magical potential of the Tarot cards. It was the work of Eliphas Levi and the French occultists that paved the way for the full integration of the Tarot that occurred under Mathers in the Golden Dawn. Runes will undoubtedly become equally important in modern magic, and they will help to unite German occultism with the occultism of English- and French-speaking nations.

CHAPTER FIVE

WHAT YOU CAN
EXPECT FROM MAGIC

Those who approach ritual magic for the first time usually harbor wildly unrealistic expectations shaped by their confused and erroneous notions of what magic is and how it works. Attracted in the beginning by the aura of mystery and the promise of power, drawn by the lure of the forbidden and the spice of danger surrounding this most ancient art, they become cynical when magic fails to live up to their fantasies. This bitter pass marks the end of progress for most students.

There is nothing unnatural in such a revulsion of feeling—we learn by doing, or attempting to do, and by making mistakes. A few who persevere in the face of barren reality reawaken to a new understanding of magic in which the boasts of the ancients seem modest. They attain a transcendent view of the universe where contradictory truths exist side by side in harmony and things are never exactly as they seem on the surface. Here I would like to give some idea of what a serious person willing to work and learn can ultimately expect to get out of magic on the personal level.

You must first be aware that you perceive the world around you in a way that is conditioned by the conventions and prejudices of society. When you look at a street, or a tree, or a flower, your awareness of that thing is not separate and unvarying but an integral part of your own mind. You shape your world by the way you selectively interact with sense impressions. The world you are able to perceive is limited by your mind and senses, but within the parameters imposed by your own human nature an amazing amount of variation is possible. This potential for differing world views is not widely known. Even philosophers and physicists possessed of the most subtle mental abilities automatically assume that their view of the world is the only view. It is this hidebound ignorance that is the greatest check on the progress of modern science.

You have the latent power to alter the fundamental nature of your universe because you, and you alone, have created that universe in the first place. Unfortunately, you did not create it independently. Your free will played a relatively small part in its composition. In building your world, you followed the dictates of your culture and all its complex web of beliefs and taboos, accepting them automatically without examination or criticism. So mechanical and unthinking was this acceptance, which began long before you possessed a symbolic concept of self or could express your ideas and feelings in language, that you assume it was inevitable, utterly beyond your freedom to choose. This is not true.

Although our view of the world is conditioned by our society before we attain control over our will, once this control is attained we do have the power to alter our perception of the world. Magic more than any other human pursuit gives us the ability to change our view of the world in useful ways. By changing our perception of the world, we actually do change the world itself. This is a great magical truth. It can only be rightly understood through the practice of ritual.

The second sentence of the Emerald Tablet of Hermes Trismegistus contains the great Hermetic maxim that governs all magical operations:

> What is below is like that which is above, and what is above is like that which is below: to accomplish the miracle of the One Thing.

It is based upon a magical view of the universe. "What is below" is the self-awareness of the individual, the microcosm. "What is above" is the greater, external world, the macrocosm. Below and above must be alike because they are created by the single mind that perceives both of them. Both macrocosm and microcosm exist within mind and must for this reason correspond. It is not the mind of some vast, distant supernatural being that holds them; it is *your* mind. You are the bridge. You have shaped the patterns.

The mystical magus Hermes Trismegistus, to whom the alchemical Emerald Tablet is attributed. —*from a 15th-century Italian mosaic*

Regular practice of ritual magic engenders a magical view of the world automatically in those who remain open to it. The mind is expanded on all levels. Perceptions that once seemed fixed and eternal begin to flow together. Fresh patterns are formed. Novel concepts arise. Things that before appeared to be static will be perceived to be in motion. Everything moves and changes. Nothing remains where it was or what it is. Nothing stays the same. You will see that each thing is linked with all other things that exist not just by the laws of physics but in a living way.

The Earth is a great, conscious being who thinks slow thoughts and is aware of what transpires on her surface. She has the power to nourish or chastise but is by nature loving and giving. You will understand that you are her child. You breathe her breath, drink her milk, play on her lap, and die in her arms. Once you know this to be true with your heart as well as your head, you will never be able to hurt her again.

Ritual will also change your view of yourself. There will no longer be "me" and "everything else." Everything else is you. You will not be able to run away from the events happening around you with a clear conscience once you know in your heart that they are a part of you. Moreover, you will come to understand that you are the center not just of the Earth but of the greater universe, which radiates away equally from you on all sides in a ceaselessly expanding sphere. You were not born into the world as an accident or a joke. You have a purpose to fulfill that is vital to the Soul of the World, as are the functions of all living things.

Magic will free you from the prison of the past by opening many doors of self-awareness. Instead of always looking back at what has happened in your life, you will learn to turn to the future and shape what will happen. The results of your actions will become increasingly clear, allowing you to direct your life more intelligently. This is the freedom that stems from knowledge. The more clearly you see, the less likely you are to stumble.

There is a price to be paid for freedom. A slave has no options, but a free person must choose a direction. A magical view of a world in constant flux, filled with conflicting and contradictory beliefs, can be terrifying. The loss of all the comforting certainties in life sets the soul adrift on a sea of shifting values. Many students of the art renounce the practice of magic not because it fails to give results but because the results it gives prove too potent to control. Treasured beliefs about the nature of reality slip away one by one. There is a strong impulse to grasp onto them with the desperation of a drowning man, turning the back on the chill, radiant beacon of truth. Many who test the waters of magic draw back from the edge because they sense where magic will lead them and are unwilling or unable to take the plunge. They adopt an attitude of skeptical

Amait, the Devourer of Souls, waits behind Thoth to receive sinners who fail the test of the Great Balance in the Hall of Osiris. A similar monster guards the threshold of magic and must be faced by anyone seeking occult wisdom, but its shape is different for each individual.

—from Papyrus of Ani, British Museum

contempt to mask their terror from their own minds. It is not deliberate hypocrisy, but self-preservation. Such individuals are constitutionally incapable of handling a magical view of the world.

Magic will always give you what you want—but not what you *think* you want. If you tell yourself that you are seeking a true awareness of reality when in fact you are frightened to death of what you may discover, your view of the world will remain unchanged. Similarly, if you pretend to be an altruistic lover of mankind but really are more concerned with exhibiting your power and attaining celebrity, your rituals to heal the sick are apt to fail.

The big question in the mind of most individuals who consider the study of magic is "Does it really work?" By this they mean "Does magic produce a desired result in the material world that may be objectively perceived by more than one person at a time?" The short answer is yes. Those who regularly practice rituals designed to improve their physical health or enhance their beauty and personality or succeed in business or gain love or heal others will certainly achieve these goals to a greater or lesser extent, depending on how strongly they are desired.

The long answer involves the nature of reality. Magic is affected by consciousness and belief. It is a product of the mind, and the mind has absolute control over its effects even when this control is exercised unconsciously. Consequently, magic usually operates on the margin of human awareness. Scrutiny and skepticism destroy it. Magicians are secretive not because they like sneaking around in the dark but because, when their rituals are known to others, they are apt to fail. Call it bad luck. It is very bad luck to tell others what you are seeking to accomplish through ritual before it has been achieved. Magic does change the material world, but usually not in plain sight. It operates when people have their backs turned or their eyes shut.

An important part of ritual magic involves communications with spirits, discarnate entities that possess a limited self-awareness and a certain degree of independent action within their own spheres. They are called ghosts, angels, elementals, incubi, demons, gods, and a host of other names according to the personalities and abilities they exhibit. At root they are a single spiritual essence that pervades the mind and can take on any form the mind imposes upon it. This is the same essence that constitutes our own souls. The fundamental difference between a human being and a spirit is that a human has a certain limited control over a corporeal body and a spirit usually does not. Growing up in bodies differentiates human souls from spirits. The body gives the soul a stability and a continuance that spirits lack, unless they are able to get it second hand through communion with a human being.

It is not necessary to communicate with spirits in order to work magic. Words of power, occult symbols such as the runes, and physical objects made into amulets can all convey magical potency. However, spirit magic is an integral part of the Western tradition. In the Bible frequent mention is made of spirit magic. "Regard not them that have familiar spirits, neither seek after wizards, to be defiled by them" (Leviticus 19:31). "And when they shall say unto you, Seek unto them that have familiar spirits, and unto wizards that peep and that mutter: should not a people seek unto their God?" (Isaiah 8:19). "And a man also or woman that hath a familiar spirit, or that is a wizard, shall surely be put to death:" (Leviticus 20:27). "Then said Saul unto his servants, Seek me a woman that hath a familiar spirit, that I may go to her, and enquire of her" (1 Samuel 28:7). "And he made his son pass through the fire, and observed times, and used enchantments, and dealt with familiar spirits and wizards:" (2 Kings 21:6).

A familiar spirit is a spirit that has formed an unusually close association with an individual man or woman. The familiars of the European witches of the Middle Ages were not really the animals they kept as pets but the spirits that possessed these animals as corporeal hosts through which they could gain awareness of the physical world. Spirits need physical eyes in order to see physical things. When a spirit enters into the intimate relationship of familiar, it becomes very easy for the magician to communicate with it.

Spirits in one form or another were vital in the early history of the major religions. When they were part of the orthodox religious hierarchy they were called angels; when they formed part of the hierarchy of some older, supplanted religion, they were called devils or demons. The god of the Philistine city of Ekron, Beelzeboul (Lord of the Earth), who was consulted by King Ahaziah of Israel in his illness (II Kings 1:2) was corrupted by the early Christians into the demon Beelzebub (Lord of the Flies). Similarly, the Phoenician Moon goddess Astarte was transmuted into the demon Ashtaroth.

Spirits are dismissed by modern Christian theologians as a delusion produced by mental instability. In Tibetan Buddhism, there is a strong esoteric current that flows from the ancient *bon* religion that Buddhism supplanted. Buddhist monks refer to spirits with contempt and regard them as obstacles on the path of enlightenment, yet among Tibetan magicians spirits are very prominent and are considered a vital part of their art. In Tibetan Buddhism itself, spirits have been domesticated, so to speak, and are used for such menial functions as guarding the temples. They fulfill a role similar to that of Christian saints. The tendency in modern Buddhism is to deny the value and even the reality of spirits altogether.

In modern high magic, spirits are used as mobile and semi-intelligent agents to assist in the accomplishment of the ritual purpose. I say semi-intelligent not to imply that spirits are stupid, but to indicate that their awareness is not the same as ordinary human consciousness. They may be likened to "smart" bombs that, once programed, find their target on their own initiative. Spirits tend to take instructions literally and have difficulty distinguishing between mental and physical reality as we understand this distinction. They have trouble with logic. They try very hard to say what human beings want to hear, and are convincing and persuasive in their assertions. This has led some occultists to regard them as deceitful, but in fact they usually have no intention to deceive.

Spirits communicate with human consciousness through the mind by affecting the perceptions directly, bypassing the physical senses. They manifest to human awareness in the forms our minds are equipped to comprehend—sight, sound, sensation, odor, and taste. If they do not use these sensory avenues, we remain unaware of their existence, apart from any intimation we may be able to gain indirectly from their actions.

To see or hear a spirit is the same as seeing or hearing any material thing. Spirits are completely real when they come into the awareness through the metaphors of the senses. When you feel a spirit touch you, it is actually felt on the skin and there is no doubt in your mind about whether or not you have felt something. However, the perceived nature of a spirit is usually different from the perception of a physical object. Spirits often have an imperfect control over the senses of the individual to whom they manifest. They may appear to the sight as diaphanous, transparent wraiths. Such airy spirits move with great quickness. Their shapes shift and mutate from one moment to another.

The touch of this type of spirit draws warmth from the surface of the skin and is very delicate. It is remarkably similar to a light breeze and has often been described in this way by those who have experienced it. Such spirits do not actually stir the air—it is the cooling effect of their touch that creates this impression. Spirits are quite capable of touching a human being inside the body as well as outside. I myself have had the interesting experience of feeling a spirit caress my heart in an experimental way, which caused a temporary irregularity in its rhythm. The sensation of being physically touched on one or another of the internal organs is distinctive and unmistakable.

While on the subject of the physical effects of a close contact with spirits, it should be mentioned that such contact frequently produces a sharp rise in blood pressure, resulting in a flush in the face and a ringing in the ears. This is what occurred to S. L. MacGregor Mathers, the head of the Golden Dawn, while he was in personal communion with the Secret Chiefs. If it were intense enough, it could easily produce the bleeding at the nose and ears

Mercury as the homunculus, a spirit created
within a sealed vessel by alchemical processes.
—From Mutus liber, 1702

that Mathers describes. I have not myself experienced external bleeding, but the rise in internal pressure is obvious.

Another effect of close contact is the aggravation of asthma and other bronchial complaints. I have a very slight tendency to be asthmatic. Under ordinary conditions it almost never manifests, but during close physical contact with spirits it is frequently evident. I mention this because Aleister Crowley was afflicted in his adult life by asthma. To alleviate his condition he took opium. It is my personal conviction that his asthma would have remained a very minor problem all through his life had he not taken up the practice of magic with such single-minded intensity.

There is the mistaken notion among many students of magic, who probably have never succeeded in forming a close bond with a spirit, that spirits are purely a mental phenomenon and exist only within the imagination. On the contrary, they can be very real to the perceptions. It is true that they exist solely in the mind, but then so does the bullet fired from the gun that kills you. Those

with weak constitutions should avoid too great a physical famil-
iarity with spirits. For others in sound health, there appears to me
to be relatively little danger, at least in the short term.

Spirits derive their forms, personalities, and identities from the
expectations and beliefs of the human beings with whom they
interact. They are dependent for their very existence upon the
minds through which they arise into manifestation. An adept at
magic can create a spirit from the primal spiritual essence, becoming its father and mother and giving it all its qualities with conscious deliberation. It is also possible to call forth into human
awareness a spirit that has already been formed by the expectations and beliefs of others. These are the gods, angels, and demons
of mythology and religion.

You can prove the existence of spirits to yourself easily enough
through the regular practice of ritual. You will find that you have a
harder time convincing others of their reality, even as a person with
normal sight might find it difficult to persuade a man colorblind
from birth of the wonderful difference between green and red. Spirits are experienced subjectively. A person who has been conditioned
by ritual will be able to perceive the presence of a spirit while
another person standing close by will see and hear nothing. Quite
naturally, the second person will deny the existence of the spirit. The
spirit does not exist for that person, and will not come into existence
until it is perceived directly or the effects of its actions are felt.

Writing about the nature of the spirit Nakhiel (also spelled
Nachiel—Hebrew: נכיאל), and incidentally about the nature of
reality, Aleister Crowley observed:

> Thus, when we say that Nakhiel is the "Intelligence" of
> the Sun, we do not mean that he lives in the Sun, but
> only that he has a certain rank and character; and
> although we can invoke him, we do not necessarily
> mean that he exists in the same sense of the word in
> which our butcher exists (Crowley 1976, 8).

Even if the spirit is able to cause change in his mind and body
or in his immediate physical environment, it is easy for the skeptic
to find some other explanation for the effect. If all the pictures
simultaneously fall off his walls, or if his hall mirror cracks, it is put
down to earth tremors or a passing train or a sonic boom, and if no

natural explanation can be conceived by the most extreme and ingenious efforts of the imagination, it is simply called an unfortunate coincidence. To the casual observer, that is what magic appears to be—a series of the most extraordinary coincidences.

In some ways the world has been growing over the centuries. More exotic machines let us see farther into space, reach deeper inside the atom, chart the electrical rhythms of the brain. In other ways, the world is shrinking. There was a time when everyone knew angels existed and was confident that miracles happened. Anything strange and wonderful might lie beyond the edge of the map where the ancient cartographers had written in clouds: HERE THERE BE DRAGONS. Now all the blank spaces on the map have been filled. There is no room for wonder. But there are other regions that lie beyond the flatlands of our physical sphere, regions vast and almost completely unexplored. The beings that dwell in these numberless extra-physical dimensions are more strange than myth.

Magic opens the doors on these other realities. It frees us from the prison of the predictable and allows us to perceive the universe beyond the physical level. The world we have been taught to see is like the two-dimensional surface of the ocean. By the art of ritual magic we are enabled to descend along the third dimension into the vastness of the deeps where the dragons live. If we are skillful we may even be able to steal a portion of their fire and return with it to the surface where it can be used for our own ends.

Some people have unrealistic expectations about magic.
—*from an illustration by Gustave Doré for Ariosto's* Orlando Furioso

CHAPTER SIX

WHAT YOU SHOULD NOT
EXPECT FROM MAGIC

Everyone who gets into ritual magic has pretty much the same goal in the beginning—they want to rule the world. They do not say it in so many words and may not even admit it to themselves, but they are thinking: Suppose I could learn to hurl lightning from my fingertips and bring the fortresses of evil crumbling down? Suppose I could foresee the future of the stock market and make a vast fortune for noble ends? Suppose I could control the leaders of the multinational corporations with my will and make them clean up the environment? Suppose I could destroy the stockpiles of nuclear weapons and bring about world peace? What a power trip! What an ego booster!

In some ways, magic shows the personality of an Oriental courtesan to the newcomer. She taunts and allures with promises of power. She tickles the imagination under the chin with infinite possibilities. Every time the sorcerer's apprentice is about to turn away in disillusionment, she flips the corner of her veil and reveals her smile. This is more than enough to keep those who have an innate talent for magic interested, even when they see their secretly cherished dreams of world domination recede into the mist.

Magic is seductive and deceiving, but not unjust. She gives far more than she takes. While she is gently pulling away the material gun she is putting a spiritual flower in its place. Instead of learning how to command the world, the magician gradually discovers ways to control his or her thoughts and passions. The world is seen as it truly is in all its beauty and complexity, and the desire to impose a selfish pattern on it through the personal will melts away like a dream. After a while, ruling the world ceases to look like such a great idea. Too much work.

You should not expect to control the thoughts and actions of others through magic, even though such domination is entirely possible. Most of the more colorful magicians were able to impose their will on receptive individuals who came into their sphere of influence. The Russian monk Rasputin possessed this power of personal magnetism and used it to gain influence over the family of the Czar Nicholas II. To a lesser extent, Aleister Crowley was able to command the wills of his followers. Dion Fortune relates in her book *Psychic Self Defense* an attempt to dominate her will made by her employer while she was a junior teacher at a boarding school. Whether or not this woman had actually studied magic, it appears from Fortune's description that she was using magical techniques.

This kind of control is only effective when applied to those who are by nature susceptible to it. A cult leader such as Jim Jones who exerts mind control over his followers to shape their view of themselves and the world, treats with coolness anyone not amenable to his will who attempts to join the group. He justifies the barring of those with strong wills from the cult on the grounds that such individuals are not ready for his teachings or are unworthy to receive them. In fact, they are kept out because the leader knows they cannot be manipulated.

Those who come under magical control do not always stay under it. Everyone has a will that is continually seeking to exert personal influence over the greater world. If you magically push someone, sooner or later they will push back. Hard. They may not even be consciously aware that they are doing it. People who seem very weak physically and emotionally may be very strong on the unconscious level. Extending the magical will over the lives of others is like building a fragile house of cards. The more complex the pattern grows, the more certain it is to collapse.

There is another factor to consider, which I mention only to the intelligent reader, as it is not likely to discourage fools. When you manipulate other people against their will, no matter what level you do it on, you are debasing your own nature and being far more repulsive than you really need to be. If, on the other hand,

The Russian holy man Grigori Efimovich Rasputin, who gained control over the family of Czar Nicholas II through his powers of occult healing and projection of the will.

you behave in an honorable way, you are acting in harmony with your own true nature and may even find happiness as a result of it. Pushing other people around gives satisfaction, not happiness. Happiness has value, satisfaction is barren.

Almost as alluring to the beginner as the promise of personal power is the prospect of limitless wealth. Most people have the idea that, if they can master magic, they can make themselves rich—otherwise, what is the good of it? For centuries, unscrupulous hack writers have pandered to this fantasy by selling books that guarantee instant riches through magic, even to those who have never worked magic before. Notable among these is *The Black Pullet*, said by A. E. Waite to be a product of the late 18th century. This amusing grimoire details the creation of a gold-finding black hen through the use of which great wealth may be amassed.

The alchemical process for transmuting base metals into gold is actually an extended ritual of high magic. It requires purification of the alchemist's body and soul, extensive preparation of materials and instruments, prayer, and a very specific set of required actions that must be carried out in a fixed sequence and manner for the transmutation to occur. The gold of alchemy was never understood by enlightened alchemists to signify material gold. It is quite clearly stated in the *Rosarium Philosophorum* (1550): "*Aurum nostrum non est aurum vulgi*" (Our gold is not the common gold). Even so, the credulous and the greedy persisted in believing they could manufacture the element gold from lead or other metals, and there were many unscrupulous "puffers," who received this name from their constant working of air bellows to feed their fires, who were more than willing to seek the secret of transmutation on behalf of wealthy patrons for a fee.

One of these was the alchemist Edward Kelley, best known for his service as crystal scryer to the Elizabethan occultist John Dee. In the course of his colorful life, Kelley had gained a close acquaintance with precious metals. It is said by some that he had his ears cut off as punishment for counterfeiting. He prided himself on his alchemical knowledge and even went so far as to write several tracts on the subject. At the gracious invitation of the Emperor Rodolph II, King of Hungary and Bohemia, Kelley was invited to prove his skill. The king provided him with funds and materials. When Kelley failed after long effort to manufacture gold and

Magic circle (left) from The Black Pullet, *an 18th-century grimoire. Note its similarity to the circle of another grimoire,* The Red Dragon *(right).*

sought to leave Rodolph's castle, the king had him cast into the dungeon and vowed he would never release him until Kelley made good on his promises. Kelley died in a daring but unsuccessful attempt to escape the hospitality of the king.

Because gold is dug out of the ground, it falls particularly under the influence of gnomes, elemental spirits of the earth. These gnomes, called *kobaloi* (wicked spirits invoked by rogues) by the Greeks and kobolds by the Germans, dwell in tunnels and chambers under the surface. Sometimes they lead miners to rich veins of ore, but may just as readily decide to kill them. The English miners call them coblyns or goblins, and sometimes knockers or tommy-knockers, from the tapping of their picks heard in the silence by solitary miners after the regular work shift has returned to the surface. There is a whole class of magical rituals designed to compel gnomes to reveal the hiding places of buried or lost treasure. Needless to say, such rituals are groundless.

The most popular way of seeking wealth through magic employs amulets manufactured for this purpose according to ritual methods. Frequently, these amulets are dedicated to Jupiter, the planet in astrology that presides over riches. In *The Greater Key Of Solomon,* it is said concerning the second pentacle of Jupiter: "This is proper for acquiring glory, honors, dignities, riches, and all kinds of good, together with great tranquility of mind; also to discover Treasures and chase away the Spirits who preside over them."

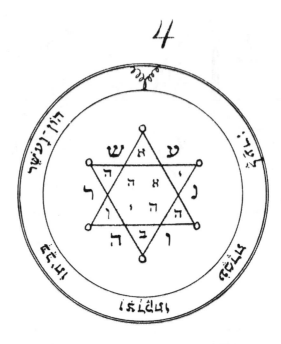

Second Pentacle of Jupiter from The Key of
Solomon the King, *as drawn by S. L. MacGregor Mathers.*

    This type of manufactured amulet is the most plausible tech-
nique of those mentioned for increasing wealth, but its successful
creation would require effort and skill, and it would not act in an
overt manner by leading its possessor to a place where a crock of
gold has been buried. If it worked at all, it would function more
subtly, perhaps resulting in a run of gambling luck or a successful
business investment. It could not be counted upon by anyone, not
even the most accomplished adept. History provides the proof of
this. Many of the greatest magicians, men like Agrippa, Paracelsus,
Dee, Mathers, and Crowley, died in obscurity and relative poverty.
If they could manufacture gold, or compel the elemental spirits of
the earth, or even create potent amulets for drawing money, why
would they not provide for their own comfort and the welfare of
their children?

    It is possible through ritual magic to create a general climate of
prosperity that will encourage luck and success in business ven-
tures and financial concerns, but it requires complete dedication to

Lucifer Rofocale, who stands over a heap of golden coins he has been compelled to uncover for the magician.
from The Red Dragon *(18th-century grimoire)*

this end. Ritual magic is not the easy road. Sometimes it can achieve goals that are not possible by ordinary, nonmagical means, but it takes hard work to gain consistent results. Magicians die in poverty because they are interested in something more than amassing wealth. Someone who is solely interested in making money should enter a university and seek a business degree. The results will be more reliable and direct, and will entail less labor.

The glamor of magic tickles all the vices, and lust is high on the list. Love magic is as old as time. The Greek poet Theocritus wrote around 290 BC:

> Even as I melt this wax, with the god to aid, so speedily may he by love be molten, the Myndian Delphis! And as whirls this brazen wheel, so restless, under Aphrodite's spell, may he turn and turn about my doors *(Second Idyll)*.

Over two centuries later, the Roman poet Virgil showed his regard for this magical poem by imitating it closely in his own *Eighth Eclogue.*

The ritual procedure described by Theocritus and Virgil is perfectly good magic, but questionable morality. What right has Theocritus' narrator, Simaetha, to tell Delphis who he may and may not love, or torment him if he chooses someone else? If she succeeds in binding the love of Delphis, does she think he will ever be truly content and happy during their future years together? Is it not more likely that he will end up hating her even though he cannot leave her? But perhaps she is thinking only about herself and the glory of conquest and the pride of possession, and does not really care whether Delphis is happy so long as she has him. Whatever this feeling may be, it would be difficult to characterize it as love, even though it usually passes under this name.

You can use magic to attract a lover, but not to compel love. Sooner or later a revulsion will occur that turns love to hate if the love has no natural foundation. If you are seeking love, you should invite it in a form that is in harmony with your essential character. First you may need to use ritual to discover who you are and what you really want. Few people see themselves clearly. Often they are attracted to someone with the qualities they admire but lack in themselves. If you already have a lover in mind, it is far better to use the art to transform your own personality and circumstances so that the other will seek out your company gladly rather than trying to compel the prospective lover against his or her inclination.

Following closely on the heels of power, money, and sex in the list of magical seductions is fame. Who is so callow among us that he or she has not fantasized about taking up the magic wand and performing a wonder here, a miracle there, to the cheering and applause of gathered thousands? Suppose you could save someone terminally ill from cancer in a showy, public way—not just anyone, mind you, but someone really worthwhile and important. Suppose you could levitate over the sports field at the next Olympic Games and light the torch with a scowl and a muttered word of power. Imagine the free publicity!

Sorry, magic does not work this way. Ask Simon Magus. He was a Gnostic magician who lived, according to the early Christian writers, in the reign of the Roman emperor Claudius (41-54 AD). His feats of magic gained many followers, but when he publicly announced that he would be translated to heaven in a chariot drawn by demons, the prayers of Saint Peter sent him crashing to

The death of Simon Magus.
from The Nuremberg Chronicle

earth a mangled corpse. This fable is a crude form of Church propaganda, but it may contain a germ of truth. It appears possible that a gnostic cult leader named Simon did announce that he would levitate his body from the top of a high building, with the result that he fell and broke both his legs. Arnobius' version of the legend suggests that, in shame over his failure, he made a second attempt and was killed.

Whenever a self-proclaimed master of the occult arts publicly asserts that he or she will at a certain time and place perform a miracle, it is absolutely certain to fail. This may have something to do with the dependence of magic upon belief, or with its inherent unpredictability, or even with the attitude of the awareness in the unconscious that directs magical operations—if we cannot be certain the higher self has a moral code, we can at least confidently state that it has a sense of humor. Anyone who loudly shouts, "Look at me! I am about to do something wonderful," is riding for a fall.

I have a confession to make—I have never levitated, walked on water, restored the dead to life, lit fires with my mind, turned myself into a wolf, or divined a winning lottery number. Maybe this makes me an inferior magician. There are certainly enough people in the world who do claim to be able to perform these and similar wonders. However, I have not seen them do so. Am I willing to say such feats are impossible? Of course not; such a statement would be rash. But I have not done them, and have never seen them done.

The main limitation on magic seems to be its lack of predictability. Wonders of a physical kind seem to occur from time to time. It is unlikely that all the stories of poltergeist phenomena and the more gross material manifestations of possession and spirit evocation are lies and delusions. The difficulty is that they do not, and by the very nature of magic cannot, happen where and when you want them to take place. It would be the wildest coincidence if you set out to achieve a specific end through ritual by a certain means and realized your purpose in exactly the time and place and manner predetermined. Magic fulfills its purpose, but in its own hidden way. It can never be bullied or rushed. It hates the limelight.

Magic has many miracles, but these are not so crude as they are presented to be in popular fables. For example, it is possible to attain invisibility through ritual practices. Magical invisibility does not involve rendering your physical body transparent to all wavelengths of light. It is rather a withdrawing of yourself from the awareness of other people so that, when they see you, they fail to notice you so utterly that later they would never believe they had seen you at all. An invisible person is one who does not interact in either a positive or negative way with others.

I remember hearing a story some years ago about a man who was a prisoner in a Nazi death camp during the Second World War. He knew he was certain to die. It was only a matter of time. Consequently, he had stopped fighting against his fate and resigned himself to death. One day he saw that the camp gate was open and, on impulse, he began to walk toward it, at each step expecting a bullet from one of the many guards who could plainly see him from their towers. It was broad daylight. There was no diversion to draw the attention of the guards elsewhere. Yet for some reason, not one of the dozens of Germans in the prison yard or on the guard towers called out to stop him as he walked through the gate and down the road to eventual freedom.

It may have been that the Germans assumed from his confident manner that he had a right to leave the camp. Or perhaps they felt a strange compassion and silently in their own minds decided that they would not shoot this single, brave man. The other possibility is that the prisoner had unconsciously succeeded in rendering himself invisible through his completely neutral and passive state of mind. This is the way real magic works, quietly and without fuss, just beyond the margins of things.

The theme of a doorway that leads from the oblivion of the flesh to the gnosis of the spirit is common in mystical literature. The seven steps indicate levels of occult knowledge.

—from Raymond Lully's Liber de Ascensu, *Valencia, 1512*

CHAPTER SEVEN

WHY MAGIC IS IMPORTANT
IN YOUR LIFE

Everyone is searching for the meaning of life—not so much life
in general, but of their own life. They want to know why they
exist and what they are supposed to do with existence. They want
to feel productive and fulfilled. Most of all, they want to be happy.

To live in a modern city is to be trapped in a great machine,
whirled round by cogs and gears, shunted from place to place in
repetitive patterns. The machine allows only one option to the poor
human rats racing madly inside its works. Either they get into step
with the gears and pushrods, or they are ground into hamburger.
The machine has no tolerance for pity, no allowance for aberration.

Those who succumb to the remorseless song of steel become
slaves, not to other men, but to the cold, calculating god of contemporary society, a god I have christened Meckanos, whose only
criterion is efficiency. Those who opt out of the system or who cannot manage to march in step with its mechanisms are destroyed.
For a while, they may enjoy frolicking between the assembly lines
while their more timid peers toil away, but sooner or later their feet
slip and, like Charlie Chaplin in *Modern Times,* they are consumed
by the social process. They end up in prisons, in mental hospitals,
or in coffins.

Magic is a hidden door that leads out of the machine. It is not a
portal to another physical place, because the machine is a state of
mind and no one can ever escape from him or herself. It opens on a
new awareness of the world where dreams can happen and where
human actions have meaning. It opens on hope and purpose.

Through ritual magic the world can be changed by changing the fundamental nature of the self and the relation of self to the world.

If you are constantly told that the world is gray and heartless, that your life is insignificant, that the dreams you dream and the feelings you feel are trivial, and if you believe this lie, you will inevitably experience a deep sense of futility. But if you realize that you are important to the world, indeed its very heart and center, and that every thought and feeling you have is significant not only to your life but to all life, and if it is pointed out to you that, at least potentially, you have complete control over your own existence, you will experience an exhilarating sense of freedom.

You must realize that, when you alter your self, you actually do change the world in a real sense. The world is not some fixed and eternal sculpture fashioned by a divine being ages ago from which you are forever separate. It is created by you from moment to moment within your mind from the substance of your mind. This act of creation occurs below the surface of your consciousness. Magic allows you to gain access to the levels that create your world so that you can to a greater or lesser extent control the pattern of that creative process.

Ritual provides the mechanism for changing all four levels of being: physical, emotional, mental, and spiritual. We all know that our feelings affect our physical health. We know that our minds, both the part we see and the part we do not see, control our feelings. What many do not realize is that there is a fourth level of spirit that determines the state of our minds, the thoughts we think and our attitudes toward life. The social norms and the intellectual climate of our culture increasingly deny the existence of this level of spirit, thereby denying access to it. If spirit falls out of balance, the mind is afflicted and gives a jaundiced assessment of the world. If the mind is warped, the feelings become unhappy. If the emotions are hurtful, the health of the body suffers.

Ritual magic permits you to wrest control over the state of the world and your place in it out of the hands of government policy-makers and big business so that you can assume personal responsibility for your own actions. Little wonder that it is universally condemned by the vested interests of the present mass-market culture. Its potential to shift power from institutions to individuals is revolutionary. For example, suppose you are running a business

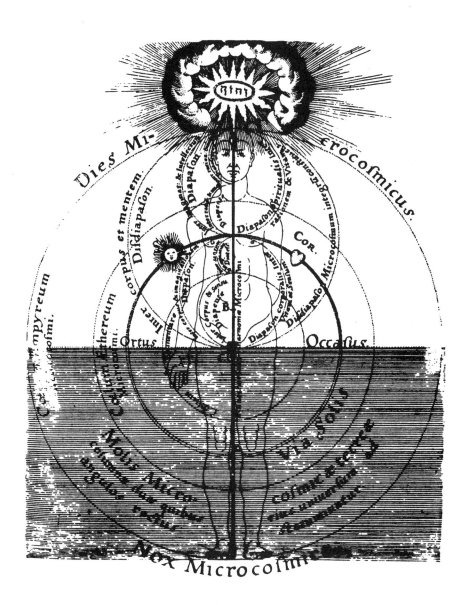

"As above, so below." The microcosm and
macrocosm as described by Robert Fludd in 1619.

and wish to open a new market for your products or services. Market analysis advises against it, lending institutions are pessimistic, other entrepreneurs in your own field laugh at the idea, government civil servants say that the political climate for such a move is unhealthy. Despite your inner conviction that the move is correct, you can find no support or backing. If you have the common material view of an external, immutable reality, you give up and bow to the collective opinion. On the other hand, if you have the magical view that you create the world with all its limits and opportunities, you set about seeing how you can change the world climate to make it receptive to your enterprise.

There are many examples of individuals who shaped their world to fit their dream. Mikhail Gorbachev is one. Before he rose to power in the Soviet Union, conventional opinion held that the Communist Bloc would endure in more or less its cold-war status for another half century. Within the space of a single momentous year, his personal vision shattered it forever. Steven Jobs, who started Apple Computer, is another example. Virtually alone, he created the personal computer industry out of his own unique vision. He used his mind to expand the world rather than allowing the world to restrict his mind. This is the magical approach to life.

Gorbachev and Jobs changed the world on a large scale, but everyone has the potential to change the world on the level of their interaction with it. An elderly person on a fixed income will change it in ways that appear small to others but are of momentous importance to that person. A poet will change it in ways that are very different than the ways of a politician. Magic is an art flexible enough to respond to the needs of rich and poor, great and insignificant, idealistic and crass.

You may object that Gorbachev is not a magician. True, he probably did not closet himself in a temple and stand in a mystic circle to do battle with the shades of Stalin and Marx. Nonetheless, he used magical techniques without knowing that they were magical. One is ritual visualization. To change yourself, it is only necessary to repeatedly visualize in your mind that you have become the type of person you long to be, and before many weeks or months you will outwardly begin to resemble that person. Success depends on the intensity of your need and your degree of willpower.

Not long ago, a woman who was reviewing a book on magic

(not one of mine) made the comment that, for her money, magic was nothing more than visualization. This was putting the cart before the horse. Visualization is nothing more than a part, a very small part, of ritual magic. It does work in ways that can at times seem miraculous, but there are many other magical techniques that are equally effective.

The channeling of spirits has in recent years become widely popular. It is used by some as a form of alternate psychotherapy. The secrets spirits reveal about deep needs and motivations can provide startling insights into personality problems. There is nothing at all new about channeling. It is only another name for spiritualism. Seeking information from spirits is as old as human history. When Saul consulted the Witch of Endor, he was going to see his local channeler.

Channeling is a small twig on the vast tree of ritual magic. Other twigs are crystal therapy, holistic healing, aura reading, laser therapy, pyramid power, chanting, biorhythms, acupuncture, acupressure, reflexology, and a host of other fads that come and go, all with one thing in common—they rely for whatever effectiveness they may possess on ancient self-transformation techniques that have been understood and used in magic for millennia.

The ultimate goal of ritual magic as a life process is the fulfillment of personal destiny. "Destiny" is the term I use to indicate the complete utilization of all the talents, abilities, potential, and opportunities that exist latently within an individual soul. Magic can help you get the most out of your life. In this way, it is similar to Eastern alternate philosophies such as yoga, Tibetan Buddhism, Zen, Taoism, and Tantra, but Western magic is different in the value it places on the present existence within the world. In general, Eastern occultism regards the world as transitory and unreal, something to turn away from in pursuit of eternal truth; Western occultism recognizes that the world is essentially a mental creation but regards actions committed in the world as real and important in their own right.

The whole focus of magic is directed at changing the world through the application of will. To bring about such transformation, whether for higher or lower ends, is the purpose of ritual magic. The most profound and useful change is the transformation of the self, and thus the world, so that the highest and best possibilities of the self are realized in the world. This is the fulfillment of destiny. In yoga and esoteric Buddhism, it is recognized that magical phenomena will occur during the lengthy process of seeking enlightenment, but the chela is cautioned again and again not to place any value in magical powers or seek them in any way lest they distract the mind away from the ultimate reality which is without form. In seeking the ultimate reality through magic, these phenomena are used in a conscious, deliberate way as instruments for perfecting the soul.

All the minor improvements in the quality of life that are brought about through the use of ritual magic, if they really are improvements, tend toward the creation of a total, fulfilled human being. They are pieces of a puzzle that make up a single, perfect image. Due to the essential oneness of world and self, outward improvements produce sympathetic echoes inwardly. Just as mental chaos can express itself in a chaotic lifestyle, so order and personal harmony in the outer life can influence for the better the condition of the soul.

One technique used is Western magic to bring about personal transformation is ritual communication with the Holy Guardian Angel, the higher spiritual intelligence that concerns itself in the affairs of an individual human being. Each person has his or her guardian spirit, which the ancient Greeks called the genius, or daemon. The daemon is always present, but usually the noise of everyday life renders its quiet admonitions inaudible. Only when the mind is in a receptive state can it hear the daemon clearly.

The Greek philosopher Socrates was famous in his own time for the careful heed he paid to the warning signals of his daemon, which he claimed to have often perceived through various signs. Always when he was in difficulties, his daemon advised him on the best course of action. Socrates would share this advice with his friends, who had many occasions to thank him for it. He was greatly puzzled as to why his daemon had not warned him when the leaders of Athens made a plot to convict him on trumped up charges of sedition against the state and forced him to drink poisonous hemlock. He concluded that it was because death is not, as everyone assumes, an evil, but a good. His daemon had no need to warn him against a blessing.

The Western method for attaining the conversation of the Holy Guardian Angel is detailed in *The Book of the Sacred Magic of Abramelin the Mage*, a grimoire in the Bibliotheque de l'Arsenal in Paris

The spirit of Virgil who guides Dante through hell and shields him from the malice of demons is a projection of Dante's personal guardian angel.
—*illustration by Gustave Doré for* The Divine Comedy

that was translated into English from its French manuscript in 1898 by S. L. MacGregor Mathers. It is extremely lengthy and involves the construction of a special ritual place in which the magician undergoes a regimen of purification, fasting, and prayer for six cycles of the Moon. The devotions require the greater part of each day and necessitate a partial withdrawal from society. It is doubtful that most students of the occult could even attempt the working due to financial constraints, let alone pursue it faithfully to its conclusion. Aleister Crowley is said to have undergone it with success.

Fortunately, communication with higher Intelligences is a major part of theurgic rituals, following the tradition of the Greek Neoplatonists. What cannot be accomplished in a single span of six Moons may at least partially be achieved over time through briefer rituals of invocation where higher spirits are invited to possess the magician within the magic circle. This is sometimes referred to as "assuming the god-form." Gods of wisdom who are skilled in magic such as the Egyptian Thoth or the Teutonic Woden are invoked in this manner. By repeatedly mingling with the essence of the god, the soul of the magician is exalted and his or her personality elevated and purified.

Another method for transformation used by Western occult schools is an entrance ritual involving a symbolic death and rebirth in which the neophyte casts off the old name that is used in day-to-day living and takes on a new magical name that represents the higher aspirations and purposes of the magician. In past times, this initiation has involved such things as the pretended drinking of poison and mock burial, but nowadays it is usually less literal in its representation. Aleister Crowley's magical name and motto in the Golden Dawn was Perdurabo ("I shall endure to the end"). Later, he called himself the Master Therion (an English adaptation of the Greek for "the great beast" of the Apocalypse).

These name changes seem frivolous and affected until their magical purpose is understood. On the surface, what can seem more ludicrous than a plain-faced, average woman named Violet Mary Firth calling herself Dion Fortune? Yet it was precisely with the intention of leaving the mundane world forever behind that the founder of the Society of the Inner Light cast off her birth name, which she associated with the unimaginative outlook and limited expectations of the drab English middle class, in favor of a name that contained, in her mind at least, the potential for wonder and excitement. She derived this pen name from her Golden Dawn motto: Deo Non Fortuna. To take on a magical name is to renounce the emptiness and failure of the past and embrace the promise of the future.

If you undertake the study of magic with the intention of always remaining exactly as you are now, with the same set of opinions and beliefs, the same outlook on the world, the same relationships with other human beings, you are apt to be disappointed. Magic does more than just affect what we regard as the outer world. It acts on the dynamic relationship between the outer world and the inner world of thoughts and feelings. It changes the world by changing you. When you deliberately freeze the pattern of your mind and refuse to allow it to evolve, you limit the power of magic to cause transformation on all levels.

The Book
of the
Sacred
Magic

Of Abra=Melin
the Mage,

As delivered by Abraham the
Jew unto his son Lamech,
A.D. 1458.

Title page of The Book of the Sacred Magic of Abra-Melin the Mage.
The artist was Moina Mathers, wife of the magician of the Golden Dawn.

Magic has always been worked for trivial personal reasons. To exact revenge against an enemy. To gain favor or love. To draw luck or money. To learn the outcome of a material event. For these and similar tangible purposes, it can be worked with great effectiveness. Many people are constitutionally incapable of aspiring after anything beneath the horizon of the physical senses. But the potential of magic extends far beyond materialism. It can not only give you what you think you want now, but can make you want something entirely different that you never before valued in the least. This is the true power of magic, at the same time awesome and terrifying.

CHAPTER EIGHT

MAGIC, THE ALTERNATE VIEWPOINT

W here in the world does magic live? It is not to be found seated at the table of the sciences. Science refuses to acknowledge any study not amenable to verification by experiment. It regards magic as a pernicious delusion that encourages sloppy thinking and erodes the educational base that supports the glorious progress of the machine age. It is not welcomed into the shelter of the churches. Historically, all the major religions have viewed magic as a devilish distraction from the legitimate labor of worship. It is not employed by big business, which demands immediate return on investment and has no venture capital to risk on such frivolous pursuits as transformation of the soul. Neither is it enrolled in the schools and universities. Scholars who write learned papers on magic treat it as a dead relic of past ages, or as a quaint superstition of primitive societies, or as an example of cultural mania similar in type to the flying saucer craze and the search for Elvis.

Magic is a disreputable outcast treated with intense suspicion and dislike by the bastions of the establishment. It wanders unloved on the fringes of our world, settling for a short time here or there until it is rousted and made to move along. All doors are slammed in its face. The bread is stolen out of its hand and the rags torn from its back. Unseeing eyes pass over it with steely indifference, and its cries fall on deaf ears.

Bored people with time on their hands sometimes take up the practice of ritual magic in a careless way as an amusement. When they find that it does not provide instant gratification of their lim-

ited desires, they abandon it, usually with the comment that they
knew all along that magic was bogus. They never really expected
it to work and they are not surprised when it fails. They even
derive a certain sour satisfaction in confirming their cynicism.

Working professionals who practice ritual in their daily lives
usually maintain a prudent silence. True, sorcerers are no longer
burned at the stake or hung as they were in former centuries, but it
does not do for people in sensitive occupations—the police or doc-
tors or airline pilots, for example—to let it generally be known that
they conduct magical rituals. Such an admission insures that they
will be labeled with the lunatic fringe and deemed unsuitable for
positions of responsibility. If they do not lose their jobs outright,
they can at least be confident that they will never be promoted.

The institutional hostility against magic is difficult to understand if magic truly is held by the majority of people to be nothing
more than a fantasy. Why get excited about an activity that cannot
accomplish any of its stated goals and therefore poses no threat?

Magic is reviled and condemned because it is viewed by the
greater mass of society as a menace to the existing power structure.
In most cases this awareness of the danger of magic is unconscious.
Ask people if they are afraid of magic and they will laugh at the idea.
Continue to talk about the subject and gradually they will begin to
look at you strangely and edge away as though they perceived a
patch of leprosy on your skin. Are they afraid of you because they
fear you are about to blast them with occult thunderbolts? No, they
just feel uncomfortable talking about magic, which is somehow dis-
tasteful to them. Since they cannot think why they dislike magic, they
transfer that dislike to you for bringing up the subject.

The world we live in is held together by a complex web of
beliefs and expectations. Change beliefs, and you change the
world. Magic has the power to transform the beliefs and expectations of those who practice it. Whether they realize it or not, people intuitively perceive the potential of magic to reform the
underlying pattern of the world. This is a frightening possibility.
The uncertainty of change terrifies the average man or woman,
who tends to prefer a known evil to one that lurks in the shadows
of the future.

Magic is revolutionary. It threatens the comforting truisms of
our culture with anarchy and annihilation. Once received into the

bosom of science, it would destroy the model of the universe constructed over centuries on the static framework of natural law. Embraced by religion, magic would undermine the essential relationship between man and God that forms the rationale of the churches. Adopted by big business, it would shatter the ethos of our consumer-driven society. All of these systems would have to reform themselves to accommodate the magical view of the world. They shun magic because they fear change.

Fear of change is why magic has been traditionally looked upon as satanic and demonic. There is nothing inherently evil about the practice of ritual magic. Magic is an art. No art can be itself evil, even though evil may on occasion find expression through its creations. It is possible to talk about an evil poet, and even an evil poem, but poetry itself can never be evil. Yet for thousands of years the authorities of the great religions regarded magic as wicked and condemned to death those who practiced it.

To the established church, magic consisted of the beliefs and rituals of the previous religion which had been supplanted and suppressed, usually as the result of military conquest. The Jews regarded the practices of the peoples they warred with and conquered as sorceries. For example, it is written of Ahaz, son of Jothan, the king of Judah, that he "made his son to pass through the fire, according to the abominations of the heathen" (II Kings 16:3). Trials by fire such as fire-eating and fire-walking are common religious rites around the world. This was not some strange torment that Ahaz was inflicting upon his son, but an accepted rite of passage from childhood to adulthood. It is only called an "abomination" in the Old Testament because it is not a Jewish rite.

Similarly, Egyptian priests resisted the contaminating incursion of magic from African tribes (it got in anyway—Bes is an African god), the Jews denigrated the acts of the priests of Egypt as sorcery while the identical acts of Moses were regarded as holy, the orthodox Greek philosophers condemned the strange mystical beliefs picked up by the Pythagoreans in Egypt as barbarian superstitions, the Romans tried and failed to ban the Egyptian gods along with the strange sorceries from Asia Minor and Gaul, the Christians called the Hermetic philosophers of Egypt foul magicians and accused the Jews of roasting Christian babies, which brings us more or less full circle.

Why has magic been so consistently regarded by Christian writers over the last twenty centuries as satanic? The explanation may lie in the nature of Satan himself. Satan, or more properly Lucifer, is before all else a rebel. He was an angel who defied the will of God and instigated a civil war in heaven. As punishment, he was cast down into a dark pit for eternity. His essential sin was defiance of established authority, the same sin that caused Adam and Eve to be cast out of the Garden of Eden.

The poet John Milton rightly portrays this original defiance of Satan as courageous and even noble:

> All is not lost; the unconquerable Will,
> And study of revenge, immortal hate,
> And courage never to submit or yield:
> And what is else not to be overcome?
> That Glory never shall his wrath or might
> Extort from me. To bow and sue for grace
> With suppliant knee, and deify his power
> Who from the terror of this Arm so late
> Doubted his Empire, that were low indeed,
> That were an ignominy and shame beneath
> This downfall;
> —*Paradise Lost*, bk. I, lines 106-16.

The Christian church lumped all defiance of divine authority under the mantle of the original rebel, Lucifer, whose bold example tempted the parents of the human race to the sin of disobedience—Adam and Eve ate the apple of the tree of knowledge after the example of the Serpent in direct defiance of God's order. In presuming to demand miracles through the work of their art rather than meekly asking for them with prayers, magicians place their wills before the will of God. Defiance of God is the primary evil from which all other sins spring. Therefore, magic must be wicked. This is the thinking of the Christian church, an opinion shared with Judaism, Mohammedanism, and other established religions.

Aleister Crowley called himself Master Therion, the Great Beast, because he perceived as his mission in life the disruption and eventual overthrow of the mores and values of Victorian middle-class society that seemed to him so hollow and hypocritical. This jaundiced view was largely the result of his suppressed and

Lucifer, the rebel against divine authority, broods on the injustice of his fate.
—*illustration by Gustave Doré for* The Divine Comedy

puritanical childhood, but also stemmed from his inherently anarchistic temperament. As his instrument for defying the authority of the church, the government, and the law of England, Crowley chose magic. Had he not been casting spells, he would probably have been throwing bombs.

The perception of magic as an evil practice stems from the view that it is in defiance of divine will as expressed in human society through the official institutions of church and state. This view is only partially correct. Magic is not so much defiant as independent. Crowley used it as an weapon of rebellion, but it may also be used as an instrument of liberation. Magicians work magic less to thumb their noses at the church than to find their own spiritual path and come to terms with their lives. Magic frees them from the bondage of social conventions that have long since ceased to nourish their hearts and minds.

To use magic only as a way of mocking convention is to limit its possibilities. It was employed in this restricted manner by the Satanists of the 18th and 19th centuries. Inverted ceremonies such as the black mass, a parody of the rite of the Catholic Church where the belly of a naked woman took the place of an altar and feces replaced the host, served to titillate the jaded palates of decadent aristocrats and lend a supernatural zest to crime. The satanic mass itself was almost wholly a literary invention, but it was based upon parodies and desecrations of Church ceremonies that actually occurred. The dilettantes of the court of the French king Louis XIV, who hired as many as 60 priests to conduct masses on the bellies of nude girls, or the members of the Hell-Fire Club founded in England in the middle of the 18th century by the rake Sir Francis Dashwood, were more intent on cheap thrills than miracles.

An identical impulse drives the Satanism of modern times. It is either a way of mocking and desecrating existing conventions or a cover for criminal activities. Teenagers who spray the number 666 on church walls or Columbian drug runners who sacrifice chickens know nothing about real magic and seldom care to learn. The practice of real magic requires discipline and hard work. Would-be Satanists often derive their craft from the garbled lyrics of heavy-metal rock musicians who themselves have not the faintest notion of what they are talking about. It is the blind leading the blind. Or they study the Satanic Bible of that self-acknowledged con artist Anton LaVey, who established his Church of Satan as a money-making venture that caters to the sensational.

The desecrations and crimes of Satanists, though they are usually just a petty nuisance, are none the less deplorable and deserve the condemnation of religious leaders. But they have nothing whatsoever to do with magic as an art of spiritual self-expression. By characterizing as Satanists all practitioners of ritual magic, priests, rabbis, and ministers betray their ignorance of the facts and do a disservice to the honorable intentions of thousands of genuinely good people who seek an alternative to the established church in bettering their lives.

Although the practitioners of magic make up a kind of secret underground, they are not drawn from any one stratum of society. The come from all backgrounds and walks of life. There are Christian occult churches, temples of the Kabbalah with strongly Ortho-

The Abbe Guibourg sacrifices a child during a black mass celebrated for Madame Montespan, the former mistress of Louis XIV of France. Her naked body serves as the altar. One of the most notorious incidents of Satanism, in fact it may never have happened—details of the confessions of those concerned were extracted under torture.

dox opinions, feminist Wiccan covens worshiping God as a woman, lesbian and gay circles, Druidic brotherhoods, groups based on the writings of anarchistic Aleister Crowley, groups founded on the rituals of the Golden Dawn, survivalists, ecologists, animal rights activists—all using ritual to further their diverse goals.

Attitudes are changing. The expansion of New Age subjects into all walks of life has carried magic along with it. Magic is ceasing to be a taboo subject and becoming a curiosity. Most people are interested in magic, even if they are afraid to admit that their interest is serious. Given half a chance, they would attend seminars and university lectures to learn the correct techniques of ritual, if such schools existed and if no one would laugh at them.

Groups presently working the Western magical tradition may be divided into two branches. The more numerous are the pagan groups that incorporate magic into the ceremonial worship of nature. Druidism, Wicca or Witchcraft, cults based upon the goddess Earth, and those derived from the mythologies of the Celts,

Greeks, and American Indians fall under this heading. The less numerous practice an abstract ceremonial magic that descends more directly from Neoplatonism and Jewish mysticism. They deal in words, symbols, and numbers and work more through the mediation of spirits to accomplish their purposes. This type of ritual is called *high magic* or *theurgy.*

It may help to grasp the difference between these two types of magic to think of the first as exemplified by the Witch, and the second as represented by the wizard. The popular mythology of these archetypal figures is not wholly inaccurate. Witches live in closer touch with nature and the earth. They rely on the healing and occult powers of herbs and stones. They are more conscious of the seasons. Wizards are occupied with words, symbols, and instruments. Their magic tends to be abstract and intellectual. For example, the Enochian magic of John Dee, which depends on words of power and angelic names, is popular with this second class of magician.

Ultimately, Witchcraft and theurgy have the same objective—the release and application of human potential through magic for the purpose of life fulfillment. This goal is not achieved all at once or quickly. Perhaps it is *never* attained to its fullest possible degree—who can say how awesomely powerful a fully realized human being would be? Rather, it is approached over time through small victories that make life a little more worth living.

Ritual magic can be conducted by an individual in solitude or with those of like mind in a group. Group ritual is favored by most people, who draw support from the other members of the circle. It is easier to learn the basics of ceremonial magic by imitation. Those who work alone often become discouraged when they find themselves pouring large amounts of energy into their rituals while seemingly getting little or nothing in return. After working ceremonial magic for a while, you become aware of the long-term cycles of the mind that extend over periods of many months. Another advantage of group practice is that it helps individuals get through the low points in their personal cycles. It is easy to become discouraged and give up. A perception of failure often turns an initial fascination with magic into aversion.

Magical groups tend to be small and closely knit with a limited patience for those who are titillated by the occult but do not wish to make a firm commitment. Usually they have neither the inclination nor the money to advertise for new members, but they can be discovered through the many newsletters they publish, from announcements in newspapers and other media of seminars and gatherings, and by talking and corresponding with those directly involved in magical activities such as occult writers, those who operate alternate book stores, professional astrologers and diviners, therapists using New Age techniques, and others similarly involved in a general way with the occult.

Persistence pays off. The best way to penetrate the outer circle of a group so that you can discover firsthand what they are really doing is to demonstrate a sincere interest. Keep calling and phoning and showing up at meetings and seminars. Take whatever opportunities to participate that may be offered. If you later find out that the group is only a money-making scam, or a front for devil worshipers, or something else that does not interest you at all, you can always politely disengage yourself.

Obviously, common sense and a certain amount of watchfulness are needed to keep out of trouble. One warning sign is the request for substantial amounts of money in exchange for occult secrets. Modest fees for lessons and seminars are not unreasonable, but take care that they do not escalate beyond the scale of fees you would expect to pay for services that involve similar expenditures of time and effort, such as exercise classes, dance instruction, and so on. Another warning sign is the use of drugs by any member of the circle, even supposedly mild drugs such as marijuana, and especially the offer of free drugs to you. There is no free lunch in this world. A third danger signal is the invitation to participate in illegal acts. If any of these things happen, leave the group.

There is no great secret waiting to be whispered into your ear. No occult lodge or Wicca circle or magical brotherhood can give you the key to magic on a silver tray. The key is within you. Some groups, if they contain intelligent and skillful leaders, may be able to help you find that key for yourself. Or they may not. Only you can decide if you are being aided in your search for truth or being led by the nose to a lie.

If you are serious about wanting to learn ritual magic, read as much as possible so that you will not be ignorant of the mechanics of the art. Most of the courses in magic offered through the mail and in seminars involve basic techniques that can easily be absorbed through books. It is not necessary to pay large fees for this primary training. At the same time, you should be attending lectures and seminars and get-togethers revolving around New Age subjects in your local region, not so much for the topics themselves as to make useful occult contacts.

Keep your eyes open for notices of clubs and study groups being formed. You may wish to attempt to start your own study group to gauge the level of interest in your community. This can be done by placing an ad in the personal section of your local newspaper inviting calls from anyone interested in meeting and talking about magic.

There is an old saw that says when the student is ready, the teacher will appear. This is only true when rightly understood. The teacher appears because the student has indicated his or her readiness by a fervent and single-minded search for the teacher, often over a considerable span of time. Do not expect your teacher to knock at your front door. You must go out and make your interest known. Those who have studied magic for many years are not only willing but eager to teach students the art, but they want to know that their knowledge will be valued. To them, it is the most precious possession in the world and deserves the highest veneration. They do not wish to make the mistake of casting it into the mud.

SECTION TWO

SYSTEMS

*A stylized Golden Dawn interpretation of the Tree
of the Kabbalah showing the ten sephiroth as spheres.*
—*from* The Golden Dawn *by Israel Regardie*

CHAPTER NINE

THE GOLDEN DAWN

The complex and rigid structure of ritual magic that developed in the Hermetic Order of the Golden Dawn is firmly based on the European medieval tradition. This is in large measure a fusion of the practical Kabbalah with Graeco-Egyptian magic as it was imperfectly transmitted through grimoires and surviving Greek, Arabic, and Latin manuscripts.

There is heavy emphasis on number magic. The names of the spirits connected with the planets along with their various sigils are derived through the association of individual letters of the Hebrew alphabet with their numerical equivalents. For example, the name of the spirit of the outermost planet known to the ancients, Saturn, is Zazel (זאזל), which in Hebrew forms the equation $7 + 1 + 7 + 30 = 45$. The simplest magic square of numbers—a square grid in which all the rows, columns and diagonals sum the same—has nine cells. The sum of all the cells equals 45. This first magic square is linked with the first planet, and the geometric symbol of Zazel, called its *sigil*, is formed by tracing the positions of the numbers in the name in order on the grid of the square (see next page).

From the Kabbalah come the methods of deriving names of power from holy texts or from numerical tables of Hebrew letters. The Golden Dawn developed its own instrument for generating graphic symbols for significant names. The 22 Hebrew letters were inscribed on the petals of a stylized rose and a line traced over the rose from one letter in the name to another, after the example of the magic squares, resulting in a figure of angled line segments. This

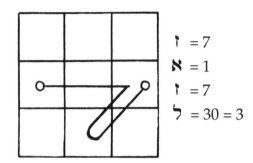

Magic Square of Saturn with Sigil of Zazel

system is unique to the Golden Dawn.

From the Pythagoreans descends the belief that certain regular polygons have specific meanings and potentials. For example, the square is regarded as the embodiment of materialism. The most important of these symbols in practical Golden Dawn magic are the triangle, square, pentagram, and hexagram. The Vault of the Adepti is in the shape of a heptagon. The regular solid bodies described by Plato also play a role in the ritual furnishings and instruments. For example, it is recommended that the Golden Dawn altar be in the form of a double cube, and the instrument of the solid cross, the 22 sides of which relate to the Tarot trumps, is formed from five cubes. The black and white lotus pillars of the temple are surmounted by small tetrahedrons.

Also strongly influenced by numerological considerations is the Enochian language, with its names of spirits and poetically beautiful calls, which are drawn from certain complex letter grids. Enochian, a language transmitted to the Elizabethan sage John Dee through spirit communications, has a numerical correspondence much the same as Hebrew and plays a significant part in higher Golden Dawn magic.

The technique for creating telesmatic images of spirits may have originated with this order. These images are created from the letters in the names of the spirits by building up a set of associations with those letters. These associations are drawn from the formalized correspondence between the letters of the Hebrew alphabet and the Tarot trumps By this method, the angel Raphael (רפאל) would be visualized with flowing golden hair because the Hebrew letter Resh (ר) means "head" and is linked with the Sun

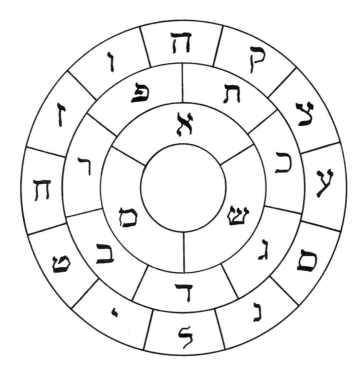

Sigil Rose of the Golden Dawn

in astrology and with Tarot Trump XIX: The Sun. He might be given a tongue of fire because the letter Pe (פ) means "mouth" and is associated with the planet Mars and Tarot Trump XVI: The Tower Struck by Lightning. In this way, a full picture of any spirit can be built up and through this image the spirit can be communicated with or evoked.

It is thanks to the Golden Dawn that the Tarot enjoys its present status and widespread use in practical occultism. The linking of the 22 Tarot trumps with the Hebrew letters resulted in a rich cross-current between the potent visual symbols of the Tarot and the magic of the Kabbalah. Although the actual esoteric Golden Dawn Tarot never received the credit that was its due, because it was copied individually by hand and kept secret, the influential Tarots of A. E. Waite, Aleister Crowley, and Paul Foster Case were shaped by its set of correspondences.

The workhorses of Golden Dawn magic are the five occult elements: Spirit, Fire, Air, Water, and Earth. The latter four are represented by the lesser suits of the Tarot, and it is from the emblems of these suits, the Wand (Fire), the Dagger (Air), the Cup (Water), and the Pentacle (Earth), that the four magical instruments of the order take their design. These instruments are described in detail and are illustrated in Chapter Nineteen. So far as I have been able to determine, they originated with the Golden Dawn.

By drawing the pentagram in certain specific ways, it is possible to evoke or banish the spirits and forces of any element at will. The particular method of drawing the pentagram does not in itself possess any inherent force but rather acts as a psychic key that accesses certain mental conditioning, and it is this conditioned response, built up over months or years of meditation upon the essential qualities of the elements, that allows them to be concentrated or dispersed. The technique of evoking or banishing the elements with the pentagram also appears to be original with the Golden Dawn. It is used widely in modern magic. Because it is so complex, it is best illustrated by the accompanying diagram. Usually, the pentagrams are inscribed on the air with the index finger or one of the magical instruments suitable for projecting the will, as though they were being drawn on an invisible blackboard.

An element is invoked by making the first stroke of the pentagram toward the point of that element, and banished by making the first motion away from that point. Spirit is invoked by two pentagrams, one active and one passive, and banished by two pentagrams.

This system is so clumsy that I was moved to simplify it. In *The New Magus* system of magic, any element, including Spirit, is invoked by beginning the pentagram clockwise from its point and banished by beginning the pentagram counterclockwise from its point. In this way, all elements can be manipulated with a single pentagram. After designing this system, I was fascinated to discover that the occult organization Aurum Solis uses the identical method—either a case of great minds thinking alike or unconscious telepathy.

The Golden Dawn developed an even more involved method of invoking and banishing the seven traditional planets through the use of the common hexagram of two interlocking triangles. To invoke the Sun by this system requires the drawing of six separate hexagrams, an operation so lengthy and awkward that the simpli-

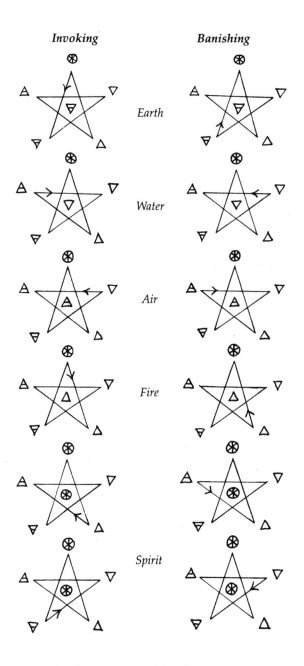

Invoking and Banishing Pentagrams

*Allan Bennett, one of the few Golden Dawn members
who seemed to have made progress in spiritual development.*

fied method described in *The New Magus* was almost a practical
necessity.

The pre-eminent symbol of the Golden Dawn is the rose-cross,
a Rosicrucian emblem. It is important to understand that the order
was Rosicrucian in its philosophy and goals. It sought to turn the
men and women who were its members into enlightened beings
with powers of awareness and self-control that would be regarded
as superhuman. Like the mythical Rosicrucians of old, they would

The rose cross as it was conceived by one of the early admirers of the German mystical order of Rosicrucians, Robert Fludd.

move through the world behind the scenes, taking control where necessary, healing the sick, and doing what good they could through their magical training.

It was recognized that the majority of the human race could never achieve such lofty spiritual discipline, so the membership was restricted to a select few, with favoritism given to those who had distinguished themselves socially or artistically. It might be argued that the real criterion was snob appeal. In any case, only a handful of Golden Dawn members ever achieved prominence in the area of spiritual development. Perhaps the most successful was Allan Bennett, who lived the creed of the order, but ultimately renounced magic as a trivial distraction and became a Buddhist ascetic. Aleister Crowley openly mocked the high ideals of the order. This contributed to his unpopularity with its leaders, who were quite sincere in their desire to save mankind from itself.

Rosicrucian elements color the rituals of the Golden Dawn. The Vault of the Adepti, a seven-sided chamber decorated with occult symbolism, was said to be the "symbolic burying place of our Founder C. R. C." (Christian Rosenkreutz—see "Concerning the Use of the Vault," Regardie 1989, 270-1), and the ritual of the Adeptus Minor grade is laden with the Rosicrucian mythos. The extreme complexity and formality of the rituals take their inspiration from the rituals of high Masonry and to a lesser extent from the rituals of the Anglican Church.

One of the most important distinguishing features of Golden Dawn magic is the belief that there is a class of superior beings that sometimes manifest upon the Earth to teach receptive human beings higher spiritual truths that are not accessible through ordinary methods of research. In the Golden Dawn, these were called Secret Chiefs. The names of the three highest are given as Hugo Alverda, Franciscus de Bry, and Elman Zata. And of course Christian Rosencreutz was also one of the chiefs. The strength of the order was the belief among its members that they were the chosen ones, that the Secret Chiefs were in direct communication with their leaders. There is a strong element here of 19th-century spiritualism. MacGregor Mathers and his wife were fulfilling much the same role as trance mediums when they transmitted the teachings of the chiefs to the order rank and file. Voluntary possession plays an important part in many systems of magic.

CHAPTER TEN

THELEMA

It was an incident of spirit visitation that gave the magic of Aleister Crowley its independent and original direction, distinguishing it from the magic of the Golden Dawn. While staying in Cairo in 1904, Crowley was informed through the mediumship of his wife Rose that he was to be an instrument of the Egyptian god Ra-Hoor-Khuit (Horus), who had been "waiting" for him. Crowley performed a ritual invocation of Horus, and, on April 8 at exactly 12 noon, he began to receive a clairaudient dictation in his temple. The voice was that of the spirit Aiwass, Crowley's Holy Guardian Angel. He wrote furiously for one hour, after which the voice abruptly ceased. The same thing happened on the following day, and the next.

The result of these three hours of inspired scribbling was the three brief chapters that make up *Liber Al vel Legis, (The Book of the Law)*. From it come the essential distinguishing features of the Crowley cult. On page 10 of the manuscript is written: "The word of the Law is θελημα. Who calls us Thelemites will do no wrong, if he look but close into the word." *Thelema* is the Greek word for "will." Thelemites reckon its letters to be Kabbalistically equivalent to the number 93. They call the teachings of *The Book of the Law* the 93 Current.

There are two statements in the *Liber Al* that stand out. The first is the infamous dictum "Do what thou wilt shall be the whole of the law." The other is "Love is the law, love under will." In both statements the concept of will is paramount. As one would expect of a new world order presided over by the Egyptian god of war, Horus, a severe discipline is demanded of the chosen ones of the new aeon. The statements can by no means be interpreted as a license to do whatever strikes the fancy, or to revel in mindless sexuality. Horus is a war god—his followers are soldiers. True will is paradoxically both freedom and servitude. It is freedom in that all other courses of action are slavery, the result of a mindless action and reaction of lower karmic forces; it is servitude in that there is only one free course for each individual from which he or she can not deviate yet still remain free.

Unfortunately, the almost monastic dedication required for a fruitful understanding and attainment of the true will has held little attraction for the majority of those who adopt *Liber Al* as their bible. All too often, "do what thou wilt" is interpreted to condone a liberal use of drugs, ostensibly for the purpose of altering consciousness, but in reality to gratify a craving for novelty and physical pleasure.

In this self-destructive course, Thelemites follow the footprints of their late master down a descending spiral. Crowley died a heroin addict, having in the course of his life willfully indulged himself in cocaine, hashish, and whatever other noxious substances offered the promise of a few hours of diversion. Disciples caught up in the 93 Current see attempts to hinder their chemical experiments as unwarranted interference in their right to pursue their true will. This results in a general contempt for the law and its instruments, which is in keeping with the attitude displayed by their leader during his life.

Crowley saw himself as the prophet of a new Aeon of Horus that would be introduced by a wave of war and destruction. This warfare was necessary to sweep away the last putrefying vestiges of the Aeon of Osiris, characterized by the duality of man-God that was the basis of Christianity and other major religious movements of this aeon. The Aeon of Horus is equivalent to the astrological Age of Aquarius, which Crowley believed had begun in 1904 precisely when he received *The Book of the Law*. Under Horus, humanity would recognize itself as one with deity. The occluding and restricting notion of a God that is otherwhere would be left behind, the way a serpent sloughs off its skin and emerges shining and renewed.

*Perhaps the most famous portrait of Aleister
Crowley. His bald head lends him a suitably Satanic aspect.*

Unicursal hexagram

Crowley thought of himself as the Great Beast who would herald the necessary destructive purging of the world. He was the prophet of the new aeon, as it is written in *The Book of the Law:* "I am the Master; thou art the Holy Chosen One." The modern Thelemites also tend to consider themselves chosen and assume a mocking, anarchistic air in their newsletters and other writings.

It is important to understand that by the message in *Liber Al* and by his own nature Crowley was essentially a destroyer, not a creator. He was not involved in whatever reconstruction might occur in the maturity of the Aeon of Horus. He was the herald of the final collapse of the Aeon of Osiris. His was the power to discover weaknesses and flaws and pull things apart. It was so much his personal destiny that he performed this function almost without being aware of it wherever he went. Those who associated with him on the personal level frequently attempted suicide or had nervous breakdowns. Crowley was not deliberately trying to

Symbol of the Master Therion

destroy these people. He merely acted as a mirror to reveal to them their own imbalances and weaknesses.

This communication from Aiwass was equivalent for Crowley to the communication that S. L. MacGregor Mathers had earlier established with the Secret Chiefs of the Rosicrucian current. It gave his teachings the blessing of a higher spiritual authority. He was not merely a man expressing personal opinions about occult questions; he was the Chosen One of the new aeon. Had Crowley not received *The Book of the Law* by supernatural intervention, it would have been necessary for him to fabricate some similar authority in order for him to successfully establish himself as the leader and prophet of a major occult current.

Crowley is associated with two magical societies. The first is the Argenteum Astrum (Silver Star), the so-called Great White Brotherhood of which the spirit Aiwass is the supreme head. This evolved out of the Golden Dawn and was based on the magical methods of the parent order. Its purpose, according to Kenneth Grant, is to "prepare humanity for the next stage of its progress, its initiation into Solar Consciousness" (Grant 1976, 133).

The second is the German Ordo Templi Orientis (Order of the Temple of the East), which practices sex magic based on Tantric methods. Occult energy is raised within the body of a woman by means of intense and prolonged sexual arousal, and at a critical moment this energy is released and channeled by the priests who surround her for the purpose at hand.

As is true of the magic of the Golden Dawn, Crowley's magic is worked mainly indoors in formal temples. Use is made of the Book of Thoth, a set of Tarot cards designed by Crowley and executed by the artist Lady Frieda Harris. The occult attributions of these cards closely follow the esoteric Golden Dawn Tarot, with the exception that arises from the statement in *The Book of the Law* that "All these old letters of my Book are aright; but ש is not the Star." Crowley assigned Tarot Trump XVII: The Star to the Hebrew letter *He* based on this hint, and gave *Tzaddi* to Trump IV: The Emperor.

A symbol that is particular to Crowley's brand of magic is the unicursal hexagram, which Crowley claimed to have invented, a hexagram drawn with one unbroken line from beginning to end. This figure has practical value in ritual magic because it can be inscribed on the air with a single motion of the hand, as can the pentagram.

Another symbol associated with Crowley is the number 666 of Revelation 13:18—"Here is wisdom. Let him that hath understanding count the number of the beast: for it is the number of a man; and his number is Six hundred threescore and six." In his youth Crowley took to calling himself the Great Beast out of sheer devilment, as an affront to his puritanical parents and disapproving mentors. Later he fitted the notion into his perception of his higher destiny, calling himself the Master Therion from the Greek *To Mega Therion* (The Great Beast). The number is occasionally found inscribed with the figure of an inverted heptagram that has a stylized phallus rising from its center.

Because Crowley took some of the mythology for his personal occult movement from the Book of the Revelation, calling himself the Beast and his lover Leah Hirsig the Scarlet Woman (see Tarot Trump XI: Lust, in the Book of Thoth), and occasionally employed

The archfiend Satan as the red dragon of Revelation 12:3, having seven heads and ten horns. Upon his back rides the Whore of Babylon. This image was central to the personal mythos of Crowley.

—from an illustration by William Blake

the image of the goat and the phallus (Tarot Trump XV: The Devil), many newspaper writers and fundamentalist preachers have confused Thelema with Satanism. However, there are clear distinctions between these two occult currents that can best be revealed by examining modern satanic beliefs and practices and comparing them with the teachings of Crowley.

CHAPTER ELEVEN

SATANISM

Satanism is a Christian phenomenon. The word has no meaning except against the backdrop of the medieval European Christian view of the universe. In the early centuries of the present era there were many pagan religions that worshiped in groves, sacrificed beasts, conducted fertility rites, and adored images. As these were suppressed by Christianity, their gods and goddesses became demons. Anything not Christian was viewed as evil. Surviving vestiges of pagan practices, such as the European Witchcraft cult postulated by Margaret A. Murray, were attributed to the leader of the fallen angels, Lucifer, who under Christian dualism has swelled into the shadowy arch-foe of God, Satan.

The God-Satan dualism is not unlike that in the Zoroastrian religion of ancient Persia between Ahura Mazda (Ormazd) and Angra Mainyu (Ahriman). It did no good for Christian theologians to argue that God was infinitely more powerful and significant than Satan—the common people feared the Devil at least as much as they feared the wrath of God. They might acknowledge that God was superior, but yet Satan was a dreadful antagonist full of tricks and wiles and mighty in evil. Moreover God was remote, concerned with ethereal matters such as the salvation of souls, while Satan was offering concrete bribes of lust, power, and wealth for service.

Historically Satanism as an organized cult does not exist. Early pagan practices called satanic by Christian writers were merely non-Christian. Heretical movements such as the Knights Templar were regarded as devilish not because they worshiped the Devil, but because they worshiped Christ in an unorthodox form. In the 18th and 19th centuries, the rare occurrences of ritual worship of Satan, such as that of the infamous Hell-Fire Club of Sir Francis Dashwood, were usually masks for the free indulgence of vice without a serious religious or magical content.

The Church of Satan, established by Anton Szandor LaVey in California on April 30, 1966, perhaps marks the first organized and publicly proclaimed worship of Satan as the arch-foe of Christ. It evolved out of a small group of occultists who met once a week in LaVey's home to study and talk about magic. The creed of the Church is one of selfishness and materialism. LaVey emphatically states in *The Satanic Bible* that his flock should never turn the other cheek, but rather should strike back when they are struck. "If a man smite thee on one cheek, smash him on the other!" (LaVey 1969, 47).

Followers are trained in how to assert their wills over others, how to manipulate people in day-to-day life through the use of flattery, lies, personal charm, sex, and intimidation in order to gain the material possessions, wealth, and status they are seeking. The Golden Rule of the Church is "Do unto others as they do unto you" (ibid., 51), and its rallying cry, taken from the first sentence of the "Book of Satan," which is the first "book" of this parody of the Bible, is "Death to the weakling, wealth to the strong!" (ibid., 30). LaVey is quite consciously striving to imitate the nihilistic tone of Crowley's *Book of the Law* in this section, but with only middling success.

The techniques of practical magic used in the Church of Satan are patterned on the teachings of Aleister Crowley and the German Ordo Templi Orientis, a branch of which Crowley headed. LaVey advocates the generation of magical force through either sexual arousal or rage as a substitute for the ritual torture and sacrifice of beasts, which he regards as a less effective magical generator. In this belief, he follows Crowley and Austin Osman Spare, the father of chaos magic. He is not opposed to human sacrifice "to dispose of a totally obnoxious and deserving individual" (ibid., 88), but says that this sacrifice is symbolic, ritually enacted. Of course, if the sacrificial victim should actually happen to die as the result of this magic, so much the better: ". . . and if your curse provokes

*The eternal battle between good and evil. Lucifer and his fallen
angels are cast down from heaven by the angelic host led by Michael.*
—*woodcut by Albrecht Dürer*

their actual annihilation, rejoice that you have been instrumental in ridding the world of a pest!" (ibid., 90).

Much use is made of satanic symbols, symbols that are deliberate inversions of corresponding Christian symbols, or desecrations of those symbols. Traditionally Satan is worshiped, not in a positive way, but by desecrating, mocking, and defiling Christianity. In LaVey's Church, this takes the form of a burlesque. Baphomet replaces the cross. The satanic altar is the body of a naked woman. The prayers mock the sentiments of Christian prayers. Priests wear black robes, and black candles are burned. An erect phallus replaces the aspergillum.

It is surprising how much of *The Satanic Bible* is taken up with Enochian magic—more than a hundred pages. LaVey derived this material from the Golden Dawn, but gives his own particular translation of the Enochian Keys that the Elizabethan sage John Dee would hardly have approved of: "Be friendly unto me, for I am the same!—the true worshiper of the highest and ineffable King of Hell!" (ibid., 162).

The primary satanic symbol is the inverted pentagram, which is a pentagram with two points uppermost. The notion that this figure signifies evil is based on the duality of its crown. In duality there is division and strife, therefore chaos, and disorder is the instrument of the Devil. Two upper points represent the mind divided. So far as I have been able to determine, this use of the inverted pentagram descends from the writings of the French occultist Eliphas Levi: "The pentagram with two points in the ascendant represents Satan as the goat of the Sabbath; when one point is in the ascendant, it is the sign of the Saviour" (Levi 1979, ch. V).

Modern occultists perceive the evil significance of the inverted pentagram as stemming from the attribution of the five elements to its points. Since the uppermost point is commonly given to Spirit or Light, the inversion of the pentagram exalts the four material elements of Fire, Air, Water, and Earth over Spirit, by implication elevating materialism above spirituality.

Very little in magic is universal. Although the inverted pentagram is almost everywhere accepted as a symbol of evil, there are groups of occultists who use it merely to signify third degree initiation, and it is also employed without prejudice in Masonic lodges.

Satanic Symbol

Perhaps these uses arose in ignorance of the link between the inverted pentagram and the Devil, which has, after Levi, been firmly established for well over a century.

The head of a goat is often inscribed in the inverted pentagram with its horns in the upper points, its ears in the middle points, and its goatee beard in the single lower point.

The relatively restrained rituals of LaVey's Church of Satan do not represent the phenomenon of Satanism as it is frequently reported in the newspapers and over the airwaves. This latter class of satanic activity involves the desecration of churches and cemeteries, usually by painting them in red with inverted pentagrams and the number of the beast and polluting them with excrements, blood, or garbage. Vandalism and arson are commonly tied to these activities, as are the torture and mutilation of animals, and occasionally the torture and murder of human beings.

Those who commit these acts are usually young persons

Goetic circle of black magic, according to the French magician Eliphas Levi.
from Dogme et Rituel de la haute magie

involved in drugs and heavy metal music who have no real idea of what they are doing or why they are doing it. They seek to gain a passing thrill by shocking their elders and outraging the taboos of their society. Satanic groups are small and endure for only a brief period of time because they are inherently self-destructive. Drug overdose, venereal disease, suicide, murder, and imprisonment all contribute to their dissolution.

The creed of this brand of popular Satanism may be summarized in a few brief statements: 1) The devil is more powerful than God. 2) Those who commit acts of evil are doing the work of Satan, and are therefore his servants. 3) Satan rewards his servants with personal power and enables them to satisfy their desires.

The second statement explains the often puzzling reports of ritual mutilation and torture of animals. Apart from the sadistic pleasure this provides, it is regarded as the devil's work and the proper function for his followers. Sin equals power. The more wickedness that can be worked, the greater will be the reward granted by the Dark Lord. There is another occult reason for torture and the shedding of blood. Pain and fear release vast amounts of raw energy

The god of the Templars, Baphomet, as conceived by Eliphas Levi in his Dogme et Rituel de la Haute Magie, *Paris, 1855-6. Interestingly, this same devilish figure is sometimes shown in depictions of the initiation into the 18th degree of Freemasonry.*

that can by certain magical operations be channeled for other purposes. However, most young Satanists have no more knowledge of magical operations than what they glean from rock lyrics, and real satanic magic is probably as rare as true Satanists.

Teenagers who play at devil worship for cheap thrills or to shock their parents sometimes discover to their amazement that, when they invoke Satan, something actually appears. Since they believe in nothing, including magic, they are astounded and terrified by their success. They renounce their ritual practices only to discover to their mounting horror that the thing they have called up from the mire of their unconscious minds will not go away. It whispers evil suggestions to them in their sleep. It brings them nightmares that wake them in howling terror. It confronts them in all its hideous reality in their bathroom mirrors. It follows them with its hand on their shoulder as they creep to school. The usual result is either a complete and sincere spiritual conversion—or suicide.

CHAPTER TWELVE

ENOCHIAN

John Dee (1527–1608), astrologer and political advisor to Queen Elizabeth I of England, was one of the greatest minds of the Elizabethan Age. His historical obscurity is in part due to the bulk of his writings languishing unread for centuries in manuscript form on dusty museum shelves. This distinction he shares with the German thinker, Albertus Magnus. But in equal measure his neglect arises from his reputation as a magician. His occult experiments doomed him in the eyes of so-called serious scholars and led to his writings being passed over and ignored. Only recently, thanks to such respected academic critics as Frances A. Yates, has he begun to be rehabilitated.

Born during the reign of Henry VIII, from childhood he demonstrated a potent intellect. At the age of 10 he had mastered Latin and read deeply in the classics. At 16 he went to Cambridge, where he immersed himself in the study of rhetoric, grammar, and logic. The following year he devoured music, astronomy, geometry, and arithmetic. Perhaps it was his aptitude for mathematical studies that inclined him in later years to a Pythagorean style of numerical magic. His *Monas Hieroglyphica*, a treatise on the ultimate occult symbol, a veritable key to all the mysteries, is based on mathematical proportions. During this formative period he also learned Greek and Hebrew, both requisite in that age for the attainment of a solid understanding of magic.

Of his system of study, Dee himself writes that it was his unvarying rule to sleep no more than four hours a night and allow himself

Title page of John Dee's Monas Hieroglyphica.

Edw: Kelly Prophet or Seer to D.ʳ Dee.   D.ʳ Dee avoucheth his Stone is brought by Angelicall Ministry

Portrait of Edward Kelley, alchemist   Portrait of Dr. John Dee, English
and seer to John Dee.   astrologer, mathematician and magician.
—from A True & Faithful Relation by Meric. Casaubon, 1659

two hours each day for meals. The other 18 hours, not counting time spent in religious observance, were all devoted to learning. Although his natural gift was for mathematics, by disposition he was most fond of philosophy and mysticism. The mingling of the two streams produced his unique scientific experiments in occultism.

Dee believed in angels, not only the holy angels of light who served the divine throne, but also the angels of wickedness cast down from heaven as punishment for their disobedience. Belief in spirits was the norm during the 16th century. It went hand in hand with a literal interpretation of the Bible, a dread of Witches and the evil eye, and the conviction that miracles were historical events. It would have been a bold intellect, and most probably an irreligious one, that could in that superstitious time scoff at accounts of the fall of Lucifer and his hellish band. Dee was pious in the true sense and accepted the holy books as he received them. This has led some modern critics to accuse him of credulity, but for Dee it would have constituted a defiance of God to question the existence of angels and devils. He cared nothing for the censure of men but remained true to his concept of deity all through his life.

A bold thinker, he conceived that great benefits might be gained for his native country of England if he could establish and maintain a communication with the good angels of God while taking care to exclude the deceits of wicked spirits. Throughout his long life, his genius was devoted to the faithful service of his beloved sovereign. Dee was instrumental in promoting Elizabeth's imperial goals through his extensive knowledge of map-making and navigation—he had studied cartography under the great Mercator himself. His life coincided with the rise of English sea power and colonial dreams—and the political intrigue and danger that inevitably accompany ambition. Magic was for Dee another tool to be placed in service to the Crown. He cast horoscopes to determine politically favorable times. When a waxen image of the queen was discovered in Lincoln's Inn Fields, he undertook to expose and counter the magic being worked against her by her enemies. Spirit communication he saw as a way to gain secrets from hostile lands and peer into the closed councils of foreign courts.

Dee's approach to communication with spirits was one of the traditional methods described in the grimoires. He relied on the aid of an instrument called a showstone to act as a kind of window on the ethereal realms. His favorite "stones" were an egg-shaped globe of rock crystal and a small, polished, black obsidian mirror. Obsidian is a very dark volcanic glass. These instruments were employed within the framework of prayers, ritual actions, and occult symbols of power, which were thought at the time to be necessary to open the showstone to spiritual influences.

Unfortunately, Dee was a terrible seer. This is often the case with those who allow their intellect to dominate their intuitive faculties. He would sit for hours staring into the stone and usually end up falling asleep. Rather than abandon his enterprise, he sought out the services of a professional scryer named Barnabas Saul. The first communication received by Saul and relayed verbally to Dee occurred in 1581. Saul reported the words of the angels Annael and Michael. He seems to have been a charlatan. After only four months he was dismissed from Dee's employ. The speculation is that Dee caught him fabricating angelic visions out of whole cloth.

Discouraged, but not disappointed, Dee obtained a replacement with whom he could carry on his experiments. Edward Kelley (1555–95) arrived at Dee's large house at Mortlake, near London, on March 8, 1582, and almost at once began to describe the most significant and detailed visions in the stones. Kelley was

Edward Kelley and a friend, Paul Waring, evoke a spirit of the dead with a necromantic ritual. It is usually, but incorrectly, said to be Kelley and John Dee in the magic circle.

—from a drawing by the English magician, astrologer, and writer of the 18th century, Ebenezer Sibly a man with a checkered past and equivocal character. Legend has it that he had his ears lopped off for coining; that is, making coins out of a debased alloy and passing them off as real currency of the realm. He represented himself as a mystical philosopher and an alchemist, and when he applied to Dee for the job of seer he was using the pseudonym Edward Talbot—hardly an indication of an honest nature. Nonetheless Dee was delighted with the results of those early sessions, and all through his association with Kelley he never lost faith in the visionary powers of the alchemist.

The scrying sessions were very like the seances of modern times in their general pattern. Kelley acted as the spirit medium for Dee, who recorded the events of the experiments on the spot in notebooks called the *Libri Mysteriorum*. Certain of the angels were easier to contact and came more frequently, especially one in the form of a little girl named Madimi, who may be likened to a spirit guide. Kelley could see and hear her quite clearly, but Dee only rarely was aware of her presence by such signs as the movement of inanimate objects. On a few occasions he seems himself to have caught glimpses of the spirits, but for the most part he was wholly dependent on Kelley's descriptions.

The sessions opened with a prayer, presumably seeking divine aid in establishing the link with the spirits and protection from wicked angels. Then the showstone was uncovered and the visions that appeared in its depths were described by Kelley to Dee, who sat nearby with pen and paper before him to record exactly all that transpired. Sometimes the angels seem to have moved out of the confines of the stone and into the chamber with the two men. The angels might hold a verbal conversation with Kelley, or they might create a kind of pantomime scene intended to convey information allegorically, with spirits filling the roles of actors.

During the early communications with Kelley, the spirits described magical instruments such as a ring, lamen, engraved table, and sigils that the two men were to make. These served as the symbolic framework of the scrying rituals that were to follow. Among these instruments was the great *Sigillum Aemeth*, an elaborate pentacle of wax inscribed with Enochian letters and names of power. This has survived the centuries, along with Dee's other occult tools, and now resides in the British Museum. The word *aemeth* is Hebrew for "truth" (אמת).

Enochian	Title	English
$\mathbb{V}$	Pe	B.
$\mathbb{B}$	Veh	C or K.
$\mathbb{b}$	Ged	G.
$\mathbb{X}$	Gal	D.
$\mathbb{Z}$	Orth	F.
$\mathbb{X}$	Un	A.
$\daleth$	Graph	E.
$\mathcal{E}$	Tal	M.
$\mathbb{L}$	Gon	I, Y, or J.
$\mathbb{G}$	Na-hath	H.
$\mathbb{C}$	Ur	L.
$\mathbb{\cap}$	Mals	P.
$\mathbb{U}$	Ger	Q.
$\mathbb{Z}$	Drun	N.
Γ	Pal	X.
$\mathbb{L}$	Med	O.
$\mathcal{E}$	Don	R.
$\mathbb{P}$	Ceph	Z.
$\cap$	Vau	U, V, W.
$\mathbb{l}$	Fam	S.
/	Gisa	T.

Enochian Alphabet

In one of the manuscript records kept by Dee, *De Heptarchia Mystica*, complete physical descriptions are provided of a hierarchy of the angels the two men were in contact with, along with their proper invocations, magical hours, sigils, and seals. One such angel described by Kelley and recorded by Dee is as follows:

> He appeared in his red apparell: & he opened his Clothes
> & there did issue, mighty & most terrible gastly Flames
> of Fire out of his sides: which no mortall Eye could abide
> to looke upon any long while. And in the marvelous rag-
> ing Fire, the word BRORGES did appeare tossed to and
> fro of the very flames.

Enochian was supposed to be the language of the angels in which they spoke and wrote before the creation of mankind. Adam before his fall also used it, but after his sin of eating the fruit from the Tree of Knowledge it was lost until its recovery by Dee, or so he believed. The name derives from Enoch, a patriarch of the Old Testament who "walked with God: and he was not; for God took him" (Genesis 5:24). More specifically, the reference is to the various books attributed to Enoch, apocryphal books concerned with the names and doings of the angels. Since Enoch is not explicitly said to have died like the other patriarchs, it was presumed that he was elevated living into heaven, where he enjoyed the conversation of the angels in their own tongue.

The first vision of Enochian was received by Kelley on March 26, 1583, when he reported seeing a book "all filled with squares." The angels did not convey the language in a straightforward way, but by means of magic squares made up of rows and columns of Enochian letters from which words were extracted. Kelley had some difficulty in describing the actual letters of the Enochian alphabet, but received aid from the angels in his transcription. As Dee notes on May 6, 1583:

> . . . when E.K. could not aptly imitate the forme of the
> Characters, or letters, as they were shewed: that they
> appered drawn on his paper with a light yelow cullor,
> which he drew the blak vppon, and so the yellow cullor
> disapearing there remayned only the shape of the letter
> in blak . . .

r	Z	i	l	a	f	A	Y u	t	l i	p	a
a	r	d	Z	a	i	d	p	a	L	a	m
C	z	o	n	s	a	r	o	Y v	a	u	b
T	o	i	T	t	z x	o	P	a	c	o	C
S	i	g	a	s	o	n m	r	b	z	n	h
f	m	o	n	d	a	T	d	i	a	r	l i
o	r	o	i	b	a	h	a	o	z	p	i
t c	N	a	b	r a	V	i	x	g	a	s z	d
O	i	i	i	t	T	p	a	l	O	a	i
A	b	a	m	o	o	o	a	C	u v	c	a
N	a	o	c	O	T	t	n	p	r	u a	T
o	c	a	n	m	a	g	o	t	r	o	i
S	h	i	a	l	r	a	p	m	z	o	x

One of the complex letter tables used in Golden Dawn Enochian magic.

Letter by painful letter, Kelley conveyed from the angels to Dee the texts of a set of invocations known as the Enochian Keys that were preserved by Dee in a manuscript written at Cracow between April 13 and July 13 of 1584 and titled the *48 Claves Angelicae*. These invocations are the main basis for the intrusion of Enochian magic into modern ritual practice. They were employed by the Golden Dawn, borrowed from this occult order by the magician Aleister Crowley, and from Crowley by the satanist Anton Szandor LaVey. Many lines of the Keys are quite poetic, as this translation of the Second Key shows:

> Can the wings of the winds understand your voices of wonder, O you the second of the First? Whom the burning flames have framed within the depths of my jaws; Whom I have prepared as cups for a wedding, or as the flowers in their beauty for the chamber of righteousness. Stronger are your feet than the barren stone, and mightier are your voices than the manifold winds; for you are become a building such as is not, but in the mind of the All-Powerful. Arise, says the First; move, therefore, unto his servants; show yourselves in power, and make me a strong seething; for I am of Him that lives forever.

The biblical echoes are frequent. The "wings of the winds," for example, is the name of an order of angels, as is the "burning flames" (see Psalms 104:3-4). In Hebrew occultism, the names of angels are based upon descriptions of their functions. A common recurrence in the Keys is the phrase in various different forms "move, therefore, and show yourselves," in Enochian *Zacare, ca, od zamran*. This is the actual command given by the magician speaking the evocation that the order of angels summoned should reveal themselves. It is given with the presumptive authority of God: "Arise, says the First; . . ." In effect the magician declares him or herself to be the agent of the Highest, and as the executor of the will of deity assumes the power of deity. In becoming the agent for a greater identity, the personality is submerged and we become that thing we serve. So Moses was enabled to work the miracles of God by surrendering his concept of self to God. So does the king of a nation speak of himself in the plural and declare himself to be the nation he serves.

A True & Faithful

RELATION

OF

What paſſed for many Yeers Between

Dᴿ. JOHN DEE

(A Mathematician of Great Fame in Q. Eʟɪᴢ.
and King Jᴀᴍᴇꜱ their Reignes) and

SOME SPIRITS:

Tᴇɴᴅɪɴɢ (had it Succeeded)
To a General Alteration of moſt S T A T E S and
K I N G D O M E S in the World.

His *Private Conferences* with Rᴏᴅᴏʟᴘʜᴇ Emperor of *Germany*, Sᴛᴇᴘʜᴇɴ
K. of *Poland*, and divers other Pʀɪɴᴄᴇꜱ about it.
The Particulars of his Cauſe, as it was agitated in the *Emperors* Court;
By the Pᴏᴘᴇꜱ Intervention: His Baniſhment, and Reſtoration in part.

Aꜱ Aʟꜱᴏ

The Lᴇᴛᴛᴇʀꜱ of Sundry Great Men

and Pʀɪɴᴄᴇꜱ (ſome whereof were preſent at ſome of theſe
Conferences and Apparitions of Sᴘɪʀɪᴛꜱ :) to the ſaid D.Dᴇᴇ.

Oᴜᴛ Oꜰ

The Original Copy, written with Dʳ. Dᴇᴇꜱ own
Hand: Kept in the LIBRARY of

Sir *T H O. C O T T O N*, Kᵗ. Baronet.

WITH A

PREFACE

Confirming the *Reality* (as to the Point of Sᴘɪʀɪᴛꜱ) of
This RELATION: and ſhewing the ſeveral good Uꜱᴇꜱ that
a Sober Chriſtian may make of All.

B Y

Mᴇʀɪᴄ. Cᴀꜱᴀᴜʙᴏɴ, D.D.

LONDON,
Printed by *D. Maxwell*, for T. Gᴀʀᴛʜᴡᴀɪᴛ, and ſold at the Littl
North door of S. *Pauls*, and by other Stationers. 1659.

Title page of Casaubon's True & Faithful Relation, *London, 1659.*

Until very recently, most of the information on Enochian magic was derived from a single book, *A True & Faithful Relation of What passed for many Yeers Between Dr. John Dee and Some Spirits*, published by Meric. Casaubon in London in 1659. The book is a straightforward transcription of a portion of Dee's magical diaries, which had fallen into the library of Sir Thomas Cotton. It was this book that generated the interest among the founders of the Golden Dawn in the use of Enochian as a secret magical language. The Keys are in the book—for example, the Second Key quoted above appears on page 101. In the last few years, occultists have begun to examine the magical works of Dee that remain unpublished, and from this additional material attempts are being made to construct a formal system of Enochian magic. Prominent in this effort are the books of Gerald and Betty Schueler. Also worth mentioning is *The Enochian Evocation of Dr. John Dee* by Geoffrey James (Heptangle Books, 1984), a compilation of some of Dee's magical writings.

Nonetheless, Enochian remains primarily an occult language used in the context of established systems of magic. As such it is very useful. Western ritual magic has, since before the time of Pythagoras, relied on barbarous names of power—words whose meaning has been lost, but which are regarded as possessing immense magical potency. The most important feature in any word of power is that it be mysterious. Once it is widely understood it becomes merely another word. It is permissible for the magician to know the meaning of the word—or at least to have a personal interpretation of the word—but it is essential that the word be unknown by the multitude of listeners.

Bearing this in mind, the value of a secret language unknown since the time of Adam becomes clear. Not just a few names, but every word of Enochian is a power word. The power of Enochian stems from its unintelligibility, but also its angelic associations and its inherent mystery. Even if the magician thinks he or she knows the meaning of the words, they are strange words, alien words that come from another dimension of time and space. The sounds are strange, even the shapes of the very letters themselves are unlike anything else that exists in the world. At least, this is the underlying and unconscious presumption of those occultists who place so much faith in Enochian as a magical language, and the source of its power.

CHAPTER THIRTEEN

WITCHCRAFT

Witches meet in covens on the *sabbats*, the eight great festivals of the year defined by the solstices and equinoxes, called the Quarter Days, and the days that fall between them, called the Cross-Quarter Days. The latter are considered to be more important. It is easiest to think of the year as a wheel, and the sabbats as eight spokes that regularly intersect its rim. They are:

Winter Solstice—December 20–23, the shortest day when the sun is lowest in the sky and weakest in our northern latitudes. The celebration of Yule around this time is a pagan observance designed to call back the Sun and restore life to the frozen earth. Christmas is essentially a pagan festival and has very little to do with the birthdate of Christ, which is unknown.

Oimelc—February 2, an old Roman festival of purification during which candles were burned in honor of the goddess Februa, the mother of Mars, to frighten away the ghosts of the dead. In borrowing this pagan rite and calling it "Candlemas," the Catholic Church attributes the light of the candles to Christ and burns them in commemoration of the purification of the Virgin Mary.

Spring Equinox—March 20–23, when day and night are exactly equal. A time when opposites are in balance.

Beltane—May 1, commonly known as May Day, a fertility festival originally intended to spur the growth of crops. The Maypole is a blatant phallic symbol. This day is said to commemorate the marriage of the God and Goddess of the Witches. The eve of this day, April 30, is Walpurgis Night.

Summer Solstice—June 20–23, the longest day and shortest night, made famous by Shakespeare's play *A Midsummer Night's Dream*, when love is in the air and strange things are possible.

Lughnassadh—August 1, also called Lammas, a harvest festival celebrating the first fruits of the field with loaves of bread baked from the early wheat. It was appropriated by the early Church and justified as the day St. Peter was delivered from prison.

Fall Equinox—September 20–23, when day and night are of equal duration. It marks the turning of the year in its long, descending arc into winter.

Samhain—October 31, better known as All Hallow's Eve or Halloween, a festival dedicated to the shades of the dead, who on this night are said to be able to revisit the earth to be with the living. Witches use it to celebrate eternal life. Originally the Celtic New Year, it was appropriated by the Catholic Church as the eve of All Saints Day, when the saints are celebrated collectively.

Between the eight great festivals fall the *esbats*, lesser occasions of meeting determined by the phases of the Moon, when the day-to-day business of the coven is enacted. Usually, esbats occur on the Full Moon, sometimes the New Moon, sometimes both. The word "esbat" was introduced into the language by the anthropologist Margaret A. Murray after the example of Estebene de Cambrue (Murray 1967, 97). It is on the esbats that works of practical magic are carried out that are designed to help a member of the coven or an outsider.

A coven in an autonomous group of Witches, usually with a High Priestess who is an older and more experienced Witch for its leader. Some covens have both Priestess and Priest to represent the Goddess and God of Witchcraft, and often these posts are shared among the coven members. The optimum number for a coven is 13, composed of a Priestess and six loving couples, but frequently they are larger or smaller, since it is difficult to maintain an exact number over time.

Due to the difficulty of gathering a group of sincere and dedicated followers of the Old Religion, modern Witches often are solitaries who practice their craft in isolation. This echoes the

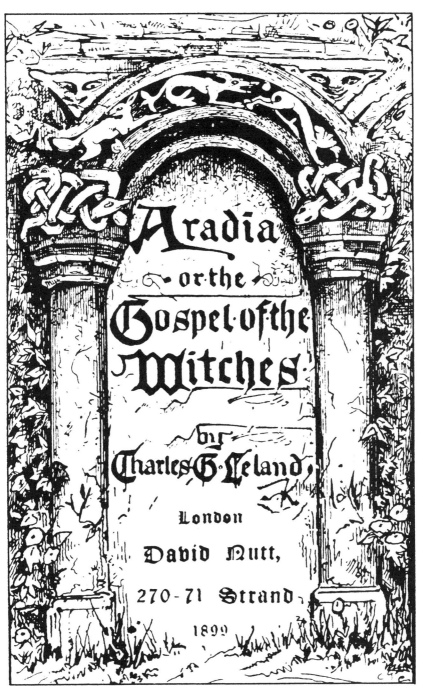

Title page from Aradia, or The Gospel of the Witches
by Charles Leland, a book that influenced Gerald B. Gardner.

*Artemis of Ephesus, one form of the Goddess that
emphasizes her life-giving and nourishing qualities.*

European tradition of the wise women of rural villages who dwelt
alone some distance apart from the group, and who were resorted
to when a cure for sickness or a solution to a personal problem was
needed. Though sometimes unavoidable, solitary practice is seldom as emotionally rewarding as group practice.

Witchcraft is performed within a magic circle. Its size varies
according to the size of the coven. Witches believe that the function
of the circle is to contain and concentrate occult force, not to protect against malefic influences outside the circle. This is at variance
with the tradition of European high magic, and it would be interesting to know where this idea originated. I suspect it was put
forth by Gerald Gardner.

A magical technique particular to Witchcraft is the raising of a
"Cone of Power," a zone of occult potency that is created within
the circle, then released toward the fulfillment of a specific purpose. Methods for raising the cone vary, but one consists of all the
coven members dancing in a ring around the High Priestess, who
stands at the center of the circle. At the climactic moment, the
dancers all fall down and direct their energies inward to the Priest-

Witch Pentagram

ess, who then transmits this focused power to the fulfillment of the magical purpose.

The Cone of Power is descended from the practice in Golden Dawn magic of circumambulation, or walking in a circle, to draw occult potency into the ritual space. Threefold circumambulation was believed to create an occult vortex that opened a passage to a higher realm of spirit, thereby inducing spiritual agents and powers to enter the magic circle and energize the ritual actions occurring within its boundary.

Witches believe in a single, all-pervading spiritual essence that is symbolically represented by a mated Goddess and God. The Goddess, whose symbol is the Moon, is usually considered to be more important in a practical sense because Her power is manifest on the Earth in the growth of crops, the health of beasts, and the well-being of men and women. She is known by many names, such as Diana, Isis, Hecate, Selene, and therefore is nameless.

Often She is called simply the Lady or the Great Mother. The God is depicted with horns, often in the form of a goat, sometimes as a stag, and is known as Pan, Osiris, and Kernunnos, but, like the Goddess, He is really nameless. Often He is called simply the Old One, the Horned One, and the Goat-foot God. His symbol is the Sun. Early Christian priests thought Him to be the devil and attributed His horns to Satan.

The Goddess has three faces that reflect the phases of the Moon. She is a young virgin just coming into Her sexual awakening in Her persona of waxing lunar disk. She is a mature, fertile woman when She represents the Full Moon. And She is an ancient crone with a bent back when She signifies the waning lunar crescent. For this reason, She is called the Threefold Goddess. This conception comes from the ancient Greek goddess Hecate, a triple lunar deity who was called Phoebe in heaven, Diana on the earth, and Proserpine in hell. She had three heads, that of a horse, a dog, and a lion.

It seems to me that the God and Goddess of the Witches represent an unusually clear expression of the female *shakti* and male *shakta* principles described in the Hindu Tantric texts. Shakti is all manifest power, all being. Shakta is the masculine seed of creation that is necessary for existence, but does not itself exist, being invisible and powerless. About the Horned God, Marion Weinstein writes: "He represents, symbolically, the initiating life-force, that spark of primal fire and the essentially phallic, creative energy . . ." (Weinstein 1981, 73). This is an excellent description of shakta.

Witches like to meet out of doors where this is possible, and those who follow Gerald Gardner's teachings practice their craft "skyclad," or naked. There is a belief that clothing can hinder the flow of occult potential. Most Witches use robes but go naked beneath them. Instruments particular to the craft are the *athame* (a special kind of knife), the cauldron of traditional Witch lore, and the Book of Shadows. A written record of magical work is common in many branches of the occult, but the name "Book of Shadows" has come to mean specifically the record of rituals and spells of a Witch.

The great symbol of Witchcraft is the pentagram with a single point uppermost. Witches often wear silver pentagrams and silver crescents, because silver is the lunar metal, and jewelry of clear rock crystal for the same reason. Their philosophy is summarized in the

The Goddess as the anima mundi (Soul of the World), the proximate minister (Shakti) of God (Shakta). This is a small portion of an engraving entitled "The Mirror of All Nature and the Image of Art" from Robert Fludd's Utriusque Cosmi Maioris scilicet et Minoris Metaphysica, Physica Atque Technica Historica, *Oppenheim, 1617.*

dictum: "An it harm none, do what ye will!" This is a modification of Crowley's "Do what thou wilt shall be the whole of the Law," of which the Great Beast would hardly have approved, since the meaning of the original is weakened and distorted in transition.

Witches show sensitivity to questions of the environment and the care of the Earth. They are generally more conscious than the average person of the phases of the Moon and the transition of the seasons. This is hardly surprising when it is realized that the Goddess is identical with Mother Nature, who was known in ancient Greece as the Soul of the World.

Besides a desire to get into touch with the Earth, another motivator of those who become Witches is a belief in the beauty, power, and holiness of womankind. Witchcraft is a celebration of the feminine principle. This attracts feminists, both female and male. Some covens, though not many, are so excessive in their zeal that they resort to the exclusion of men. These may be composed of lesbians, but often are made up of heterosexual women who simply want an art and a religion that is wholly theirs, untainted by male dominance.

In my experience, I have found Witches to be the friendliest and most decent human beings I have ever had the good fortune to meet. They are sensitive, cheerful, willing to give love without receiving it, and very down to earth. I wish there were more Witches in the world. We need them.

CHAPTER FOURTEEN

DRUIDISM

There is much in common between the modern Druidic movement and Wicca. Druids worship in groves of oak trees and sometimes in stone circles. They wear white robes. The mythology of Druidism is mainly Celtic. Modern Druidic festivals are the same eight festivals of Witchcraft described above. During rituals, there is chanting and singing, and a consecrated liquor called the waters-of-life is shared to symbolize the union of all things in nature. The creed of Druidism may be summarized as a reverence for the Earth Mother in all her natural manifestations.

Druidism in America seems to have started as a kind of philosophical joke. In 1963, some of the students at Carleton College in Northfield, Minnesota, organized the Reformed Druids of North America as a protest against enforced attendance at religious services. When in 1964 the religious requirement was abolished, much to the horror of the university and the amazement of many of the original founders of the movement, the Reformed Druids did not dissolve but flourished, becoming more and more a legitimate pagan religion with the passage of time.

There is also a loose organization of groves known as the New Reformed Druids of North America with an eclectic membership that includes or has included in its history groups of Zen Druids, Norse Druids, Wiccan Druids, and most unlikely of all, Hassidic Druids. Since Druidism was a purely Celtic phenomenon, it is difficult to know how seriously to take these exotic hybrids. If Druidism is to survive as a vital subcategory of modern paganism

153

it seems to me that it must move closer to its historical roots. This same view was expressed by the Arch-Druid Isaac Bonewits in his *Druid Chronicles* (Berkeley: Drunemeton Press, 1976).

Merlin was a Druid, as well as a seer, and Druids are associated with the gift of second sight and skill in divination. The most Druidic method of divining is with the ogham sticks, 20 symbols carved into sticks of wood that stand for the letters of the Old Irish alphabet. They have individual names, just as do the Teutonic runes. Each "few" or letter of ogham stands for a kind of tree.

In Irish legend, the Druid Dalan uses four yew wands cut with ogham characters to divine the whereabouts of Queen Etain, who has been carried off by the god Mider. This tale provides a hint about the method of divination employed by the Druids, which may have been similar to that used by the German shamans with the runes. Likely the fall of the ogham sticks was read by the Druid according to their position and relationship to each other, and according to which of the ogham characters, or sets of characters, fell uppermost.

Druids were also able to perform weather magic. In the epic tale *Cattle-Spoiling of Cualnge,* the Druids "raise their eyes towards heaven, observe the clouds, and hurl spells against the elements, so that they arouse strife amongst them and clouds of fire are driven towards the camp of the men of Ireland." They are said by early Christian writers to have opposed the progress of both Saint Patrick and Saint Columba by calling up a mist to obscure the way.

The curse of a Druid was a powerful weapon, held in such dread that Druids were able to stop a battle merely by rushing between the two hostile armies. When the Romans under Sueto-nius Paulinus invaded the island of Anglesea, a band of Druids confronted them and, with hands raised to the heavens, poured forth powerful curses upon the heads of the Roman soldiers. For a short time the Romans quaked in terror, but when the ground did not split open nor the heavens rain flames, they gathered their courage, put the Britons to flight, and then cut down the sacred oak groves in Anglesea. Before the battle of Culdremne, fought in 561, a Druid is reported to have erected an *airbe druad,* apparently a kind of magic circle of protection, around one of the armies.

It seems certain that Druidic magic in large measure consisted of chanted words of power. This may be deduced from the fact that

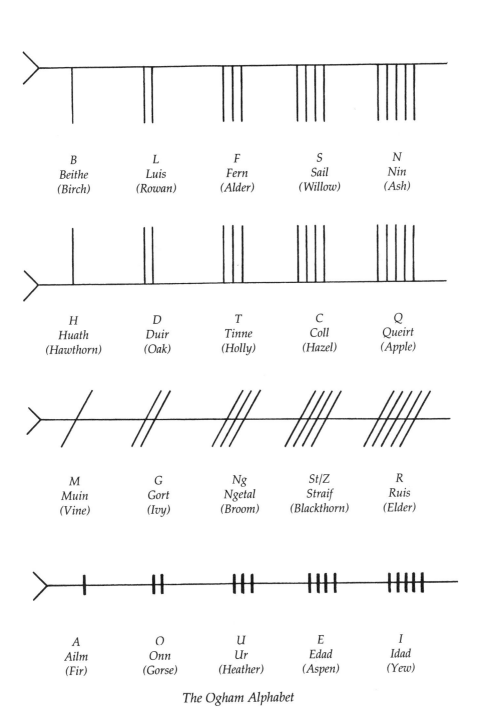

The Ogham Alphabet

The king consults his Druid Merlin.
—*from the* Chronicle *of Peter of Langtoft*

all the secret wisdom of the Druids was taught orally, from the reputation for great learning enjoyed by the order, and from the strong link between the Druids and poetry. Even after the Druids had ceased to be workers of magic, they continued as bards to counsel kings and provide teachings in history through their immense skill as poets and musicians.

In addition to divination and magic, Druids were famed for their skill in healing through the use of herbs. In legend, the hero Cuchulinn is given a potion that enables him to forget a fairy woman who has enchanted his mind. This is probably a poetic echo of the more material healing powers of the actual living Druids, who were sought out for all physical complaints. Druids were also noted for their wisdom. When Saint Patrick came to Ireland, a Druid was acting as tutor to the daughters of the high-king, Laegaire. The course of study of a novice Druid was extremely rigorous and extended over as much as 20 years.

Druids believed in the immortality of the soul and that souls

A The Stones call'd Corfstones, 12 Tonn Weight
24 foot high, 7 broad, and 16 round
B The Stones call'd Coronetts, of 6 or 7 Tonns
C The place where Mens bones are dug up.

The massive blocks of Stonehenge were fabled to have been erected by the Druid Merlin.

—from Britannia *by William Camden, 1586*

returned to Earth and were reincarnated many times. This greatly surprised the ancients, who speculated that Druids had been influenced by the teachings of the Greek philosopher Pythagoras, who held similar views. They were entrusted with enforcing the law and had the power to execute criminals or condemn men to exile, which in those days was an almost certain death sentence.

Potent symbols of Druidism are the golden sickle and the mistletoe. In ancient times, the Druids would go into the forest and seek out mistletoe growing on a mighty oak tree. This oak symbolically represented the world tree so common in shamanism. They cut the mistletoe loose with a golden sickle and caught it as it fell onto a clean white cloth, taking care that no hand touched and defiled it. Two bulls of perfect whiteness were sacrificed on the spot where it fell. The parasitic mistletoe embodies rebirth and renewal because it grows green on the stark, frozen boughs of the oaks in the dead of winter and survives even though its roots are far above the nourishing earth. Because it grew on the sacred oaks, it was regarded as a gift from heaven.

Modern Druids do not worship trees, but the life principle of the Goddess that flows through and sustains the trees, along with every other living thing. Their philosophical orientation is a curious mix of the simple, natural values of the earth and the changing seasons, the growth of plants, the health of beasts and humans, which stems from their reverence for Mother Nature, and at the same time an intellectual and analytical approach, often very witty and even cynical in its expression, that grows out of the Druidic tradition of learning and wisdom.

In ancient times the Romans looked upon Druidism as a horrifying cult of human sacrifice. There can be little doubt that Druids did sacrifice their condemned prisoners to their gods. The method may have been similar to that depicted in the cult film classic, *The Wicker Man*, where the unfortunate victim is burned inside a giant human figure of wickerwork. However, modern Druids emphasize a loving and gentle attitude toward all living things that is similar to the Buddhist reverence for life. Druids dislike killing anything, especially trees, and go to great lengths to nourish life in all its diverse forms. It is significant that Saint Columba refers to Jesus Christ as his Druid.

CHAPTER FIFTEEN

SHAMANISM

Shamanism is the root of all magic. It flourishes around the globe in many forms, but always with a startling unity in its essential beliefs and practices. It has existed in much the same state since the Stone Age and shows no signs of dying out anytime soon. Recently there has been a quickening of interest in shamanic magical techniques in the West, but modern shamanism is still in a formative state and has yet to coalesce and harden into a distinct and viable occult movement with its own unique set of rituals and an explicit manifesto.

The shaman is a special kind of healer with the power to call back souls who have wandered from their bodies during serious illness, or in the event of death, to conduct souls safely to their final place of rest. Shamanism is characterized by the ability to enter a trance state in which the soul is freed from the confines of the body and is able to journey at will in the three realms of heaven, earth, and the underworld. It involves a close communion with spirits who provide information to the shaman or power to accomplish magical effects.

The most potent of shamanic symbols is the world tree. Many shamanic rites of initiation involve climbing a tree or pole that represents the single eternal tree at the axis of the universe that has its upper boughs in heaven and its roots in the underworld. The ash Yggdrasill of Norse mythology is the best known example of the world tree. When Woden was suspended from Yggdrasill in his search for the runes, and underwent fasting and ritual mutilation

The Tree of Death upon which corpses were hung to be devoured by
ravens. A shamanic image representing the sublimation of the flesh into spirit.
—from the Travels of John Maundeville, *London, 1499*

to produce a visionary state, this was a shamanic ritual. The world
tree appears in many startling guises. The cross upon which Christ
was crucified is one of its forms, and the inverted Kabbalistic Tree
with its boughs sunk in the earth and its roots in heaven is another.

Shamans often discover their vocation, and even receive their
initiation, in the form of dreams and visions. It is possible to deliberately set out to become a shaman, but traditionally those who go
in quest of shamanism are considered to have less power than
those who are chosen by the spirits. Usually a specific dream or
vision signals a vocation for this type of magic.

For example, in one of my own dreams I stood in a circular
clearing that contained only a single tree stump in its center. The
stump was tall and very old. All the boughs and bark had long
since been worn from the trunk by wind and rain, and the spiral
grain of the wood was eroded in deep ridges that curved up
around it. My body was not as it is now, but smaller and hairy all

Paleolithic shaman dancing in the skin of
a stag. A detail from a cave painting in France.

over the naked limbs, almost apelike. With excitement and wonder
I climbed the weathered stump and stood swaying on its rounded
point to look out over the tops of the trees of the forest. I felt a great
sense of euphoria, as though I had accomplished a feat of daring
and significance, and remember growing afraid that in the intoxi-
cation of my victory I might sway and fall back to the earth. Then
I awoke.

I record this dream because it is quintessentially shamanic. It could be interpreted to mean that I have already received a dream initiation by spirits, or at the very least that I possess a natural aptitude for shamanism. Historically shamans are usually men, although there seems no reason why women should not pursue this type of magic. The exclusion of women is a cultural phenomenon and has nothing to do with the ability of women to enter trance states and commune with or command spirits. Frequently shamans are abnormal in some way. They may be epileptic, or homosexual, or sickly, or highly nervous, or at least predisposed to solitude and retreat.

The primary instrument of shamanism is the drum. The shell of the drum is cut from the world tree—that is, from a tree that has been mystically selected to represent the world tree—and the skin of the drum is that of an animal that bears a magical relationship to the shaman. When the drum is struck it is the voice of the beast that speaks. Beating the drum opens a channel through the central axis of the world that connects heaven with the underworld. After its making, the drum must be empowered and awakened. This may be done by sprinkling it with beer or other alcoholic spirits. This is interesting in view of the practice of feeding the drums of Voudoun.

All shamans are shape-changers. This is a natural function of their mastery of astral projection, for when the soul is freed from the envelope of the flesh it becomes plastic and is easily molded by the imagination into any desired form. The costume of the shaman almost always includes feathers to symbolize the shaman's power of soul flight. This is true both of the shamans of North America and Central Asia. For example, the ritual dress of the priests of the ancient Bon religion of Tibet includes eagle feathers.

Primitive shamans are not too particular how they induce the necessary trance state that allows them to leave their bodies and communicate with spirits. Often alcohol, nicotine, peyote, or other drugs are employed in conjunction with rigorous fasting and physical exhaustion brought about by chanting and dancing. Such practices are dangerous and take a cumulative toll on the health of the body. Modern followers of the path of the shaman would do well to think twice before resorting to such drastic trance induction methods.

Each shaman has a familiar spirit, called an *ayami* in Siberian shamanism, that fulfills the role of wife or husband. The bond

Siberian shaman wearing antlers and a feathered robe.

between shaman and spirit spouse is a genuine and enduring love bond. The relationship is sexual. The ayami is teacher and helper to the shaman as well as lover. These celestial wives tend to be jealous of earthly females and often try to turn the shaman away from physical love with living women. The are seductive and very beautiful. One shaman writes of his ayami: "My wife on earth/ Is not fit to pour water on thy hands" (Eliade 1964, 77).

No man or woman can be said to be a true shaman who has not successfully undergone an ordeal that traditionally involved ritual death, often by horrible means such as dismemberment, and spiritual rebirth. During this experience, the terror and pain are completely real. It is a test of will and of courage. One well known example is the corpse-sitting ceremony of the Tibetan Buddhists, borrowed from the Bon religion, where the monk sits alone in a graveyard on the chest of a corpse in the middle of the night until a host of terrible demons come and tear his body into small pieces.

This is a purely subjective experience, but so real that it sometimes results in madness—see the account of one such unfortunate monk in Alexandra David-Neel's *Magic and Mystery in Tibet* (New York: Dover, 1971, 157-63).

Of all the shamanic instruments of magic, the runes are the most potent. In recent years, they have grown so much in popularity that they now constitute a separate branch of modern occultism. Ritual rune magic will be examined in the next chapter.

CHAPTER SIXTEEN

RUNES

Runes are letter-symbols, each with its own name and meaning, that were first developed and used among Germanic tribes living in northern Italy as early as the 4th century BC. Wandering German mercenaries carried them across the Alps and spread them throughout Europe. In later centuries, they found their way in various modified forms into Scandinavia and Iceland, where they were reduced to 16 characters, and England, where their number was increased to 33, but it is the original and most ancient German *futhark* of 24 runes that is magically the purest of the rune alphabets. This elder futhark, as it is sometimes called, is becoming the standard rune alphabet of modern occultism.

Runes are completely Teutonic in origin. This cannot be said for any other surviving system of magic. The Kabbalah is Semitic. Druidism is Celtic. The ceremonial magic of the grimoires is Graeco-Egyptian. Tarot cards may or may not have some gypsy connection, but in any case underwent their early development in Italy; they may be characterized as southern European. Tantra and yoga trace their beginnings back to India. Shamanism takes its model from the indigenous practices of American Indians and other surviving native cultures. Witchcraft is either Celtic, or, in its variant form where Diana is worshiped as the Goddess, Greek. Only the runes speak to the racial memory of the peoples of Germany, Holland, Denmark, Sweden, Norway, England, and connecting geographical regions.

The need for a Teutonic current was felt in occult circles even before the runes had become widely known. It led Raymond Buckland to compose *The Tree: The Complete Book of Saxon Witchcraft* in 1974 for pagans whose racial heritage lay in the north. This pseudo-grimoire of what its author calls "Seax-Wica," purporting to be a genuine Saxon Book of Shadows first written during the Witch persecutions of the Middle Ages, was compiled tongue-in-cheek by Buckland. Much to his surprise, the book was received quite seriously by many frustrated Witches with Teutonic roots. It contains a brief treatment of the runes and encouraged the impulse that led to their present revival as a viable system of magic.

The revival received a further boost from *The Book of Runes* by Ralph Blum (Oracle Books, 1982), a system of divination by runes that was accompanied by a pouch of 25 ceramic "rune stones." Although Blum's book was marred by a host of inaccuracies, including the very practice of putting the runes on small tiles for divination and the inclusion of a blank so-called "Rune of Destiny" representing karma, it found wide public acceptance, in part due to the attractive way the book was packaged, but also because people were eager to learn about the runes. Unfortunately, it fixed the runes in the minds of most occultists as purely an instrument of divination. Nothing had been written about active rune magic, the use of the runes as instruments of ritual to bring about willed purposes.

The publication of *Futhark: A Handbook of Rune Magic* by Edred Thorsson in 1984 made available practical techniques of rune magic set against a background of solid historical information about the runes. Thorsson may be regarded as the leading light of the rune revival in America. He is the head of the occult organization known as the Rune-Gild, founded in 1980, and has authored numerous books on the subject of rune magic and related topics, such as the ogham tree alphabet of the Celts. His skill as a linguist and his academic background lend his writings more authority than is often the case with popular occult writings.

A weakness shared by many books on the subject of runes that have appeared in the last few years is the assertion, either explicitly voiced or merely implied, that the techniques of magic in their pages are historically accurate. The authors want you to believe that the magic they describe is identical to the magic worked by the German shamans in the forests of Europe 2,000 years ago. This is not true. All modern rune magic is based upon conjecture. The

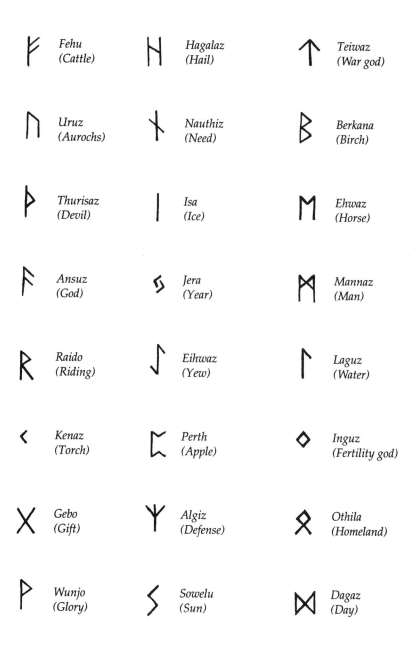

ᚠ Fehu (Cattle)	ᚺ Hagalaz (Hail)	↑ Teiwaz (War god)
ᚢ Uruz (Aurochs)	ᚾ Nauthiz (Need)	ᛒ Berkana (Birch)
ᚦ Thurisaz (Devil)	ᛁ Isa (Ice)	ᛖ Ehwaz (Horse)
ᚨ Ansuz (God)	ᛃ Jera (Year)	ᛗ Mannaz (Man)
ᚱ Raido (Riding)	ᛇ Eihwaz (Yew)	ᛚ Laguz (Water)
ᚲ Kenaz (Torch)	ᛈ Perth (Apple)	◇ Inguz (Fertility god)
ᚷ Gebo (Gift)	ᛉ Algiz (Defense)	ᛟ Othila (Homeland)
ᚹ Wunjo (Glory)	ᛋ Sowelu (Sun)	ᛞ Dagaz (Day)

The Elder Futhark

ancient techniques of the rune shamans have been lost in time and can never with certainty be recovered.

The rune magic of the present takes two forms. The first is an attempt to reconstruct the ancient shamanic rune rituals based upon the hints that survive in manuscripts, the forms of rune relics which seem to have had an occult function, and the parallel practices of other shamanic cultures around the world. There is a wonderful unity underlying the superficially diverse magic of shamans separated both in distance and in time. In my own work, *Rune Magic* (Llewellyn, 1988), I have attempted to rediscover the essential methods of the lost Teutonic rune masters by uniting these threads.

The other less praiseworthy tendency has been to take the structures and techniques of modern ritual magic, give them a Teutonic gloss, and claim that they are the genuine beliefs and methods of the ancient shamans of northern Europe recovered from the wreck of the past. One example is to claim that the rune masters of old possessed a formal pattern of the universe made up of spheres connected together with channels or pathways, each related to a particular rune, upon which the soul could ascend or descend. This runic Tree of Life is clearly no more than an imitation of the Tree of the Kabbalah. Similarly, the suggestion that ancient shamans performed a kind of yoga in which their bodies formed the pattern of individual runes is without the least foundation historically. The Germans in the time of the Caesars knew nothing of yoga. Yet both these propositions, and many others equally false, are put forward by contemporary writers concerning the runes.

A clear distinction should be made between the honest attempt to integrate runes into the mainstream of Western occultism and the deceitful practice of putting rune terminology, or labels from Norse mythology, upon modern magical techniques and passing them off as the resurrected lore of the ancients. To staple the beak of a parrot onto the nose of a cat and stick a few feathers under its tail does not make it a parrot.

This pernicious practice of claiming ancient authority where none exists has tainted the entire course of the magical revival. The founders of the Golden Dawn believed that, if they could not claim to be in psychic communication with Christian Rosencreutz, no one would take their magic seriously. Gerald Gardner and Alex Sanders both felt compelled to maintain that they had received

Sorcerer bound by the power of runes.
—*from Olaus Magnus,* Historia de gentibus septentrionalibus, *Rome, 1555*

their training at the hands of an hereditary survival of the European Witch cult—claims which are so patently bogus that it is hard to believe either man would have the audacity to make them. It is sad to think that the same course is being followed in the resurrection of rune magic.

If you realize that everything said by any author about the techniques of using runes for purposes of magic and divination is conjecture on the part of the author, you are unlikely to be misled. This is not to imply that such conjectures are valueless. Intelligent attempts to reconstruct the methods of rune magic based upon a solid analysis of surviving historical fragments in the light of existing shamanic practices may possess great potency. Even the mere re-labeling of magical techniques with Teutonic or rune names will not rob those techniques of their effectiveness. But nobody, not the greatest magician nor the most erudite researcher, knows for certain what the old rune masters did.

The Nazis' adoption of the *Sigel* rune, which has the shape of a lightning bolt, as the emblem of the notorious SS, as well as their use of the swastika, has led many to suspect that rune magic is evil and promotes racism and violence among those attracted to it. The swastika is not a rune, but is a prominent shamanic symbol of the

Teutons representing the hammer of Thor. It is one of the pre-runic symbols upon which the runes were formed.

The involvement of the Nazis with magic generally and with the runes in particular was much less than some sensation-seeking occult writers would have their readers believe. But even if the Nazis did use rune magic and employ rune symbolism, this is hardly reason to condemn the runes themselves. To vilify the rune Sigel because it was the emblem of the SS makes no more sense than condemning the letter A because it stood as the sign for adultery in old New England. Similarly the swastika, which is thousands of years old, should properly be regarded as a symbol of solar force rather than of the Third Reich. Perhaps when enough time has passed this will come to be so.

Undoubtedly runes attract white supremacists with occult inclinations. This is to be deplored but cannot be helped. No one can prevent an evil human being from using a tool for evil ends. A more legitimate fascination for the runes exists among those of northern European ancestry seeking their magical and religious roots. The gods of the runes are the gods of their distant forebears and would be their own gods but for the advent of Christianity, just as the gods and goddesses of the Witches would form the pantheon of the Celts but for suppression by the Church. Surely a Swede or an Anglo-Saxon has as much right to study the mysteries of the runes as a Jew does to learn the ways of the Kabbalah, and as much right to take a hereditary pride in that knowledge without being accused of being a Nazi or a bigot.

The traditional manner of using the runes appears to have involved carving or marking them on a surface and then evoking their potentials through chants, ritual gestures, visualization, and the sacrifice of blood, which was in ancient times believed to "feed" the runes. To ask something of the runes, it was necessary to give something in return. As the poet of the *Havamal* puts it, "a gift demands a gift." The nature of the magical effect depended upon the combination of runes carved, and the rune object thus created became a talisman of power that could be placed in the location where the magic was to be realized, or at least directed to that place by an act of will. This was known as "casting the runes." Of course, casting also referred to the random scattering of rune staffs in divination, from which certain runes were then selected blindly in a ritual manner and read according to their individual and collective meanings.

In modern rune magic, it is no longer considered necessary to spill blood to feed the runes and awaken their power. Other fluids of the body may be used, and red pigment forms an acceptable substitute when the mind of the magician is suitably trained and focused. Nonetheless, there remains in rune magic a certain wildness and danger that perhaps can never be entirely tamed, since it is an essential factor in the makeup of the rune gods. Rune magic possesses a raw, elemental force hewn from the harsh necessity of the bitter snowbound northern winters. The Teutons were, and are, a sullen, mystical, severe race given by turns to strange dreams and bloodthirsty rages. Civilization and Christianity have only partially succeeded in subduing this barbarian strain, which lurks near the surface in those of northern blood. The runes mirror the essential savagery of the peoples who created them, and like their makers are not easily tamed.

Symbol of Baron Samedi
from Voudoun Fire *by Melita Denning and Osborne Phillips*

CHAPTER SEVENTEEN

VOUDOUN

Voodoo, or more properly Voudoun, is an evolution of African shamanism and so bears many of the characteristics of shamanism that are common around the world. The *houngan* (priest) uses a sacred rattle called an *asson* to summon departed souls back from the Island Below the Sea, where they spend a year and a day after death in a kind of purgatory. The rattle is completely shamanic. Voudoun also relies on sacred drums, which must be baptized and fed to give them power. In the center of the *peristyle* (ceremonial enclosure) stands the *poteau-mitan* (centerpost), representing the intersection of the crossroads where the world of the living meets the world of the dead. This centerpost is another version of the world tree. Trees play an important part in Voudoun. They are looked upon as natural vessels for the *loa,* or gods.

In its essence, Voudoun is a religion of ancestor worship. The loa were formerly the souls *(gros-bon-ange)* of the dead, though their human origins have long since been lost in time. When men and women die, their souls travel to the land of the dead deep under the waters of the ocean, a place that is in every respect the mirror opposite of this world. Here they wait for a year and a day until they are called back by the Voudoun rites and made to reside in a *govi,* a clay vessel shaped with a "mouth" that enables the soul to speak and advise the living. The most powerful and wise souls eventually are absorbed by the loa. Each person has a special loa, usually the one by which that worshiper was first possessed, called the *maît-tête* (master of the head). It is said in Voudoun that the character of a person is the character of his or her loa.

These are not abstract concepts but regularly proved to the worshipers of Voudoun by the personal experience of possession. The loa "mounts" an individual worshiper in much the way a man mounts a horse, for a time displacing the human identity and taking control of the body. During possession, the mounted worshiper exhibits all the personal characteristics of the loa in control, qualities by which that loa is recognized and distinguished.

Possession is a completely real phenomenon. There is no need for the *houngan* and the *mambo* (priestess) to fabricate it, because it occurs regularly under well-understood circumstances. I emphasize this because I am sure that some readers will hold the mistaken belief that possession, apart from a few hysterical outbursts on the part of overexcited worshipers, is a prearranged deception between the priests and the worshipers who are possessed. This is not so. Whatever the mechanism of possession, it is more than an hysterical response and does not involve duplicity. The spirits rise from the earth through the souls of the feet of the dancers, a sensation that cannot be mistaken for any other—see the fascinating firsthand account of Maya Deren in Chapter Seven of her great work, *Divine Horsemen* (New Paltz, NY: McPherson & Co., 1984).

The loa of Voudoun have their roots in Africa. Each has a distinct personality, specific powers, its own region of authority, and an emblem called a *vever* that is drawn on the earth with flour. Some of the more important loa are:

Marassa—the Divine Twins, who are the first children of God. When they possess someone, that person at once takes on the personality of a child. The original dead, they are the primal source of all the loa, and in some respects they are considered to be stronger than the loa. They are always saluted first, and there is a saying: "Pappa Marassa is the one who must be fed before all the gods." If this natural order of precedence is overlooked, no works of magic will prove successful.

Legba—originally a Sun god, in Voudoun he is God of the Crossroads. The centerpost is sometimes called *poteau-Legba,* and without his sacred tree at the gate there can be no *hounfor* (ceremonial place). He comes in the form of a bent old peasant smoking a pipe who walks with the aid of a stick. His sacred color is white.

The Tree of Life in the Bible is essentially the same as the poteau-mitan, or centerpost, in the ritual enclosure of Voudoun.

Carrefour—Across from Legba on the same gate sits Carrefour, who commands the darkness and the demons of the night. Unless he is rightly propitiated, he can loose misfortune and evil spirits on the world. His name is a word of power to protect against evil. He comes in the guise of a strong young man who holds his arms wide in the form of a cross. No one dares to whisper or smile in his presence. God of the darkness and the Moon, he is one of the patrons of magic.

Ghede—Lord of Resurrection, he rules the road along which the souls of the dead pass away and the loa approach. Anyone wishing to gain knowledge of those who have died or converse with them must go through Ghede. Since he possesses all the knowledge of past ages, he is the wisest of the loa. In many respects, he resembles the Egyptian Thoth, and indeed Ghede is the protector of children and the greatest of the divine healers. He comes as a trickster who is mischievous and enjoys shocking with obscene words and gestures. His form is usually that of a starved wandering beggar who asks for food. The symbolic color of Ghede is black.

Baron Samadi—Ghede in his more terrible aspect of God of the Grave, he has a skull-like face and eyes that never shut, not even when fiery liquor in thrown into them. Only he can drink his special drink of rum mixed with 21 of the hottest spices without choking. As the divine gravedigger, he sings a weird, hysterical song that chills the blood. It is Baron Samadi who digs the grave of one who is about to die and who animates the dead to create zombies. Often he sports formal black evening wear, a top hat, a cane, and dark glasses and smokes a cigarette or cigar. He is another of the loa who preside over magic.

Damballah—the ancient serpent who encircles the Earth. He is the patron loa of the waters that fall from heaven and of the streams and rivers they nourish. Those possessed by this loa fall on the ground writhing or plunge into a trough of water, and climb trees where they stretch across the boughs hissing. They eat eggs by cracking the shells with their teeth. Damballah is so ancient and vast that he is treated with respectful reverence. He seldom answers questions except with an inarticulate hissing.

Agwe—God of the Sea, who rules the produce of the waves. His sacred colors are white and bright blue. His habits are reserved and dignified. When he comes, he immediately seeks water, and he speaks in a gurgling voice like rising bubbles. He is said to carry on a perpetual feud with Ogoun, Lord of Fire.

Ogoun—Lord of the Thunderbolt and of fire, originally he was the patron of iron workers and the makers of weapons of war, but in Voudoun he has come to be a kind of political figure. In all of his aspects, he is the hero. When he is called, the houngan pours rum upon the earth and sets it on fire, then leads this tongue of fire after him by trickling a stream of rum on the ground. He is the protector of the hounfor. His special instrument is the saber or the poor man's substitute, the machete. Often, to show his courage, he puts

Wrought-iron cross of Baron Samadi showing the initials of the god.

The Ouroboros, an encircling serpent with its tail in its mouth, is the alchemical version of Damballah.

the hilt of the saber on the ground and rests the entire weight of his body on its point without being cut. His sacred color is red.

Erzulie—the Goddess of Love, she comes as a highly refined and beautiful lady who delights in luxuries and is always giving gifts. Usually, she mounts the most attractive woman present. Her first act is to wash her face and comb her hair, then dress herself in the finery that has been provided. She carries with her an air of gentile nobility, and is a coquette who always pays much more attention to the men present than to the women. She wears three wedding bands: for Damballah, Agwe, and Ogoun. Her symbol is the pierced heart. Convinced that her many lovers have all betrayed her, sooner or later she always begins to weep and must be consoled. Eventually she is so overcome with grief that she becomes rigid with her arms widespread, and must be carried to a bed, where she falls into a gentle sleep.

Voudoun is the best known of the African-based cults of Central and South America, at least by reputation, but in North America it often degenerates into superstitions having to do with magic oils, powders, scents, and candles, which are sold in large quantities by occult shops. These materials have no relationship with legitimate Voudoun beyond the name that is attached to them. All of these African-based cults are strongly shamanic, and all rely on spirit possession as their vitalizing heart.

Verver of Erzulie

A magician evokes a legion of spirits.
   —*engraving by Petrini from a painting by David Teniers*

SECTION THREE

PRACTICES

The Hebrew Alphabet and Its Golden Dawn Correspondences

Letter	Meaning	Trans.	Value*	Path	Sign	Tarot Trump
Aleph א	Ox	A	1	11	🜁	The Fool
Beth ב	House	B, V	2	12	☿	I. The Magus
Gimel ג	Camel	G, Gh	3	13	☽	II. The High Priestess
Daleth ד	Door	D, Dh	4	14	♀	III. The Empress
He ה	Window	H	5	15	♈	IV. The Emperor
Vau ו	Nail	O, U, V	6	16	♉	V. The Hierophant
Zayin ז	Sword	Z	7	17	♊	VI. The Lovers
Cheth ח	Fence	Ch	8	18	♋	VII. The Chariot
Teth ט	Snake	T	9	19	♌	VIII. Strength
Yod י	Hand	I, Y	10	20	♍	IX. The Hermit
Kaph כ	Fist	K, Kh	20, ך 500	21	♃	X. The Wheel
Lamed ל	Goad	L	30	22	♎	XI. Justice
Mem מ	Water	M	40, ם 600	23	🜄	XII. The Hanged Man
Nun נ	Fish	N	50, ן 700	24	♏	XIII. Death
Samekh ס	Prop	S	60	25	♐	XIV. Temperance
Ayin ע	Eye	Aa, Ngh	70	26	♑	XV. The Devil
Pe פ	Mouth	P, Ph	80, ף 800	27	♂	XVI. The Tower
Tzaddi צ	Hook	Tz	90, ץ 900	28	♒	XVII. The Star
Qoph ק	Ear	Q	100	29	♓	XVIII. The Moon
Resh ר	Head	R	200	30	☉	XIX. The Sun
Shin ש	Tooth	S, Sh	300	31	🜂	XX. Judgment
Tau ת	Cross	T, Th	400	32	♄	XXI. The World

*Some Hebrew letters have a final form that occurs at the end of words. It has a higher numerical value.

Chapter Eighteen

Preparation for Ritual

It is unreasonable to skim through a ritual in a book, repeat the words in a halting and uncertain voice while reading from the page by candlelight, and expect to achieve anything. No one would be foolish enough to presume that they could pick up six eggs and juggle them in the air without some prior training in the matter. Yet for some reason many people have the idea that magic must be easy or it must not work at all. The notion that they fail in their first attempt because they have insufficient skill seems never to enter their heads.

Two preliminaries are needed to work ritual magic success-fully: means and ability. You must create the appropriate environment and tools for the ritual both in the external physical world and the internal world of your own mind and body, which are at root one place. You must possess enough skill at the time of the working to realize the potential of the ritual.

Liken it to playing a violin. If someone stands you on a stage in a concert hall before an audience and passes you a Stradivarius, you are not going to know what to do with it unless you have studied and practiced for years. On the other hand, if you have been playing classical music since the age of seven and at the last minute you break your instrument, there is nothing to do but whistle. The prerequisite for the practice of any art, magic included, is a trained method and a medium through which that method can find expression.

Skill is largely acquired by trial and error. Most magicians are self-taught. They may have had a teacher while absorbing the fundamentals, but beyond the most basic mechanical level of ritual they learn by doing. Skill only comes with practice. The magical maxim of Aleister Crowley was "Invoke often." Constant repetition will itself reveal the most efficient and elegant way of ritual working as unnecessary actions are gradually eliminated. Rituals worked frequently become streamlined. Once skill is attained, it must be retained. Regular practice prevents the details of rituals from being forgotten. It is surprising how easy it is to remember a ritual you practice every night, and how difficult it is to remember one you stopped working a month ago. The body has its own physical memory, as every dancer knows.

To achieve success in ritual magic, it is vital to know in advance what you wish to do and the way you intend to do it. Blindly fumbling around the magic circle with the vague hope that inspiration will strike, or that the gods will take pity on you and lead you by the hand to the fulfillment of your desire, is not a fruitful approach in spite of its popularity.

In the beginning you will be working with published rituals such as the two that are given later on in this section. There are thousands of rituals composed by modern occultists for various purposes and preserved in books, many of them practical and very beautiful. Such public rituals must be memorized and thoroughly understood before being attempted. Later, when you gain enough knowledge to compose your own personal rituals for specific life goals, you must write them down in what is usually called among Witches a Book of Shadows—a magical workbook. This serves the duel function of preserving the rituals for later years and insuring that you actually know what you wish to accomplish. You will find that you cannot write a ritual down unless it is clear in your own mind. It will lack direction and make no sense.

A Book of Shadows has other uses. If you wish to teach magic to other people you can instruct them through your own early rituals that you have proven to be effective. Also, an examination of the magical record in later years can give remarkable insights into your own psychological process. You will be able to see not only the way you approach the solving of your problems, but also the areas and aspects of life that have concerned you and occupied your energies.

Rituals are worked primarily on the astral level but receive their stability and force from the material level. For example, the magic wand must be created and made real in the imagination if it is to have power. The wand of wood merely provides a stable foundation upon which to base the wand of mind, as the body is only the earthly expression of the soul. Just as the soul would dissipate and be lost without the vessel of the body, so the mental wand would waver and fade unless sustained by the material wand.

The essential instrument of magic is the body of the magician. If ritual is to be expressed through the body with full effectiveness, physical vigor and purity are needed. Exercise moderately to maintain a general state of health and avoid vices such as smoking, drinking, drugs, and gluttony. All forms of excess are harmful and hinder the attainment of the optimum physical state for ritual magic. Hatha yoga is the best type of conditioning exercise for magic. It is not generally appreciated that yoga was developed centuries ago as the physical foundation for the attainment of magical powers, or *siddhis*. The exhibition of siddhis is considered a sign of progress on the path of enlightenment, although too great a preoccupation with the siddhis is regarded as a hindrance to higher attainment.

Magical purity involves pureness of purpose, the wholehearted dedication to a specific goal. All superfluous pursuits are set aside and the mind and body are focused intensely on a single object. Any thought or feeling or habit that adulterates magical purity weakens the will by distracting it away from its ritual desire.

This is why the diet is regulated in yoga. When the belly is constantly full of heavy foods difficult to digest, the process of assimilation requires large amounts of energy and attention. Even though you are not aware of it, a portion of your mind is involved in overseeing digestion and is distracted by it. Effective rituals are greatly hindered where there is no control over the diet.

While engaged in serious ritual work, one meal in the middle of the day is best. It should be made up of light foods such as cooked grains, beans, nuts, vegetables, fruits, fish, and poultry. Avoid sugar, grease, strong spices and sauces, beef, pork, and in general any food that remains for a prolonged time in the stomach and is difficult to digest. At other times, small amounts of fresh fruit, salads, cereals, and milk products may be eaten if desired to keep the stomach from becoming empty, although you may find this unnecessary. There is no need to starve, but you should strive for a feeling of lightness during the period of ritual practice. A diet suitable for yoga is also ideal for ritual magic.

Purity of purpose is symbolized by purity of the body. It is useful to bathe before each ritual as a way of deliberately casting off the contamination of ordinary daily life. On a more mundane level, if you are clean, you will not be distracted by an itch at a crucial moment in the ritual. This may seem a trivial consideration, but it really is not. The more you strive to focus your will, the more your mind is drawn to every little sensation in your body. It should be noted that cleanliness is stressed in hatha yoga and in the ceremonial practices of most religions. Ritual washing is not mere superstition but has a sound magical basis.

To further minimize distraction, loose clothing is worn during ritual work. Anything that constricts, binds, or irritates, such as tight jeans, shoes, a belt, a wristwatch, or jewelry should not be put on unless it is a ritual garment manufactured for a specific magical function. In the latter case, it actually helps to be physically reminded that you are wearing your ritual apparel, since it is an aid in elevating your mind from a normal to a magical state of awareness. Most ritualists make or purchase special robes in harmony with the goals of their work. The manufacture and consecration of the ritual robe, sash, and other garments is itself a magic ritual that, properly done, dedicates the self to the higher purposes of the art.

Usually nothing is worn under the robes of the art. Gerald Gardner went farther than this and instructed the Witches who followed him to meet in their covens and worship "skyclad" beneath the Moon. This alone is responsible for most of the rumors linking the occult with sexual perversion. Gardner himself was a practicing nudist and had only the noblest intentions in ordering his followers to work their magic naked. He wanted them to cast off their veneer of civilized pretension with their clothes and get back into touch with their own bodies and the natural world.

Working nude has some virtues. So much of our artificial social identity is bound up in our clothes, when we cast them off we become better able to perceive our essential being. Unfortunately, the drawbacks of working naked outweigh the advantages. Most people simply cannot disrobe and be at ease in the company of a group of others of both sexes. Nudity is a distraction both to the

Four Witches disrobe in preparation for ritual work.
Witches are often depicted skyclad in older illustrations.
—engraving by Albrecht Dürer

members of the group and to any outsiders who might chance to observe its activities. Also outdoor rituals become physical ordeals except in the mildest of weather.

Sexual abstinence is recommended in serious ritual work. The considerable energy that goes into sexual thoughts and feelings can then be sublimated and channeled toward the fulfillment of the ritual purpose. Although it is never openly admitted, the reason Catholic priests are forbidden to marry is the same reason that the priests of Isis remained chaste—chastity heightens magical potential and allows a more intimate communion with gods and spirits.

Obviously this does not apply to tantra rituals, where sexual energy is deliberately generated so that it can be consciously transmuted for magical ends. In tantra, the desire that naturally arises for a lover is directed at a god or goddess who possesses the higher virtues the magician seeks to possess, and a spiritual union is achieved with the deity that has as its material foundation a physical union.

It is best not to conduct rituals when sick, or during recovery from an operation or serious injury while the body is still weakened. Ritual magic requires large amounts of raw physical energy and can be debilitating to those who undertake it without a full reserve of vital force. A cold or flu can be aggravated into pneumonia or complete physical collapse. With exhaustion comes mental depression and a sense of futility that is inimical to the successful working of magic. Rituals tend to remain impotent or to go sour and have destructive consequences when attempted by the sick.

By the same token, it is unwise to attempt ritual work while severely depressed or mentally ill. To work effectively, the magician must remain balanced on the astral level. This balance is represented by the four occult elements of Fire, Air, Water, and Earth, which find expression in the body through the sanguine, choleric, phlegmatic, and melancholic humors. Too much Fire in the mind leads to rashness and carelessness. Dominance of Air results in instability and vague dreaminess. Water heightens irrational emotional responses of fear and desire. An excess of Earth produces dullness and inertia.

It is useful to have a special place set aside for regular rituals that is easy to get to, private, quiet, and comfortable. A small room is completely adequate for solitary working. It serves as the ritual temple and should as much as possible be furnished in harmony

Sexual union figures prominently not only in eastern tantra but also in western alchemy, where it may or may not have been purely symbolic.
—*from* Rosarium philosophorum, *1550*

with the type of magic that is being worked. For example, nature magic would be encouraged by green and brown colors; flowers and flower patterns; natural fabrics in rugs and draperies; a large window or skylight to admit the radiance of the Sun, Moon, and stars; wood paneling; an open fireplace; and so on. Any furnishing not in harmony with the ritual work must be excluded, and in general anything that is unnecessary and liable to distract the eye should be taken away.

Most rituals are done standing and require movement for such things as inscribing the magic circle and invoking the guardians of the four quarters of the heavens. Ideally the floor should have an open area large enough to set an altar at the center and still leave space to walk around it. Sometimes a stylized magic circle is drawn permanently on the floor around the altar. There are many elaborate designs for magic circles to be found in the medieval grimoires, but all physical circles are only foundations for the true circle, which is inscribed in occult fire upon the ether of the astral world.

You should realize that the ritual place where you practice the art of magic is primarily useful for creating the proper emotional atmosphere and for insuring stillness and privacy. The actual ritual temple is constructed over a period of weeks or months in the imagination by repeated visualizations. The physical temple may correspond exactly to the astral temple or may differ from it significantly. This is a matter of choice. It is in the astral temple where the magic circle is drawn and the ritual actually worked. The actions of the magician in the temple of the material world only mirror these astral events. It is vitally important that you grasp this truth.

Successful construction of the astral temple is one of the most difficult tasks in ritual magic, yet it is essential to effective working. Begin by visualizing in your imagination the space and proportion of the temple you have chosen to make in the astral world. Then concentrate successively on the details of its furnishing. As previously considered features of the temple grow hazy in the memory and begin to fade, go back and consider them again, striving to make everything as tangible as possible. Use the senses of smell, touch, and hearing as well as sight.

It is best at first to stick with something simple and familiar. A room about the same size as the one you are actually using but furnished in an ideal manner, perhaps with more luxury than you can afford, is a good way to begin. Later, when you wish, you can construct more elaborate temples in the imagination. If you are working with other occultists to build up the astral temple, you can feed each other details of its design to reinforce it in your minds. When you clearly know what your astral temple looks like from all angles, you must then project yourself mentally into it during your rituals with as great a degree of reality as your powers of visualization permit. While your body stands and moves in your physical chamber, your mind and emotions are surrounded by the temple you have built in the astral.

The process of building the astral temple is itself an excellent exercise in visualization and can be attempted by anyone who wishes to strengthen the visual imagination and improve perception of the astral world. Set aside a certain time each day when you can sit or lie quietly with your eyes closed and mentally construct your temple. Any architecture from any period of history may be used provided you are able to see it in your mind with utter clarity. To work ceremonial magic effectively, it is desirable to be able to see the astral temple with greater inner precision than you can recall a familiar physical space such as your own living room.

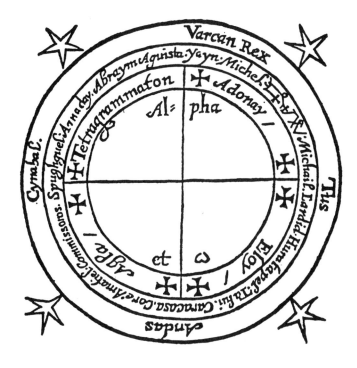

A circle designed for working rituals
in the first hour of Sunday in the spring of the year.
—*from* Magical Elements *by Peter de Abano*

In passing, it might be mentioned that the temple at Jerusalem constructed by King Solomon and destroyed by the Babylonians in 587 BC has been rebuilt countless times in the astral by Jews and Christians based upon the detailed account of its formation in I Kings 6-7. There can be no doubt that this mentally recreated temple has been the stage for numerous rituals of both a magical and religious nature. Due to the long history of its occult associations, it is the most potent astral temple of all for the magic of the Kabbalah. Even though it was physically destroyed more than 25 centuries ago, it has never ceased to exist. Paradoxically, the only way to obliterate it may be the construction of a new Jewish temple on its ancient site above the Wailing Wall, something extreme orthodox Jews in favor of such a temple might do well to consider.

An important preparation for ritual is the ability to maintain an occult silence. Eliphas Levi places silence as the final element of his famous motto: To Know, to Dare, to Will, to Keep Silent. He relates it to the eagle, symbol of Scorpio and the element Water, and to the fourth letter of the Tetragrammaton, יהוה. In doing so he has, in my view, made an error. This motto, which has great currency among modern occult groups, is nothing less than a concise exposition of the magical formula. It is written out of its proper sequence, but when rearranged its true nature is revealed:

1) To Dare (Desire or Wish) = Lion = Red = Fire = *Yod*
2) To Know (Form or Conceive) = Eagle = Blue = Water = *He*
3) To Will (Actualize) = Angel = Yellow = Air = *Vau*
4) To Be Silent (Refrain from Action) = Bull = Black = Earth = *He*

The ability to be silent is the ability to still the emotions and banish doubts and fears before, during, and after rituals. It is especially vital to be able to turn the mind to other matters while the magic of the ritual you have previously conducted is working. Since magic is a mental art, doubts after the fact can actually destroy a successful ritual. If you are not careful, you can make and then, without intending it, immediately unmake your purpose by worrying and fretting over whether the ritual has been effective. Because this doubt is automatic, it extends to a deep unconscious level and has great power. It becomes in itself a counterritual. The effect is the same as if you had said in a magical way during the ritual "do this," and then immediately afterwards had muttered, "I've changed my mind; don't do it after all."

Stilling of desire and expectation after rituals is not easy. To understand why, try not to think of a pink elephant. The moment you tell yourself that you must not think of it, you are thinking of it. In the same way, when you tell yourself after a ritual that you must not worry about its effectiveness or think about its outcome, you have already defeated your expressed purpose.

Silence requires a kind of mental trick that can only be successfully achieved with practice. After a ritual, the magician must assume with complete inner conviction that the purpose of the ritual is already fulfilled. There is no need to worry or think about something that is an accomplished fact. Nor is there any impulse to do so. If your name is Mary Smith and you know your name with utter certainty, you will not be able to doubt it or wonder about it or worry that it may be something else. You can pretend to doubt your name, but your doubt will only be play-acting and will lack conviction.

Not only your own doubt but also the doubt of others can destroy the working of your rituals. This is why laughter, mockery, and scorn were understood in ancient times as an antidote to Witchcraft. If you confide your purpose to others, their skepticism can hinder or block its fulfillment. This is true in everyday life as well as in magic. If you tell other people before the fact that you are going to achieve a certain goal, as likely as not unforeseen obstacles will arise. Fiction writers are a superstitious lot. Few novelists will describe a book they intend to write in the future for fear that in some occult way its revelation will destroy it. Their reticence is governed by an unconscious adherence to the magical law of silence, even though they are not aware of the reason for their behavior. To them it is simply bad luck to reveal a future project.

Immediately before beginning any ritual, it is useful to sit quietly for a short period and empty the mind of all thoughts directed to matters either past or future. Allow yourself to exist in the present without memory or expectation. This period of silence permits the gathering and focusing of the will upon the purpose of the ritual, which has by this time already been composed and learned. No conscious effort should be involved. If you attempt to deliberately direct the mind at this time by rehearsing all the things you must do during the ritual, the benefit of this pre-ritual silence will be lost. The quiet time just prior to erecting the magic circle aids in making a transition from ordinary consciousness to magical consciousness, when you cease to be the name you are called by other people during the day and become the secret magical name representing your adepthood.

In making the opposite transition from magical identity to everyday identity, a similar period of silence is recommended after the conclusion of the ritual. This will help your mind return to a state of ordinary awareness. It is poor practice to conduct rituals so late at night that you are exhausted and immediately fall asleep after you finish. This will often result in nightmares. If you do happen to have bad dreams after ritual work, and these are common, do not worry about them. They are only dreams and have no power to harm you directly.

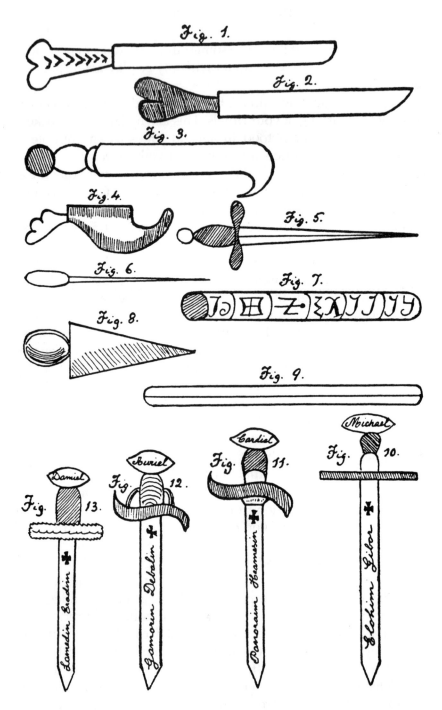

Some of the instruments of a magician, according to the Grimorium Verum.

CHAPTER NINETEEN

INSTRUMENTS OF RITUAL

The underlying assumption of ritual magic is that, if you represent a circumstance or act out an event in your mind, it can be made to come to pass in the world. This is what James G. Frazer calls the Law of Similarity: "From the Law of Similarity, the magician infers that he can produce any effect he desires merely by imitating it" (Frazer 1951, 12). He speaks of material links with the subject of the ritual by means of nail parings, hair, and such under his Law of Contagion but largely ignores the essential connecting link, the mind of the sorcerer. It cannot be emphasized too strongly that magic acts in and through the mind. The external instruments of ritual are only sensory aids for the benefit of the magician.

Externally every ritual consists of a fixed set of gestures, movements, and words within a deliberately circumscribed arena or stage. Common features are songs, chants, dances, special postures, and controlled breathing. Some or all of these aspects may be internalized, particularly if the magician is working alone. They are still performed, but they are enacted on the stage of the imagination with such intensity and clarity that they seem almost to be physical. Since the audience for magic is the magician and discarnate spirits that perceive the world through the mind of the magician, it is not strictly necessary to externalize a ritual, although this is usually found to be easier and more effective. We tend to believe only what we can touch.

The basic tool chest of Western magic is made up of a few surprisingly simple instruments which function on the astral plane.

Usually they have their material correspondences. As the physical instrument is manipulated in the ritual place, the astral instrument follows and reflects its action in the astral temple. To the magician, who strives to actualize the astral temple as vividly as possible, it is the astral instrument that leads and the instrument of metal or glass or wood that follows. It is possible to use the astral instruments without using the material, but this requires a more developed visual imagination and is seldom as effective.

The essential tools of ritual are the circle, the altar, the lamp, the four elemental symbols, the wand, the sword, the ring, the robe, the sash, the circlet or cap, the lamen, the materials of purification, and, in Wiccan rituals, the athame or knife.

Many other materials that vary with the nature of each ritual are used to affect the mind and create a harmonious atmosphere conducive to the realization of the magical desire. Incense, flowers, colored lights, mood music, cakes or bread, wine, statues, and images can be effective when employed with good judgment. Also used are nonmaterial tools such as words of power, chants, songs, dances, hand and body gestures, and visualization of incorporeal symbols such as chakras and pentagrams.

Circle

The magic circle is drawn in the astral world about the magician and the place where the ritual is being worked. Often it is inscribed in the air above a physically marked circle on the floor of the ritual chamber. This physical circle is not the magic circle. The magic circle does not actually exist until it is made in the astral by a deliberate act of will. It forms a division between the magical place and the ordinary world and sets the interior space apart from the exterior. This allows the area inside the circle to hold a heightened charge of magical potency. Because it is a pure space devoted to magic, it permits the manifestation of subtle spirits that could not be readily perceived in the ordinary world.

Equally important is the protection the circle offers against the intrusion of chaotic forces that seek to disrupt communications with gods and other higher spiritual beings, and even to harm the magician in emotional and physical ways. In modern Witchcraft, the circle is usually understood to be an instrument for concentrating magical force until the moment of its ultimate release at the climax of the ritual. The function of the circle as a protective ring is

A magician stands inside a triple circle inscribed with what are supposed to be occult symbols invoking a spirit with a wand of ten segments, corresponding to the ten sephiroth. Note the magical sash as his waist.
—*from Flammenberg's* Der Geisterbanner, *1797*

downplayed. This is mainly a difference in emphasis. In ancient and medieval magic, the prime function of the circle was protection. Medieval adepts were more conscious of the potential dangers from malign spirits than their modern counterparts seem to be, perhaps because their faith in the reality of magic was more literal.

The circle is projected mentally from the right hand, either through the extended index finger or through an instrument such as the wand or athame. The right side of the body is the side of projection, the left side the side of reception. The circle must always be drawn upon the air in a sunwise direction (with the motion of the Sun) from its center point at the heart of the magician and visualized as a flaming band of light that sustains itself at the heart level. Even if the magician is not actually standing at the center of the circle during its projection, it should be understood that the center of the circle is the center of the self. The circle becomes an extension of the body of the magician.

For convenience the circle is made of a size great enough to enclose the ritual place. A single ritualist working without an altar in a confined space might project a circle of six feet in diameter by rotating on the center point. This is the rough human measure, equal to the span of an average adult male's arms and his height. Smaller men, women, and children might wish to make a slightly smaller circle in harmony with their personal dimension. With an altar at the center of the ritual chamber, a circle of nine feet in diameter is desirable to permit easy movement around the altar.

Whatever its size, the circle should always be large enough to comfortably hold all who work within it. A coven of 13 will need a roomier circle than a solitary magician. Since it is projected upon the astral, it can be made larger than the actual physical chamber—large enough to enclose an entire house, for example. This is useful when providing magical protection for a place.

The circle must never be casually broken. Even though incorporeal it is magically real. Unless it is treated as an impassable barrier it will fail to protect the magician as it should. At the beginning of a ritual it is formally extended sunwise from the heart center through the right index finger or magical instrument held in the right hand; therefore at the close of ritual it must be reabsorbed by tracing it widdershins (against the course of the Sun) with the left index finger, or a magical instrument such as the wand held in the left hand. It must never be stepped through. To disregard the substantiality of the circle it to weaken it and render it a less useful tool.

The necessity to reabsorb the circle was not understood by the Golden Dawn, which simply allowed its magic circles to dissolve into the ether after use. Most modern magicians do not reabsorb the circle. However in my own work I have found it essential to unmake the circle as deliberately as it is made if the circle is to possess its full potency.

Altar

At the center of the circle is placed the altar, which magically represents the center of the universe and the center of the self. It is the working surface of ritual, the focal point for power and awareness. In the Western occult tradition the altar usually is in the shape of a double cube, conveniently two by two by four feet in height. The best material is natural, unhewn stone. For practical reasons this is almost never available, although the late Witch Alex Sanders used an outdoor masonry altar painted with the seal of the Moon and, for balance, the character of the spirit of the Sun, named Sorath. He also used an altar in the form of a large flat stone erected upon other stones. I strongly recommend that a natural stone of an appropriate occult nature, magically energized, be enclosed in the altar.

Usually the altar is wood. It is useful to make a cupboard inside it to hold most of the ritual instruments when they are not in use. This preserves their purity, conserves their occult potency, and keeps them collected together within easy reach. A large bedside table often makes an ideal altar. The drawer at the top serves to hold the smaller instruments and materials, the space beneath to store vessels of consecrated water and oil.

All the symbolism of the altar, its square top, its cubic or double-cubic shape, the stone that composes or is contained within it, emphasize that it is the material foundation that supports the magical work and causes it to be realized in the world. The altar is the fixed place, the earthly buttress where power is manifested. If magic is worked without a material altar, the heart-center of the magician becomes this fixed support at the center of everything.

Frequently there is not enough space in the ritual chamber to move around the altar. When this is the case it is usually put in the east, considered the most auspicious direction because it marks the rising of the Sun. There is no fixed law on the placement of the altar, and in different systems of magic it is found variously at all four cardinal points. When the altar is placed at one of the quarters of the heavens, the magic circle should either be mentally expanded around it with the altar at its center, or the altar should be imagined set like a precious jewel in the ring of the circle. The altar must never be outside and apart from the circle.

Lamp

The spiritual focus of the circle is the flame of the lamp, even as the foursquare altar is its material focus. Always lit during rituals, the lamp resides on the middle of the altar top or is suspended in space over the altar. The ideal height for the lamp is the level of the heart, because the absolute magical center of the circle inscribed on the air at heart level is the invisible point where the triangular flame of the lamp tapers up and vanishes into infinity. A brass or ceramic oil lamp is considered most appropriate, but frequently a candle flame is employed in place of a lamp. Electric light is discordant and should never be used on the altar.

Some groups, following the ancient Egyptian, Greek, and Roman examples, may want to maintain a perpetual flame on their altars. This should only be done under conditions of complete safety to guard against fire hazard. Alternately, a flame can be maintained during the entire course of an extended ritual working, which may take days, weeks, or even months. Regardless of when the physical lamp is lighted, the lamp in the astral temple of the mind is never put out. This is the true occult perpetual lamp.

The flame draws the awareness of those working the ritual. They direct their prayers to it and meditate upon it. The nondimensional mathematical point where it disappears into infinity marks the doorway through the veil of unknowing, which the ritual is designed to open. Conceive the flame as burning at your own center of being and throwing its light across your circle of self. When the circle is filled with light, the self is purified and exalted.

Purification

Once the lamp has been lit and the magic circle projected from the heart center upon the space of the astral temple, the interior of the circle must be purged with the materials of purification. These

The four elemental instruments

represent one or more of the occult elements. Some groups purify with all four elements. Fire is physically represented with a match or candle flame, Earth with salt, Water with water, but there is no really satisfactory physical symbol for Air. Sometimes a feather is used, or a smoking incense stick, or the breath. For this reason in my personal rituals I often omit Air and use the three ancient materials of cleansing: salt, water, and flame.

The salt, previously blessed and consecrated to its purpose, is cast in small pinches at the four cardinal points of south, west, north, and east. Circumambulation, or motion around the circle, is always in a sunwise direction. The water, likewise consecrated, is sprinkled from the fingertips or from an aspergillum made from a pine cone, sprig of mistletoe, or other appropriate object, similarly at the four quarters. The purifying flame is waved three times in the air in turn at each of the corners of the circle. Usually this entire act of cleansing is accompanied by a prayer expressing its purpose.

Most people have no idea how to consecrate a substance or object, but this ancient procedure is not difficult when you remember that it is designed to dedicate the thing consecrated to a higher purpose. Religious methods of consecration provide useful examples. A priest of the Catholic Church makes ordinary water holy by dedicating it to the service of Christ. In learning from these patterns, do not make the mistake of thinking that consecration is a Christian procedure. Priests of Egypt were consecrating objects and substances long before Jesus was born, and long before Moses. The Catholic Church merely imitated pagan rites of consecration that were being used all around it in the early years of its formation.

The simplest way to consecrate your water, salt, and the candle, match, or lamp that will provide your flame is with a prayer that banishes any unwanted associations and dedicates the materials in the service of the art. This should be addressed to whatever spiritual being or deity you have chosen to preside over your rituals. You may be working under the auspices of Thoth of Egypt; or Apollo of Greece; or Danu of the Celtic tradition; or Woden, if you are practicing rune magic; or the nameless High God of all personified by your own higher self. The name of your tutelary god or spirit is a name of power in your rituals.

Purification of the circle is most effective when the magician is pure, undistracted by everyday concerns, knowing his or her purpose clearly, and possessed of a quiet confidence. In ritually cleansing the magic circle, you are cleaning the house of spirit so that the light of spirit will descend and reside within it. This is a sacred act. It has been stressed by writers such as Israel Regardie and William Gray that the purification of the circle is the most important part of any ritual because it clears the stage for what is to follow. When done negligently, the work that comes after it will lack a solid foundation and likely prove futile.

Elemental Symbols

Much of modern magic is done through the mediation of the four occult elements of Fire, Air, Water, and Earth. These determine both the type of energy that accomplishes the work and the avenue through which it acts. A clear understanding and proper use of the elements is vital. Each element is represented in the Golden Dawn system of magic by its own material symbol, which is placed atop the altar beside the lamp in the appropriate elemental quarter.

Fire is embodied in a short rod about nine inches long. This has a specific ornate design is the Golden Dawn system, but the details are not really essential. It is the shape of the rod that is most important. The nature of elemental Fire is in accord with this strongly phallic symbol. Use the rod for magic involving acts of

South

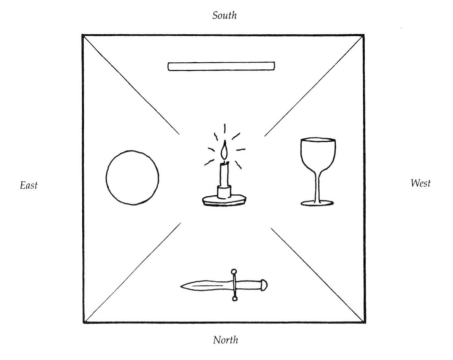

East

West

North

Placement of the instruments on the altar (New Magus *system*)

will and conflict. The rod of Fire is placed on the south quadrant of the altar.

Air is embodied in a short dagger. Again, it is the associations of the blade—its flashing quickness, its piercing qualities, its brightness—that are important, not details of the design or the names of power inscribed upon it. The difference in tone between a rod and a dagger says much about the essential difference between elemental Fire and Air. The dagger is completely distinct from the athame of Witches and the sword of ceremonial magic, both of which are described later. Use the dagger for intellectual magic such as the making of sigils. In the Golden Dawn system and its derivatives, the dagger is placed on the east quadrant of the altar. In the system described in my book *The New Magus*, the dagger is placed in the north.

Water is embodied in a cup or chalice. It should be rounded and womblike, enclosing and protective. It is also more harmonious if the cup is made of a watery or at least of a natural material. Blue handblown glass is good, as is earth-tone ceramic. The cup may be decorated with the symbols and names of spirits associated with elemental water, but this is a secondary consideration. Employ the cup generally for works relating to love, the emotions, dreams, visions, desires, and scrying. It is placed on the west quadrant of the altar.

Earth is embodied in the disk or pentacle. This is a flat disk painted with the earthy colors black, brown, dark green, and dusty yellow. Usually it is wood for ease of manufacture, but stone, ceramic, or red clay is more appropriate. It must not be too large to conveniently hold in the hand—four inches in diameter is a good size, because four is the most material number. Use the disk for magic that involves physical matters of accumulation, manufacture, and dispersal, especially money matters. In the Golden Dawn system the disk is placed on the north quadrant of the altar, but in *The New Magus* system in the east.

As far as I know, the use of these four elemental symbols originated with the Golden Dawn and received its inspiration from the symbols of the number cards of the Tarot. The Golden Dawn was the first occult organization to fully integrate the Tarot into modern magic. Formal instruments of the four elements were not used in medieval magic and are not strictly necessary. However the use of these symbols has become almost universal. It is important that they be designed to harmonize with the sensibilities of the magician who will actually use them, not merely according to some arbitrary standard.

Lamen

The lamen is the grand symbol of the art. Usually it is worn suspended around the neck. Its overall design and constituent parts express the philosophy of the type of magic being worked and the ultimate authority for its working. There is a wide variation in the design of lamen from one system of magic to another, but it is always the supreme symbol of power and, as such, can be used to compel unruly spirits and protect the magician from their malice. The Golden Dawn lamen is an extremely colorful and complex rose-cross that is also an instrument for the manufacture of spirit sigils in the Golden Dawn system. The famous Grand Seal of Solomon, without which it was said no magical operation could be brought to a

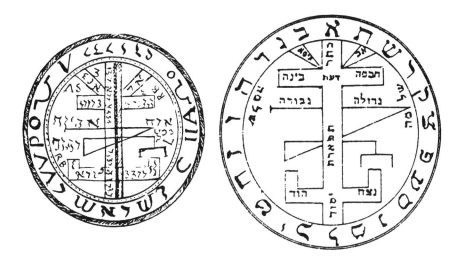

The Lamen, or Seal, of Solomon as it appears in the 18th-century French manuscript Zekerboni *(left) and in MacGregor Mathers' "corrected"* Key of Solomon *(right).*

successful conclusion, is an ancient example of the lamen.

Robe

It is customary for the magician to put on a special garment for ritual purposes. Since it is kept pure and apart, only worn after the magician has cleansed his or her body, donning it is akin to putting on a cloak of light. It helps to raise the consciousness to a higher awareness of the spiritual world and shields the magician from discordant influences. Usually the ritual garment is a robe, since this is simple to make and inexpensive to buy. The form is not so important, but it must be comfortable and feel comfortable to the wearer. It is a second magical skin and should have long sleeves and a low hem so that it completely encloses the body.

Natural fabrics such as linen and cotton are best. Avoid synthetics and silk, which is a magical insulator. Colors tend to have specific emotions bound up with them that run to the primal root of human response. For example red is usually the color of violence and rage in western symbolism. It is possible to design a robe for a specific class of magic by color, but for general rituals white or a balanced combination of the three primary pigment colors red, yellow, and blue is most useful.

Cap

The cap is an extension of the robe, but it also functions to attract and retain spiritual potency in the head. Often in modern magic the cap is dispensed with. The Golden Dawn cap is a simple piece of cloth called a *nemyss* that falls softly over the head. The ideal form of cap is doubtlessly the cone. It is not accidental that in popular mythology both the wizard and the Witch are depicted with conical headgear. The cone symbolically draws potential from its mathematical point down its length to actualize it in a circle— exactly what the magician seeks to do in the magic circle during ritual. Indeed the magic circle may be conceived as extending upwards as a cylinder to infinity, which from the visual perspective of the magician working inside it would cause it to appear to taper in a long cone to a vanishing point. All magic in the circle is worked under a great cone, and the conical hat is only a physical expression of this truth.

Unfortunately the conical hat has very evil associations that most people probably never think about, let alone wonder how such associations came to be. Not only is it the hat—in folklore, at least—of the evil Witch, it is also the dunce cap of ignorant students. It is the cap which the heretics and sorcerers of the Middle Ages were forced to wear when they were paraded through the streets of Spain on their way to their executions at the auto-da-fé. It is the headgear of the infamous Ku Klux Klan. The magician must decide if he or she is strong enough to buck such a lengthy tradition of ridicule and contempt. If a conical cap feels stupid or uncomfortable, it probably will not be an asset during ritual.

Circlet

Really a variation on the cap, the circlet is a band that goes around the head at the level of the forehead. Traditional designs have the raised Egyptian cobra in front, but a ruby or other red stone representing the focus of will at the occult third eye between the eyebrows is effective. My own circlet is in the shape of a serpent swallowing its tail, which is a symbol of infinity similar to the cone. Just as the cone vanishes up into a mathematical point, so will the serpent pass into itself to nothingness. As a practical matter, the constant pressure of the circlet against the center of the forehead is useful in focusing the awareness on the occult third eye, the center of will. Hindu mystics accomplish the same focus of attention through the use of colored-pigment designs, which vary according to the sect of the wearer.

Wand

The quintessential magical tool is the wand. It serves to project the will of the magician and is in fact the physical embodiment of his or her magical will. It should be made of wood cut from a living tree, about as thick as the thumb and as long as the space between the fingertips and the elbow. Some woods are favored for the wand—hazel is traditional. Oak is also good, since it is the wood of Zeus and an attractor of lightning.

Ideally, the wand should

Both witches and magicians were commonly depicted in conical hats.

always be cut and fashioned by the magician. It is the most intensely personal tool of the art and is used for virtually everything. Drawing the circle, forming sigils and symbols in the astral, invoking and compelling spirits, projecting the will into talismans and other objects, all is done with the wand. Over time it will gather a magical charge through use that is clearly perceptible when it is held.

Sword

Less useful but still necessary for operations of evocation involving demons and lower spirits is the sword. This is similar in function to the wand, but whereas the wand has a neutral nature, the sword is overtly offensive and projects power to dominate and hurt. It is supposed to be entirely made by the magician, but probably not one in a thousand ritualists has actually fashioned the blade by hand. It is considered an acceptable compromise between utility and expediency to procure a short sword or long knife and, after thoroughly purifying it, consecrate it by anointing it with olive oil that has been itself consecrated with prayer and words of power. I myself use an old British army bayonet that is shaped like a sword, hilt and all, and find it effective due to its military associations.

Athame

A tool used by Witches that combines the functioning of both wand and sword is the athame, or magical knife. It is an all-purpose instrument used for making the material objects of ritual, for drawing the circle, and also for projecting power. Some Witches even use it in their cooking! They explain that, since magic embraces all of life, cooking is an integral part of the art and this is no profanation.

The magical knife is quite old. In medieval times, it was divided into two—a knife with a white hilt used for all common purposes, and a knife with a black hilt used for drawing magic circles and compelling spirits. This distinction is still frequently observed by modern Witches. The white- and black-hilted knives are in some ways analogous to the wand and sword of high magic.

Descriptions for the making of the white- and black-hilted knives occur in one of the oldest Western grimoires, *The Greater Key of Solomon*. They involve the slaughter of innocent animals, a poor way to begin a spiritual quest, but they show the ancient lineage of the Witch's athame. All methods described in the grimoires must be looked at critically, since they are often needlessly involved and difficult. Modern magic tends to be more straightforward—and as a consequence more practical.

Ring

The ring fits over the index finger of the right hand and acts as a sort of magical magnetic coil, magnifying the force of the will that passes along the extended index finger. It also serves as a miniature representation of the magic circle and protects its wearer from harm. When the wand is held in the right hand, the ring should be worn on the index finger of the left hand for balance.

The best form of ring is a plain gold or silver band a bit broader than the usual wedding ring. By it the magician is wedded to the art of magic. It is customary to inscribe the ring with names of power such as the Hebrew יהוה, the divine Tetragrammaton. As

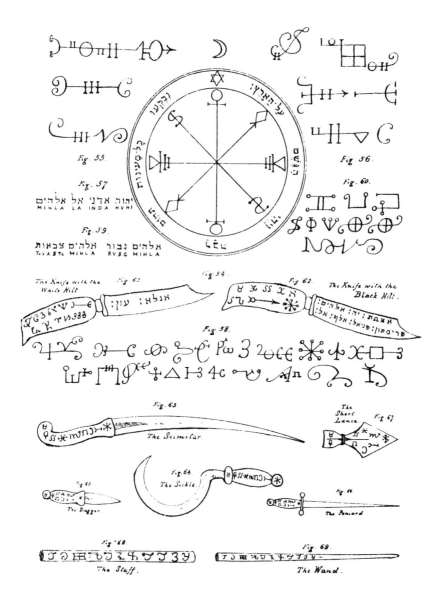

Black- and white-hilted knives from **The Key**
of Solomon, *along with other magical instruments.*

is true of all the instruments, there is no exact pattern for the ring. Its shape and inscription depend on its intended use and the personality of its maker.

Several rings may be fashioned for specific purposes. An individual spirit can be made to reside in a ring and its power utilized when the ring is put on. The ancient Greek magician Apollonius of Tyana was said by his biographer, Philostratus, to possess seven rings named after the seven traditional planets. The rings were a gift from Iarcas, leader of the Brahmans of India. Apollonius wore each of the rings in rotation on the day of the week related to its planet.

Sash

The sash, like the ring, is a variation on the magic circle. It closes the robe and is wound three times around the waist before being tied or clasped in front. To put it on is to don a threefold occult circle of protection. If it is wound around the waist sunwise it attracts and focuses solar force within the body. There is no set form or color for the sash. White linen is an excellent material to use for this purpose. Sometimes in Wicca covens the sash is tied to the wand and used as the radius when inscribing the magic circle in the earth. When joined end to end and set on the ground it can itself function as a personal circle for the solitary ritualist, who stands within its circumference. Echoes of the magic potency of the sash survive into modern times. The title belts of professional sports descend from it, as do the colored ranking belts of martial arts such as judo and karate.

CHAPTER TWENTY

RITUAL TO AWAKEN
MAGICAL AWARENESS

Everyone learns best by doing. The ritual given below is representative of the rituals worked in modern magic. It should be used as a general pattern indicating the essential elements and sequence of rituals, and will also be of some value in awakening a magical perception of the world, which in no small measure consists in just being aware that it is possible to see the world in a new way. Because few readers of this book will possess a full set of ritual tools, it has been designed not to require any instrument except the flame. It can be worked in any private place where there is half an hour of quiet. The structure of the ritual is based on my own *New Magus* system of magic, but it can easily be adapted to the Golden Dawn system by inverting the elements attributed to north and east.

Wear loose, comfortable clothing of neutral colors. Take off your watch, jewelry, shoes, and anything that hinders a free circulation of blood or irritates the skin. It is best if you bathe before beginning, or at least wash your hands and face. Remember, you are trying to invoke a spiritual awareness into the temple of your body.

Place a candle on a low table such as a bedside table, plant stand, or other support so that the candle is just below waist level. Light the candle. Take a few minutes to collect your emotions. When you feel inner tranquility, stand facing the south with the candle in front of you. Raise your arms wide and lift up your head in the traditional posture of invocation. Look into infinity and focus your attention upon an imaginary distant star overhead.

Speak this cleansing prayer, which is drawn from the 51st Psalm, part of which is used in the Golden Dawn rituals:

> *Have mercy upon me, O God.*
> *Blot out my transgressions.*
> *Wash me thoroughly from my iniquities*
> *And cleanse me from my sins.*
> *Purge me with hyssop, and I shall be clean;*
> *Wash me, and I shall be as white as snow.*
> *Create in me a clean heart,*
> *And renew a right spirit within me.*
> *Thou, who art the Crown*

(touch your forehead with your right index finger)

> *And the Kingdom,*

(touch your groin)

> *The Power*

(touch your left shoulder)

> *And the Glory,*

(touch your right shoulder)

> *And the everlasting Law,*

(touch your heart center)

> *Amen.*

(point to the flame)

As you speak this cleansing prayer founded in the magic of the Kabbalah, visualize a cascade of clear, sparkling water falling upon your head and body and refreshing you while washing away all your cares.

The Magic Wand to be used in Invocations by the Chrystal.

Gold

On

Tetragrammaton

write or engrave on the other side Ego Alpha et Omega.

Two Holy wax Lights used in the Invocation by the Chrystal.

The true size & form of the Chrystal which must be sett in pure Gold, & the same names & characters as in the model here given.

The magic Circle of a simple construction in which the operator must stand or sit when he uses the Chrystal

Tetragrammaton

ADONAI

Elohim

The Tripod on which the perfumes are put. & may be either held in the hand or sett in the earth.

מיכאל

El. Elohim. Elohe. Tzabaoth. Elion. Eserchie. Adonai. Jah. Jehovah. Jaday. Jod. Sherv.

Michael

The Lamen, or Holy Table of the Archangel Michael.

Pub. ...... b.Allen.

Lighted candles are used on the altar for many magical operations. The pair shown here, from Francis Barrett's *The Magus*, 1801, are for scrying in a crystal.

Turn sunwise on your own axis and mentally project from your extended right index finger a blazing circle of white light that hovers in the astral shadow of the place where the ritual is being conducted. Try to picture this circle clearly at the level of your heart, the energy that composes it growing out from your heart center down your right arm and out your fingertip. Be sure to join the end of the circle with the beginning in your mind. If necessary, mentally expand the circle as you project it to include the ritual place.

Speak these words as you project the circle:

From my heart of being I extend this flaming circle of power. Let no evil or discordant influence enter herein nor abide within its boundary.

Once again facing the south, stand with your feet together and your arms spread wide, making a cross with your body. Visualize a massive column of red flame rising from the earth just beyond the limit of the circle and extending up into infinity. Concentrate upon it and speak these words:

Before me Michael, Lord of Flame, the lion of the south.

Without moving, visualize behind you in the north a similar column of yellow fire. Speak these words:

Behind me Raphael, Lord of Air, the angel of the north.

Visualize in the west a column of blue fire beyond the circle. Speak these words:

On my right hand Gabriel, Lord of Water, the eagle of the west.

Visualize in the east a column of green fire beyond the circle. Speak the words:

On my left hand Uriel, Lord of Earth, the bull of the east.
The four surround me,

(raise your hands slightly above the level of your head)

Fire above,

(lower your hands to the level of your waist)

Water below;

(bring your palms together in a prayer gesture over your heart)

I am the heart of the four; I am the center of the universe.

Visualize a cross made of three beams of light radiating from its point of intersection in your heart center. The vertical beam of the cross is red and runs between your feet and through the top of your head to infinity. The horizontal beam running under your shoulders is blue. The horizontal beam which enters your chest between your clasped palms and exits your back is yellow. Your heart center blazes with a clear white light that fills your entire body as if it were a glass vessel.

Sit upon the floor before the candle and contemplate the flame. Let your breathing be light and regular. Be aware of the turbulence in the air and wait for it to be completely stilled, so that the flame rises straight up in a cone with hardly a flicker. You should be far enough away to prevent your breath from disturbing it. Try to become tangibly aware with your mind of the body and substance of the flame from all angles. Involve yourself with it. Imagine that you are surrounded by it, and that it does not discomfort you in the least. The sensation is like being encased in an upwardly flowing teardrop of sunlight.

Gradually let your breaths grow deeper and longer without forcing them or straining yourself. Remain relaxed. As you inhale fully, hold your breath for five or ten seconds and direct your awareness solely upon the uppermost point of the flame, where it vanishes into nothingness. Try to focus like a microscope of infinite power ever more finely upon the exact place where the transition between flame and space occurs.

When you release your breath, let your mind once again embrace the entire body of the flame. The next time you inhale, again halt your breath for a few seconds and focus upon the tip of the flame. Try at each stoppage of breath to get ever closer to the elusive vanishing point.

It is vital to the success of this technique that you do not strain yourself by trying to breathe too deeply or retain your breath too long. If you end up short of breath, that is where your attention will be and the whole purpose will be defeated. It may require several practices before a light, effortless rhythm of breaths and retentions can be established. I cannot stress enough that the actual length of the retention, or number of retentions, is of no importance whatsoever. Only the rhythmic shifting of your awareness from the body of the flame to its vanishing point is of significance. At each focus upon the tip of the flame, try for at least a fraction of a second to direct all your perception and will upon the dimensionless margin where it disappears out of the universe.

After a few dozen breaths, and before you even start to grow tired either mentally or physically, stand up facing the south. Raise your arms in the gesture of invocation, saying in a calm but confident voice:

I give thanks for the successful fulfillment of this ritual to awaken a true perception of the Light of Spirit.

Extending your left index finger to the magic circle in the south, rotate upon your own axis widdershins—to the left—and mentally reabsorb the ring of astral flame into your heart center as you speak these words:

I hereby absorb this flaming circle of power into my heart of being, returning this ritual place to its former level.

Facing the south once again, cross yourself as you did in the opening of the ritual, speaking these words:

> *May the grace of the Light*
> *Guide and protect me,*
> *Who art the Crown*

(touch your forehead)

> *And the Kingdom,*

(groin)

The Power

(left shoulder)

And the Glory,

(right shoulder)

And the everlasting Law,

(touch your heart center)

Amen.

(point at the flame)

Clap your hands together four times and spread your arms wide with your fingers splayed, saying:

This ritual for awakening an awareness of Light is well and truly completed.

Blow out the candle and relax for a few moments before turning your energies to any other task. Do not try to go over the ritual in your mind. Just be passive and let it work itself upon your unconscious.

I chose this ritual because it is not dangerous, and so requires no banishing formula. Since it is worked primarily in the astral by visualization, it can be done without magical instruments. However it is still a very potent ritual. If you work at it each day for several weeks you should notice subtle yet unmistakable changes in your awareness. The ritual purpose has deliberately been left unspecific in order to promote those transformations most natural to each individual. A general stirring of higher perceptions, as well as an increase in vitality, are to be expected. Other effects will depend on the personality and abilities of the person using the ritual. For a lasting change it should be worked regularly for several months.

Leaves cast into the sea become a fleet of ships.
—from an illustration by Gustave Doré for Ariosto's Orlando Furioso

CHAPTER TWENTY-ONE

RITUAL TO ACCOMPLISH
A WILLED PURPOSE

Western magic is worked through natural objects called amulets and talismans. Amulets are carried or worn on the body to provide protection. Talismans have a more general function. They may or may not be carried, and they accomplish specific goals other than merely providing protection. Amulets frequently consist of natural objects such as stones, plants, bones of animals, seeds, hair, and so on. Talismans more often are constructed through the use of symbols, sigils, images, and letters. If natural substances are presumed to have efficacy in magic, it can be seen that the power of a talisman is increased when it is inscribed upon or physically united with an appropriate material in harmony with the magical purpose.

The following ritual is designed to empower a talisman and cause it to commence working. Its general pattern can be used for any ritual of empowering. Details will vary according to the specific type and function of the talisman. As an example, the construction of a solar talisman to attract peace, harmony, and good fortune into a house is described. This ritual is based upon the system of magic described in *The New Magus*, but it can easily be adapted to the Golden Dawn system.

All work is best done on a single Sunday, the day of the Sun. If possible, the actual construction of the talisman should be commenced at dawn. The first hour of any day is always the hour of that day's planet. It is not strictly necessary to observe astrological times in the making of talismans, but doing so helps to focus the

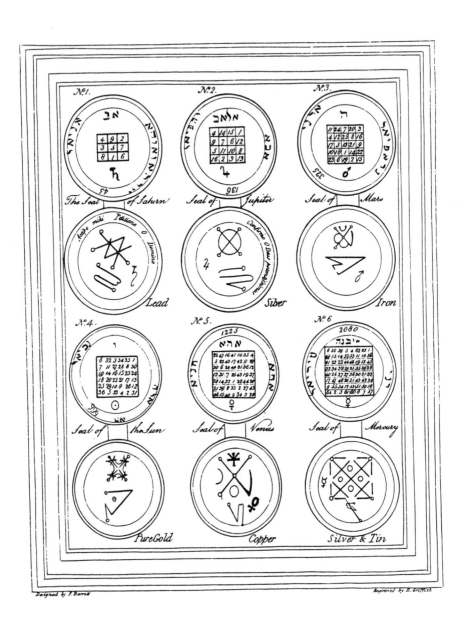

Talismans formed from the magic squares of the planets and their related seals and sigils, with significant numbers, divine names, and names of spirits.
—from The Magus *by Francis Barrett, 1801*

Solar talisman: front and back

mind on the magical desire and strengthens the overall unity of the ritual. Materials should be gathered and preparations made before the day of the working. Be sure to keep everything in a clean, private place and tell no one what you intend to accomplish.

On a three-inch circle of yellow paper or blond parchment, draw or paint in gold a large, masculine, solar face in a Sun of the type that is frequently seen in old woodcuts. The face should be fat with health and smiling with good cheer. From the circle of the Sun, draw or paint 16 wavy solar rays. If you own a deck of Tarot cards, you will see a similar face on the card of the Sun. Make sure your Sun is smiling and has 16 rays—different Tarots show different faces. Sixteen is the four-square number of physical realization.

The best drawing instrument is a pen of the type sold in photography and stationary stores for writing in gold on photographs. These pens dispense a thin line of gold pigment that dries quickly and does not smear. Alternately, a gold crayon or gold-colored pencil may be used. If you use gold paint and a fine artist's brush, be sure the paint is quick drying.

After the Sun face has dried, draw on the back of the circle of paper a medium-sized triangle with its point uppermost, as shown in the accompanying illustration. At the top point of the triangle, make the symbol of the Sun. At the right point, the symbol of Leo, which is the Zodiac sign of the south and of the Sun. At the left point, the seal of the Intelligence of the Sun, Nachiel. Finally write in the center of the triangle in Hebrew characters from right to left the banner of Tetragrammaton that accords with the south and with Leo, יההו. (There are 12 permutations of Tetragrammaton called banners, one for each sign of the Zodiac.)

As you can see, this talisman is based on the magic of the Kabbalah, which lies at the heart of so much of the Western occult tradition. The shape of the seal of Nachiel is drawn from the Kabbalistic square of the Sun, and the name Nachiel is numerically 111, a solar number also extracted from the solar magic square.

To get ready for the actual ritual, place a square table in the south of your ritual chamber, or at least so that it is in front of you when you stand facing the south. On the table, you will need a small pitcher of liquid honey, a clear glass bottle that can be tightly stoppered or capped—the little liquor bottles given out by the airlines are ideal, but a tiny spice or pill bottle will work. Make sure the bottle is clean and remove the label. Also have ready a white candle in a holder, a yellow candle in a holder, three sunflower seeds, a dish of salt, and a goblet of water.

Preparation is important. It is best that the salt is sea salt or natural rock salt and the water for the goblet has been collected from a fresh running spring, stream, or river. Before the Sunday of the ritual, the honey that will be used, the candles and holders, the empty bottle and its cap, and the sunflower seeds should be cleansed by sprinkling them three times with the water drawn from the stream or spring. As you cast droplets of the water from the fingertips of your right hand, speak the words:

By this clear, pure water, I cleanse these instruments of the art from all contamination and dedicate them wholly to this work of the Sun, in the name Yod-He-He-Vau.

If you have no other choice, tap water can be used, but it should itself be consecrated with prayer under the authority of the divine name of the south before it is employed for cleansing. Spring water is a pure, natural product of the earth and is magically clean to begin with.

Draw in the air over the gathered materials the Hebrew letters of the name IHHV (יההו), from right to left, using your wet right index finger. Then leave the materials that will be used in the ritual exposed to the morning sunlight for about an hour. Hold in your mind the thought that they are absorbing the golden light the way a dry sponge sucks up water. This will charge the materials with solar virtue.

On the Sunday of the ritual, ideally just before noon when the Sun is approaching its highest point in the sky, place the white candle in its holder in the center of the table that will serve as an altar and the yellow candle in its holder on the south side of the table. Also in the south, put the pitcher of purified and Sun-charged honey to the right of the yellow candle and the three sunflower seeds to the left. The dish of salt goes on the east side of the table, the goblet of fresh water on the west side, and the circular paper with the smiling face of the Sun uppermost in the north.

Cleanse and prepare yourself, light the white and then the yellow candle, then stand before the altar facing south. Close your eyes and relax. Try to empty your mind and calm your emotions. Passively contemplate the task you undertake. When you are ready, clap your hands together sharply three times and raise your arms to heaven. Speak the declaration of intent:

This ritual for charging the talisman of the Sun with solar virtue is well and truly commenced.

Speak the cleansing prayer and draw the Kabbalistic cross upon your own body. Extend the magic circle from your heart center through your right index finger as you turn on your axis sunwise, mentally including the altar in the circle. Spread your arms and invoke the four guardian angels of the quarters, Michael, Gabriel, Raphael, and Uriel, and visualize the cross of three beams of light extending through your heart center. All these preliminary steps have been described in detail in the previous chapter.

Having established the circle, you must cleanse it of discordant influences to make it magically a blank slate that will receive the impression of the solar virtue. This may be done symbolically by banishing the four quarters with the banishing pentagrams of the elements, or physically by purging the quarters with the materials of cleansing, or by combining both techniques. Here, for the sake of simplicity, the circle is cleansed only with salt, water, and flame.

The ritual of banishing by pentagrams can be found in *The Golden Dawn* and many other magical texts.

Take the dish of salt from the altar. Cast a pinch three times to the south across the altar top, saying:

With salt I cleanse the region of the south.

Repeat this procedure in turn to the west, north, and east, saying

With salt I cleanse the region of the west.

And so on at each quarter.

Replace the salt on the altar and take up the goblet of water. Dipping your fingers into it, lightly sprinkle a few drops three times toward the south, saying:

With water I cleanse the region of the south.

Repeat this cleansing in turn to the west, north, and east, altering the words as needed.

Replace the goblet and take up the yellow candle. Raise it in the air to the south across the altar and wave it up and down three times so that the flame flickers, saying:

With flame I cleanse the region of the south.

Repeat this formula in turn to the west, north, and east. Replace the yellow candle on the altar. This completes the cleansing of the circle.

Rotate on your own axis, or walk three times sunwise around the circle if you have enough room to place the altar at the center. Visualize a great vortex of golden light swirling down in a funnel shape, its focus the tip of the flame of the white candle at the center of the altar. Will everything upon the altar to be suffused with this radiance so that it shines. Speak the words:

By this threefold turning I fill this circle with the radiance of the Sun.

Remember, magic is worked in the mind. Make your physical circumambulation of the circle only a reflection of what is occurring within the bounds of your astral temple, which you must be able to clearly see in your imagination. As much as possible, be yourself present in your astral temple, and regard your physical body as only remotely imitating the actions you perform in the astral.

Take up the yellow candle again and, with its flame, draw in the air directly above the altar the four Hebrew letters of the banner of Tetragrammaton that lies in the south. These are the letters in the center of the triangle on the back of the paper circle. Hebrew is written from right to left, so begin with the letter on the right. Visualize the four letters flaming with golden yellow light on the air. Speak the words:

> By the most potent name Yod-He-He-Vau, banner of the south, I hereby infuse this talisman with the strengthening, harmonious, and joyful virtue of the Sun. So by this virtue shall it gather happiness to the place and persons who possess it.

You will notice that all statements made during the course of the ritual are wholly positive. There must be no doubt or ambiguity, either in the actions and words of the ritual, or in the mind of the magician, or the working will surely be futile.

Return the yellow candle to its place on the altar in the south. Hold the paper circle over the altar upon your hands with the solar face uppermost and visualize golden light flowing into it. When it radiates so strongly it can hold no more, roll it up and slip it into the small glass bottle. After it drop in the three sunflower seeds. The sunflower is one of the most solar of plants. Fill the bottle with liquid honey and tightly cork or cap it. Honey is perhaps the most strongly solar substance on earth. Take the yellow candle and drip wax across the cork or at the place where the cap joins the glass neck of the bottle to make a yellow wax seal. Then hold the honey-filled bottle over the flame of the yellow candle and slowly heat it until you can feel a mild warmth. Take care not to overheat it or you may crack the bottle. Imagine the bottle glowing with golden light. When you feel the honey has absorbed all the solar virtue it can hold, set the bottle on the north side of the altar.

Rotate on your axis or walk around the circle three times widdershins to close the magical vortex. Visualize the golden funnel of light fading from the air, but continue to see the radiance shining forth from the honey-filled bottle. Speak the words:

By this threefold turning, I restore this circle to its former state.

Reabsorb the magic circle into your left index finger by turning on your axis or walking around the circle widdershins and repeat the Kabbalistic cross over your body as described at the close of the previous chapter. Stand facing south with arms upraised and speak the closing declaration:

By the authority of the most potent name Yod-He-He-Vau, this ritual for charging the solar talisman with golden light is well and truly fulfilled.

Clap your hands sharply together four times and cross your arms upon your chest with hands closed. Bow your head and shut your eyes, and stand for a few moments with complete inner stillness.

Extinguish the candles, first the yellow, then the white. Put away the materials used in the ritual with care. They have been purified and consecrated by use and should be treated with respect. If you later discard them, do so with full awareness that you are returning them to the Earth. Wash the talisman bottle clean of any honey you may have spilled on its outside and wrap it for safekeeping in blue or purple silk or white linen.

When you are ready to use the talisman, it should be unwrapped and placed in the corner of a cupboard, closet, or other place where it will remain undiscovered and undisturbed, as close as possible to the center of the house you wish to harmonize. After that, it is best to completely forget that it exists. Magic works in silence, both mental and verbal. Do not speak of the talisman.

CHAPTER TWENTY-TWO

THE MAGICIAN'S LIBRARY

Although magic is a living art that exists only when it is practiced, its ideas and techniques are embodied in a relatively small library of source books. These books have had and continue to have great influence in shaping the beliefs and methods of modern pagans, Witches, and ceremonial magicians. To study them is to gain a solid grasp of what magic purports to be about and where it comes from.

Unfortunately there is a great deal of derivative writing in the marketplace that is based upon these few seminal works. Some of it is excellent, but the sheer bulk of it tends to obscure the primary literary fountains of inspiration from the awareness of the newcomer to Western magic.

The following reading list contains some, but by no means all, of the most vital sources. Also included are a number of excellent secondary works that will help the beginner make sense of the primary texts. The books are graded in three levels of difficulty to ease the absorption of the information they contain. Most are readily available either from booksellers or through secondhand bookstores and libraries.

This is very much a subjective list. At various times I have studied all these works and found them to contain valuable insights and useful techniques. Another writer might well compile a completely different list, but you may rest assured that the study of all of the works that follow is well worth the effort.

LEVEL I

The books on this level are all accessible and require little or no previous study. They provide an introduction to some of the most important ideas in magic.

Preparation

The Kybalion by Three Initiates. Chicago, IL: Yoga Publication Society, 1940.

An extremely odd work which introduces seven basic occult principles that govern the universe and the human mind. At first glance it seems simplistic, but it has a strange power of resonance and remains in the memory long after the book itself has been filed away.

The One Year Manual by Israel Regardie. York Beach, ME: Samuel Weiser, 1981. Formerly published under the title *Twelve Steps to Spiritual Enlightenment*, Sangreal Foundation, 1969.

A program of exercises extending over one year designed to awaken magical awareness and prepare the mind and body for more advanced rituals. Regardie was a follower of Aleister Crowley.

Theory

Transcendental Magic: Its Doctrine and Ritual by Eliphas Levi. New York: Samuel Weiser, 1979.

A. E. Waite's 1896 translation of Levi's *Dogme et Rituel de la Haute Magie*, first published in 1855–6, had a strong influence upon occultists in England and America. All the main figures in the Golden Dawn had read and admired Levi's work, although from a modern perspective it appears vapid and unfocused. Nonetheless it is an important milestone in the development of magical theory.

Positive Magic by Marion Weinstein. British Columbia: Phoenix, 1981.

One of the best general treatments of magic by a modern Witch. This is a good book to study if you have any lingering worries that all magic is evil. Weinstein teaches a gentle, loving way into the art.

Real Magic by Isaac Bonewits. Berkeley, CA: Creative Arts, 1979.

A sensible introduction to modern magic that makes an effort to take away the fear and mystery.

Practice

Applied Magic by Dion Fortune. London: Aquarian Press, 1962.

An easy overview of some basic ideas of Western ritual magic. It is colored by the background of its author, but it offers useful insights into the mindset of one of the members of the original Golden Dawn and the founder of the Society of the Inner Light.

The Inner Teachings of the Golden Dawn by R. G. Torrens. London: Neville Spearman, 1972.

The title is misleading. This is really a kind of student's notebook on *The Golden Dawn* in which all the basic esoteric information in the larger work is compressed and logically arranged for easy comprehension. Very useful for gaining an overview of the Golden Dawn system of magic.

Witchcraft

Lid Off the Cauldron by Patricia Crowther. York Beach, ME: Samuel Weiser, 1985.

A readable account of what modern Witches actually believe and what they do when they gather together, written by a practicing Gardnerian Witch.

The Alex Sanders Lectures. New York: Magickal Childe, 1984.

A set of lectures composed by Sanders and some of his followers around 1970 to introduce students to his personal brand of Witchcraft. A bit shallow, but significant because of its source and purpose.

Tarot

A Complete Guide to the Tarot by Eden Gray. New York: Bantam, 1972.

A very good basic introduction to the Tarot cards designed by A. E. Waite in company with the artist Pamela Colman Smith. The Tarot is an important pillar of Western magic.

The Pictorial Key to the Tarot by Arthur Edward Waite. New York: Samuel Weiser, 1980.

Originally published in 1910, this book was written by Waite to explain his Tarot deck, which remains the most widely used deck today despite its many shortcomings.

The Tarot by S. L. MacGregor Mathers. New York: Samuel

Weiser, no date.

The first edition of this slim pamphlet was published in London in 1888. It is a simplistic examination of the Tarot strictly as a device for divination, but it is important because its author was a founding member of the Golden Dawn.

Kabbalah

The Ladder of Lights by William G. Gray. Great Britain: Helios, 1971.

The clearest, simplest, and best introduction to the Kabbalah of modern magic, which is not quite the same as the traditional Kabbalah of Jewish mysticism.

A Practical Guide to Qabalistic Symbolism by Gareth Knight. New York: Samuel Weiser, 1980.

A compendium of the relationships and correspondences between the magical Kabbalah and the Tarot. Very useful as a quick reference. Gareth Knight is a pseudonym for Basil Wilby, a former member of Dion Fortune's Society of the Inner Light.

LEVEL II

The books on this second level are more involved and theoretical in their examination of magic, and for this reason more difficult. You will find here the most important texts that give the actual practical techniques of ritual.

Preparation

Concentration by Mouni Sadhu. London: Mandala, 1977.

Basic but effective exercises to transform consciousness and prepare the mind for higher work. It leans to the Eastern tradition but is truly an excellent work.

Initiation into Hermetics by Franz Bardon. Germany: Dieter Ruggeberg, 1971.

Despite the really execrable translation into English from the German, this is the best book of exercises designed to prepare the mind for high magic that I have ever read. It is very potent.

Theory

The Tree of Life by Israel Regardie. New York: Samuel Weiser, 1973.

Written under the influence of Regardie's apprenticeship to

Aleister Crowley, this is a complete analysis of the Golden Dawn magic as Crowley adapted it to his own thinking, and is not, as the title implies, merely a book on the Kabbalah.

The Key of the Mysteries by Eliphas Levi. London: Rider, 1959.

Translated into English by Aleister Crowley for his periodical *The Equinox*, in my opinion this is Levi's best work. It gives his understanding of magic in a highly compressed set of epigrams.

Practice

The Golden Dawn by Israel Regardie. St. Paul, MN: Llewellyn Publications, 1982.

This is the magical bible of the Western tradition. Composed of the original Golden Dawn order papers, it is huge, expensive, almost impossible to read except in small bits, but absolutely essential for anyone seriously studying magic. Shortly before his death, Regardie revised it and added additional material, and it continues to be revised and corrected—my own work on the magic squares and seals of the planets is included in the latest revision.

The Magical Philosophy by Melita Denning and Osborne Phillips. St. Paul, MN: Llewellyn Publications, 1974.

A vast, five-volume set that gives the entire system of magic worked within the occult organization Aurum Solis. The methods described here are very much in harmony with the magical techniques of *The Golden Dawn*, and the two works are best studied together for purposes of comparison.

Magical Ritual Methods by William G. Gray. New York: Samuel Weiser, 1980.

Advanced techniques of ritual. This is a practical text that not only gives rational explanations but describes how to make magic happen.

Inner Traditions of Magic by William G. Gray. New York: Samuel Weiser, 1978.

An excellent companion to the book above, its approach is more theoretical, yet it stays down to earth. All of Gray's books are firmly based in the Western tradition of ceremonial magic.

Witchcraft

Witchcraft Today by Gerald B. Gardner. New York: Magickal

Childe, 1982.

First published in 1954, this is *the* book that started the modern revival of Witchcraft. In fact it is not a very good book but it must be read.

Meaning of Witchcraft by Gerald B. Gardner. New York: Magickal Childe, 1982.

A follow-up of the previous work published in 1959 to satisfy growing interest in Witchcraft.

Aradia, or the Gospel of the Witches by Charles Godfrey Leland. New York: Samuel Weiser, 1974.

Written in 1899, this examination of supposed Witchcraft survival in Italy was one of Gardner's sources when he composed his Book of Shadows containing modern Witch rituals.

The Spiral Dance by Starhawk. San Francisco: Harper and Row, 1979.

A complete and practical treatment of modern Witchcraft by a modern Witch.

Tarot

The Tarot by Paul Foster Case. Richmond, VA: Macoy, 1975.

The writings of Case on the Tarot are very highly thought of by many occultists. Case was for a time head of the Golden Dawn in North America. Later he founded the occult school known as the Builders of the Adytum, or B.O.T.A.

The Symbolism of the Tarot by P. D. Ouspensky. New York: Dover, 1976.

Ouspensky was a student of occultism and for a time the disciple of the charismatic Russian mystic, G. J. Gurdjieff. His insights are significant.

Introduction to the Study of the Tarot by Oswald Wirth. New York: U.S. Games, 1983.

Wirth, a friend of the occultist Stanislas de Guaita, designed a set of the 22 Major Arcana cards of the Tarot based on the descriptions of Eliphas Levi.

The Tarot of the Bohemians by Papus. New York: U.S. Games, 1978.

This work concentrates strongly on the relationship between the Tetragrammaton and the Tarot. Gerard Encausse (the author's true name) was a friend of de Guaita and a fervent admirer of Levi. A fine book, quite unjustly underrated by some modern occultists.

Kabbalah

The Kabbalah Unveiled by S. L. MacGregor Mathers. London: Routledge and Kegan Paul, 1962.

A translation of part of Knorr von Rosenroth's *Kabbalah Denudata* (Latin, 1677-84) by the leader of the Golden Dawn. It was extremely influential on later occult writers and magicians.

Q.B.L. or The Bride's Reception by Frater Achad. New York: Samuel Weiser, New York, 1972.

Achad was an American follower of Crowley, who considered his pupil brilliant but ultimately incorrect in his conclusions on the Kabbalah. This book describes a new system for assigning the 22 paths on the Kabbalistic tree to the Tarot trumps.

The Egyptian Revival by Frater Achad. New York: Samuel Weiser, 1973.

A further examination of the Kabbalah of modern occultism as it relates to the Tarot.

LEVEL III

The books on this highest level are generally esoteric or are important source books upon which later occult writings were based. They will be of more interest to the serious student than to the beginner.

Preparation

Samadhi by Mouni Sadhu. London: Mandala, 1971.

More advanced exercises for opening the higher awareness than were given in the author's book *Concentration*. All of Sadhu's works are excellent.

Book Four by Aleister Crowley. Texas: Sangreal, 1972.
An exposition of Crowley's experiments with yoga.

Liber Aleph, The Book of Wisdom or Folly by Aleister Crowley. California: Thelema, 1962.

A set of meditations on the art of magic written by Crowley for his son. Very concentrated, very insightful, very good. One of Crowley's best works.

Theory

Tertium Organum by P. D. Ouspensky. New York: Vintage, 1970.

A great work by perhaps the most brilliant Western occultist of all, it shatters the narrow materialistic view of time and space. This is required reading for anyone who wants to see how magic might actually be able to work in the world.

A New Model of the Universe by P. D. Ouspensky. New York: Vintage, 1971.

Ouspensky examines from a critical and analytical perspective such things as the fourth dimension, yoga, dreams, hypnotism, and the myth of the superman. Less difficult than the work above.

Practice

Magick in Theory and Practice by Aleister Crowley. New York: Dover, 1976.

This is Crowley's textbook on magic, where he sets forth his basic understanding of the art and his theories to explain how magic works.

The Practice of Magical Evocation by Franz Bardon. Germany: Dieter Ruggeberg, 1975.

The best book I have read on the ceremonial evocation of spirits. Bardon knew what he was talking about. The complex spirit system he gives should be used as an example, not followed slavishly.

The Book of Pleasure by Austin Osman Spare. Canada: 93 Publishing, 1975.

Spare presents some of his techniques in what has come to be known as chaos magic, along with his spirit hieroglyphs and automatic drawings of spirits. A strange and difficult work, but fascinating. Spare deliberately wrote it in a way that would obscure his meaning.

Witchcraft

The Witch-Cult in Western Europe by Margaret A. Murray. London: Oxford, 1967.

First published in 1921, this work gave a scholarly impetus to the theory that Witchcraft was the survival of an ancient goddess cult. It has since been dismissed by the academic world but enjoys credence in occult circles.

The God of the Witches by Margaret A. Murray. London: Oxford, 1979.

An elaboration of the ideas Murray expressed in her earlier work. No one can claim to understand the origins of modern Witchcraft without having read Murray.

Witches by L. C. Lethbridge. Secaucus, NJ: Citadel, 1968.

An interesting and knowledgeable look at the theory of Witch-cult survival in Europe.

Geography of Witchcraft by Montague Summers. Secaucus, NJ: Citadel, 1973.

An historic overview of Witchcraft in Europe by individual countries. Summers was fanatically opposed to magic but is generally accurate.

Tarot

The Book of Thoth by Aleister Crowley. New York: Samuel Weiser, 1974.

Crowley's analysis of the Tarot symbolism, intended to accompany his own Tarot deck which he designed with the artist Frieda Harris.

The Book of Tokens by Paul Foster Case. Los Angeles, CA: Builders of the Adytum, 1968.

A set of meditations written by Case in 1934 to awaken a magical awareness of the Tarot. This book impresses other occultists much more than it impresses me, but it is historically important.

Kabbalah

The Kabbalah by Christian D. Ginsburg. London: Routledge and Kegan Paul, 1970.

First published in 1863, this work was a strong influence on MacGregor Mathers and the other leaders of the Golden Dawn.

The Kabbalah: The Religious Philosophy of the Hebrews by Adolphe Franck. New York: Bell, 1940.

Another early work (published in French in 1843) that influenced Mathers.

777 and Other Qabalistic Writings by Aleister Crowley. York Beach, ME: Samuel Weiser, 1987.

A collection of Crowley's Kabbalistic writings.

Kabbalah by Gershom Scholem. Jerusalem: Keter, 1977.

A general background by the foremost authority on the Jewish (as opposed to the Western occult) Kabbalah. An excellent source of factual information.

The Holy Kabbalah by A. E. Waite. New Hyde Park, NY: University Books, 1975.

Widely recognized as Waite's greatest work, this book examines the history and literature of the Kabbalah.

THE PRAYER OF
HERMES TRISMEGISTUS

This prayer occurs in the *Divine Pymander* of Hermes Trismegistus, the semi-divine authority to whom most of the Hermetic writings are ascribed by their anonymous authors. It is a hymn to the highest God who is without attributes. Hermes makes the vital philosophical point in the prayer that the only suitable sacrifice to this supreme divinity is inner stillness. This is a profound mystical insight.

The earliest version of the hymn occurs in an Egyptian collection of Christian prayers on a scroll of papyrus dating from the 3rd century. However Hermes was not a Christian. His sophisticated understanding of the essential nature of God and the universe makes much early Christian theology seem naive and simplistic by comparison. Not surprisingly, the early Christian fathers raided the Hermetic books for ideas that they could turn to their own purposes. The prayer is thought to have been originally written sometime during the 2nd century.

The awkwardness of the translations from the Arabic and Greek versions of the prayer have led me to paraphrase it and cast it in the form of a simple ritual. Although some precision of meaning may be lost, it is much easier to speak the words of the paraphrase as a living communion with the Light.

The amalgamation of the prayer with the divine fivefold name יהשוה (Yeheshuah) is wholly my own innovation. Since the Hebrew letters of this divine name can be assigned the occult elements and the four cardinal points, it helps to ground the prayer and give it structure.

The Hermes prayer ritual was previously published in the 1991 edition of *Llewellyn's Magickal Almanac,* but I wished to repeat it here because I find it so useful in my own ritual work. It can be completed in a few minutes. Repeated daily working will encourage an increase of optimism, vitality, and inner harmony. It is most effective done at night under a starry sky on a hill or other high place.

Prayer of Hermes Trismegistus

Face south. Raise your arms wide in a gesture of supplication with your palms forward and gaze southward into infinity. Speak the first verse:

> *Holy is God, the Father of All.*
> *Holy is God, the Will become Law.*
> *Holy is God, the Lamp of Love.*

Place your left hand over your heart-center and, with your right index finger, inscribe at heart level the Hebrew letter *Yod* (׳) so that it floats upon the air in the south. Put your palms together in a gesture of prayer over your heart and contemplate the south for a few moments.

Turn to the west. Raise your arms in supplication to the west and look into the infinite distance. Speak the second verse:

> *Holy art Thou, the Word into Flesh.*
> *Holy art Thou, the Shaper of Mountains.*
> *Holy art Thou, by Nature not formed.*

With your left hand over your heart-center, inscribe largely the Hebrew letter *He* (ה) in the air of the west using your right index finger. Join your palms in prayer over your heart and contemplate the west.

Turn to the north. Raise your arms in supplication and look northward into infinity. Speak the third verse:

> *Holy art Thou, Power beyond knowing.*
> *Holy art Thou, Worth beyond measure.*
> *Holy art Thou, above all praises.*

With your left hand upon your heart, inscribe largely with your right index finger the Hebrew letter Vau (ו) in the air to the north at heart level. Join your palms together in a gesture of prayer over your heart-center and contemplate the north.

Turn to the east. Raise your arms in supplication and look eastward into infinity. Speak the fourth verse:

> *Accept this sacrifice from a pure soul and a yearning heart.*
> *Ye Nameless! Ye Formless! I praise Thee with Silence.*

With your left hand upon your heart, inscribe largely in the air to the east the Hebrew letter He (ה) using your right index finger. Join your palms in a gesture of prayer over your heart-center and contemplate the east for a few moments.

Then place your left hand upon your heart and raise your right index finger to your lips in a gesture of silence. Cross your hands and forearms upon your breast at the wrists with your fingers extended stiffly. Bow your head and try to still all movement within yourself, even your thoughts. Present this silence, a sacrifice of the mind, to God.

Turn back to the south. Raise your arms heavenward with the palms up and fingers spread wide in a gesture of invocation. Look up into the infinite space above you. Speak the fifth verse:

> *Shed down Thy Light upon me; shower down Thy Light to the dark*
> *corners of the Earth.*
> *I believe in Thee and bear Thy witness; I walk with Thee into Fire.*
> *Blessed art Thou, Lord of Creation, All in One and One in All.*

With your left hand to your heart-center, inscribe upon the air over your head the Hebrew letter Shin (ש), using your right index finger. Place your palms together in a gesture of prayer over your heart and contemplate the heavens.

Raise your hands still joined to your forehead and press the second segments of your thumbs against the domed part of your skull, where it curves outward just below the hairline. Speak the word:

> *Amen.*

Lower your joined hands to your face and touch the end segments of your index fingers to your lips. Speak the word:

Amen.

Lower your joined hands to the level of your heart-center. Press the base parts of your thumbs against your sternum. Speak the word:

Amen.

Allow your hands to fall to your sides, and spend a few moments visualizing the five letters of the name that represents spirit incarnated into human flesh as these letters flame upon the air all around you.

GLOSSARY

ACUPRESSURE—A form of physical therapy in which certain occult nodes recorded in the literature of acupuncture are pressed or manipulated without being pierced by needles.

ACUPUNCTURE—A traditional art practiced primarily in China, in which needles are inserted into occult nodes in the body to deaden pain or produce other beneficial effects.

AEON OF HORUS—The age of oneness between human beings and God that follows after the Aeon of Osiris where human-God was a duality. According to Aleister Crowley, it began in 1904 with the dictation of *The Book of the Law* and is coeval with the astrological Age of Aquarius.

ALCHEMY—The art of transforming by magical and physical practices that which is base into that which is precious. The central rite is the Great Work, the purification and exaltation of the human soul.

ALEXANDRIAN WITCHES—Modern Witches who follow the teachings and use the Book of Shadows composed by Alex Sanders.

ANGEL—Literally, "messenger" of God. Angels are the intermediaries between God and humankind. They bear teachings, warnings, and messages of all kinds from heaven to Earth and carry out the orders of God.

ASSON—The sacred rattle of Voudoun, used to summon the *loa*, or gods.

ASTRAL TEMPLE—The place of ritual working that is created in the astral realm, or imagination, by repeated intense acts of visualization and meditation. The true temple of which the material temple is only a reflection.

ASTROLOGY—The art of reading the future and hidden events from the relative positions of the stars and planets at a given time and from a given place upon the Earth.

AURA—A halo of colored light observed by some sensitive or psychic individuals around the bodies of human beings, beasts, and even plants. The colors are said to indicate definite emotional states. Since they are not seen with the physical eyes, they cannot be recorded by machines.

AUTO-DA-FÉ—A grotesque kind of festival mounted by the Spanish Inquisition in which accused heretics, whose only crime was adherence to their faith, were publicly paraded through town in special costumes, beaten and humiliated, and then burned alive.

BINDING—To bind a spirit means to secure its obedience through the authority of divine names and the threat of punishment. An occult symbol may act as a seal upon the binding, and the spirit may be confined to a certain place or within a specific object.

BIORHYTHMS—The regular rhythmic cycles of the body, which may have an amplitude of days, weeks, or even months, and which vary in intensity from individual to individual.

BLACK MAGIC—Magic that is worked for evil purposes or that involves malign actions or agents.

BLACK MASS—A satanic parody of the mass of the Catholic Church in which the body of a naked woman serves as the altar and excrements replace the host. It had its origins in decadent France but was so rare as to be virtually mythical.

BON—The shamanic religion of Tibet before the coming of Buddhism, which officially supplanted it. In fact many Bon beliefs and practices were absorbed into Tibetan Buddhism, giving it a unique, magical character.

BOOK OF SHADOWS—A collection of rituals, prayers, charms and other magical bits of information compiled by a Witch or group of Witches. It varies from coven to coven. The Books of Shadows of Gerald B. Gardner and Alex Sanders serve as guides for their followers.

BUDDHISM—A religion and philosophy of life based on the teachings and example of Gautama Siddhartha, an Indian prince who lived during the 6th century BC. Buddha means "enlightened one" and was applied to Gautama as a title of respect. Buddhism teaches freedom from attachment to worldly things.

CALLS (KEYS), ENOCHIAN—Invocations to the Enochian angels dictated to John Dee through his seer, the alchemist Edward Kelley. The calls were used extensively in the magic of the Golden Dawn, Aleister Crowley, and Anton LaVey.

CATHARSIS, MAGICAL—The release of magical potency at the climax of a ritual. It is usually accompanied by an emotional release, and in some forms of magic by physical climax. The catharsis of Greek tragedy was no more than a pale echo of the original magical catharsis of the Mysteries.

CHAKRAS—Occult energy centers of the body. *Chakra* means "wheel." In Western magic, the most important are usually said to be seven in number and located along the spine from the perineum to the crown of the head. Opening the chakras results in the attainment of various magical powers.

CHANNELING—The process by which a spirit takes control of a medium, or channeler, and speaks through the mouth of that person. Identical to the practices of trance mediums, but it tends to dispense with the traditional paraphernalia of the seance.

CHANTING—The rhythmic repetition of sounds or words to induce an altered mental state and produce a magical effect.

CHAOS MAGIC—Magic based on the presumptions that the universe is uncertain and that natural laws are not everywhere and always constant.

CHELA—Eastern term for a student of spiritual and occult matters who learns mainly by imitating the guru, or teacher.

CLAIRAUDIENCE—The auditory perception by the conscious mind through the unconscious of sounds, usually voices, transmitted by an unknown agency.

CLAIRVOYANCE—The visual perception by the conscious mind through the unconscious of objects or scenes transmitted by an unknown agency.

COLOR THERAPY—The use of colors to induce mental and emotional changes, usually for a therapeutic purpose.

CRAFT, THE—Witchcraft, with emphasis on the craft part of this pagan religion.

CROSS-QUARTER DAYS—The four most important Witch festivals of the year that fall exactly between the solstices and equinoxes and thus form the figure of a cross on the wheel of the year. They cross the Quarter Days.

CULT—A group of fanatical admirers who form a devoted attachment to and follow the teachings of a charismatic leader or set of ideas.

CUNNING MAN—The solitary male Witch who healed, gave advice, told fortunes, and dispensed charms to the inhabitants of rural villages in Europe.

CURRENTS, OCCULT—An occult current is a coherent set of beliefs and practices based either on a historic tradition, such as druidism, or the revelations of a prophet purporting to have a supernatural authority, such as Aleister Crowley.

DAEMON—In Greek myth, an intermediate spirit between men and gods. Daemons such as the one that guided Socrates act as counselors and guardians to human beings.

DEMON—In Christian folklore, an evil spirit under the authority of Satan. Modern practice tends to distinguish "demon," the evil spirit, from "daemon," the guardian angel of the Greeks, by spelling.

DESIRE, RITUAL—The emotional motivation that gives rise to and drives a particular ritual expression. The ritual desire is what the ritualist seeks to fulfill by conducting the ritual.

DESTINY—The complete and perfect fulfillment of human potential.

DEVIL, THE—Satan, the chief foe of God.

DEVILS—An alternate name for the legions of demons in Hell that serve Satan.

DIVINATION—The art of revealing by occult practices the future or matters that are hidden. The types of divination are too many to mention, but Western occultism favors astrology, palmistry, the Tarot, and more recently the runes.

DRUIDISM—An ancient Celtic brotherhood of scholarly priests that underwent a modern revival in Minnesota in the early 1960s. Druids worship in groves and venerate the Goddess through trees, especially the oak. Like modern Witches, they believe in reincarnation.

EASTERN OCCULTISM—The magic of India, China, Tibet, Japan, and other nations of the Far East. Its range is roughly coequal with that of Buddhism.

ELEMENTAL—A spirit formed from one of the four magical elements: Fire (Salamander), Air (Sylph), Water (Undine), and Earth (Gnome). The names of the four classes of spirits come from the German occultist Paracelsus.

EMPOWERMENT—The assumption of responsibility and control by the individual over his or her life. Also, the giving of power to a person, place, or thing.

ENCHANT—The act of casting a magical spell, especially through the use of muttered, recited, or chanted words of power.

ENOCHIAN—An occult language with its own distinct alphabet that was received by John Dee through his seer Edward Kelley during a series of seances around the end of the 16th century. Dee supposed it to be the language of the angels.

ESBAT—A lesser gathering of Witches for the purposes of celebration and works of magic. It usually occurs on the nights of the full or new Moon.

EVIL EYE—The projection of malefic occult force through the glance. Persons, beasts, and growing things "overlooked" by the evil eye are believed to wither and die.

EVOCATION—The calling forth of spirits into visible and sometimes tactile presence. Usually evil spirits or demons are evoked inside an equilateral triangle beyond the limit of the protective magic circle that surrounds the magician.

EXPERIMENTAL METHOD—The measure of truth used in science. A hypothesis is arrived at through research and observation, then tested by further observation and the use of experiments to determine its validity. If replicable experiments support the hypothesis, it may then be developed into a theory. An experiment is not considered valid unless it can be successfully reproduced.

FAMILIAR—A spirit that has established a close relationship with a human being, usually of a beneficial or benign nature. Often the spirit communicates through the physical body of a pet animal such as a cat.

FATE—The end result of the actions of life, either good or bad.

FEW, OGHAM—One of the characters of the Celtic tree alphabet called ogham.

FUTHARK—A word made up of the first six rune characters in the German rune alphabet: F-U-Th-A-R-K. Other rune alphabets are called by slightly different names due to variations in the pronunciation of the letters. The English rune alphabet is known as the *Futhorc*.

GARDNERIAN WITCHES—Modern Witches who follow the teachings and use the Book of Shadows composed by Gerald B. Gardner.

GHOST—The soul of a dead person that is bound to Earth, usually to the specific locality where it died, or to its former home, or its place of burial.

GNOMES—Spirits that live in the depths of the Earth. Traditionally they are said to guard buried treasure.

GNOSIS—A total gestalt comprehension of the universe and the relationship between God and humanity. The goal of members of the Gnostic sects that flourished in the early centuries of the Christian era.

GOBLINS—Evil spirits noted for their ugly appearance and malicious habits.

GOD-FORM—The outer expression of a god. The magician takes on the characteristics and powers of a god by invoking the god through ritual. This was known in the Golden Dawn as assuming the god-form.

GODS—Powerful, immortal, spiritual beings who command the lesser spirits and living creatures of the Earth and are worshiped by humanity with prayers, offerings, sacrifices, and the erection of temples and images.

GOVI—A clay pot in Voudoun into which the soul of a dead relative that has been called back from under the waters of the sea is made to reside and respond to questions.

GRIMOIRE—Literally, "grammar" of magic, from the French. A book of magical practices, usually anonymous or pseudonymous. The word may have been introduced into English by A. E. Waite—at least, the *Oxford English Dictionary* cites Waite as its first source.

GROS-BON-ANGE—The souls of the dead that are venerated in Voudoun worship.

GURU—Eastern term for a teacher of occult and spiritual matters who instructs mainly by example.

HEPTAGRAM—A star of seven points drawn with a single, unbroken, reflecting line. Its points are related to the seven traditional planets of astrology.

HEXAGRAM—A figure formed by two overlapping equilateral triangles. Also called the Shield of David, it is the Jewish symbol. In modern magic, it is used to invoke and banish the spirits and powers of the seven ancient planets.

HEXAGRAM, UNICURSAL—A hexagram that is drawn with a single, unbroken, reflecting line. Used by Aleister Crowley and his followers.

HIEROPHANT—Originally the high priest of the Greek Mysteries at Eleusis. More generally, any priest of the Mysteries who reveals sacred secrets to initiates.

HIGH MAGIC—Ceremonial magic involving the actions of gods or heavenly spirits. The Greeks called it *theurgy*, which literally means "god work." Its opposite is *goety*, ceremonial magic concerned with evoking demons and the souls of the dead.

HIGHER SELF—What you really are, as opposed to what you think you are. The purest identity of the individual stripped of all transitory veils.

HOUNFOR—Distinguished from the peristyle, or ritual enclosure, of Voudoun, *hounfor* is a more general term that means all the physical area, ritual equipment, and persons under the immediate authority of the *houngan*, or priest. As such, it is equivalent to the Christian parish. It may also be used in a more restricted sense to mean the small chamber adjoining the peristyle that contains the altar of one or more *loa*.

HOUNGAN—A male priest of Voudoun who presides over the rites and gives counsel and magical aid to worshipers.

HUMORS—The four elemental qualities that make up the human body. When they are in balance, health results; imbalance creates sickness.

HYPNOSIS—The techniques for inducing a trance state in another person or persons during which the will and judgment are temporarily and partially placed in abeyance and become subordinate to the will of the hypnotist. Often it occurs without the knowledge or consent of the entranced individual, the result of a sudden shock or rhythmic sounds and gestures.

INCUBUS—A spirit that comes in masculine shape to have sexual union with a mortal woman, often against her will and usually while she is asleep. The plural is *incubi.*

INITIATE—A person who has undergone, or is about to undergo, the primary rite of entry into an occult organization or current.

INTELLIGENCE—A spirit usually said to reside in the heavens. Intelligences are benign spirits of considerable power.

INVISIBILITY—The withdrawal of involvement by an individual from the exterior world to so great an extent that other people and even animals fail to notice the presence of that individual, or notice but immediately forget.

INVOCATION—The calling of spirits into an object, such as a crystal, or into a human being. Mediums and channelers invoke spirits. It is done by a magician to obtain intimate communication with a spirit or to assume a portion of the spirit's power.

KABBALAH—A Jewish mystical philosophy, the central doctrine of which concerns the emanation of the world from the godhead in the form of ten divine names or spheres of light. The practical Kabbalah is a magical system based on numbers, divine names, and words of power extracted from the Torah.

KARMA—A very important concept in Hindu philosophy that is used to justify apparent injustices in the world. Karma is cause and effect extended to its widest possible scope. By karma a crime in this life may be punished in the next. By karma every action, however small, has its inescapable consequence. Sooner or later each good action is repaid by good, and each evil action by evil.

KOBALOI—Greek word meaning wicked spirits invoked by rogues, the origin of the German kobold and English goblin.

KOBOLDS—Mischievous Earth elementals that inhabit German households.

LAMEN—Originally a plate of metal upon which occult names or symbols were inscribed, in modern magic it has come to mean the symbol of occult authority worn by the magician about the neck during rituals. Inscribed on it are the most potent words and signs of the magical current followed by the magician.

LEVITATION—The occult suspension of a physical body without apparent support. Usually applied to the suspension of a human being. Christian saints, Hindu yogis, and Victorian spirit mediums were sometimes credited with this ability.

LOA—Gods of the Voudoun religion of Haiti. They are descended from the practice of ancestor worship, but their beginnings are lost in the past. The singular of *loa* is also *loa*.

MACROCOSM—The greater world, or universe. Distinguished from the microcosm, with which it corresponds.

MAGIC—The art of causing change in the manifest world through the Unmanifest. Definitions of magic differ widely.

MAGICAL NAME—A name given to an initiate, or chosen by one who is self-initiated, to signify the death of the old life and the birth into the magical life.

MAGNETISM, ANIMAL—A universal fluid postulated by Friedrich Anton Mesmer (1733-1815) that renders human bodies susceptible to the influences of celestial bodies and other human beings. It manifests itself in the body with opposite poles of force similar to those of the magnet.

MAÎT-TÊTE—Literally the "master of the head." Each worshiper in Voudoun has a special loa, usually the one by which the person was first possessed, with which the person enjoys a more familiar relationship.

MAMBO—A priestess of Voudoun. In some parts of Haiti she is considered lower in status than the *houngan*, or priest, but her role is similar.

MANA—A Polynesian word for the occult essence that pervades the universe and gives objects, words, animals, people, and places their magical potency. Mana is the force or energy of magic.

MEDITATION—The act of turning the mind inward with focused attention. There are many forms of meditation which are distinguished by the immediate object the mind focuses itself upon. Meditation upon silence seeks stillness of the mind, whereas meditation upon a specific idea or problem necessitates mental activity.

MICROCOSM—The lesser world, man, which in the Middle Ages was believed to correspond in every respect with the greater world, called the macrocosm. This correspondence was used to explain many magical effects.

NATURAL LAW—A sequence of events in nature that has been observed to occur without variation under the same conditions. Natural law is the basis of the experimental method in science, and is dependent upon cause and effect.

NEMYSS—A simple ritual headgear of Egyptian origin used by members of the Golden Dawn, consisting of little more than a piece of folded cloth.

93 CURRENT—What the followers of Aleister Crowley call their cult. Its holy book is Crowley's *Book of the Law*, its creed his infamous "Do what thou wilt shall be the whole of the Law."

OGHAM—A magical alphabet of the Celts composed of 20 letters called *fews*, each standing for a different kind of tree. It is very simple in appearance, being made up of short vertical or diagonal strokes set against or across a horizontal line.

OLD HORNY—An affectionate name for the horned male consort of the Goddess of the Witches. Early Christian priests mistook this pagan god for Satan.

OLD RELIGION—Another term for Wicca, or Witchcraft, which many occultists believe to be the descendant of an ancient pagan Goddess religion.

PARAPSYCHOLOGY—The investigation of the mental processes of paranormal events such as telepathy, telekinesis, and so on.

PENDULUM—The motions of a pendulum, a small weight at the

end of a short length of thread or fine chain, are often used to communicate with spirits.

PENTACLE—An occult diagram, usually circular in shape, that is either inscribed on parchment or metal to form a talisman or marked on the ground to act as a magic circle.

PENTAGRAM—An occult figure in the shape of a star with five points. Also called the pentalpha because it can be formed by five capital As. It is used to invoke and banish the elements.

PENTAGRAM, INVERTED—Usually considered to be the symbol of Satanism, it indicates the exaltation of duality over unity and of the lower four elements above the quintessence, Spirit.

PERISTYLE—The sacred enclosure of Voudoun rituals.

POTEAU-MITAN—The centerpost that stands in the middle of the ceremonial enclosure for Voudoun rituals. It is a form of the world tree so common to shamanism.

PSI—Short for psi-phenomena, or psychic phenomena, it embraces all forms of paranormal manifestation believed to be caused by the action of the mind.

PYRAMID POWER—The supposed occult virtue concentrated inside pyramidal structures by their triangular planes. It was believed by some to heal the body, restore vigor, sharpen razor blades, and effect other wonders. A variation on the idea of the cone of power of Witchcraft.

QUARTER DAYS—The solstices and equinoxes, which fall at quarter intervals around the wheel of the year.

REFLEXOLOGY—Based on the notion that the body is one interdependent whole, it is a form of remote massage. By massaging certain points on the hands or feet, therapeutic effects are assumed for the internal organs and other parts of the body that are connected to these points via the nervous system.

REGRESSION, PAST LIFE—A hypnotic technique in which a person in trance is led to imagine that he or she is remembering events that occurred in past lives, when the soul of the person inhabited other bodies. Often the regressed person and even the therapist conducting the regression do not realize that a trance state has been induced or that suggestions are being given.

REINCARNATION—The rebirth of human souls into other bodies, either human or animal, after death.

RITUAL—A formalized series of actions both mental and physical by which magical potency is released and directed toward the fulfillment of a specific desire.

RUNES—Angular glyphs used both as magical symbols and as letters of writing by the ancient peoples of northern Europe.

SABBAT—Also spelled Sabbath. The general gathering of Witches for the purpose of worship, it occurs on the eight pagan festivals of the year recognized in Wicca.

SATANISM—The worship of Satan, the arch-foe of Christ, through such practices as the black mass, sexual perversion, drug taking, violence, mutilation, killing, and sacrilege. True satanic rites are parodies of Christian rites.

SCHOOL, OCCULT—A general term to describe an organized occult tradition that has a specific magical teaching. It may or may not have an actual physical center where students are instructed.

SECRET CHIEFS—Supernatural beings who preside over the Rosicrucian current and communicate occult teachings to men and woman who seek to follow this path. The head of the Golden Dawn, MacGregor Mathers, was said to be in communication with them. Aleister Crowley also claimed a psychic link.

SHAKTA—The male seed or spark of light that impregnates the womb of the universal goddess, Shakti, and allows her to give birth to all things. It is viewed as a god in tantric doctrine. Shakta does not himself exist, but he enables existence.

SHAKTI—The universal power of realization that creates and sustains the world from moment to moment. In tantric doctrine it is viewed as a fertile goddess who gives birth to all existing things, both material and immaterial.

SHAMANISM—The religion of the primitive peoples of northern Europe and Asia, and more generally of primitive cultures around the world. Key features include animism, possession, soul travel, oracular revelations, and shape changing.

SHAPE-SHIFTING—The magical ability to assume the forms of beasts or other human beings with the soul while it is astrally projected from the body. Occasionally these altered shapes are seen by other people, who mistake them for bodies of flesh.

SHOWSTONE—A crystal globe used for divination and scrying. The magician uses the stone as a focus to induce a trance that causes images to appear in the depths of the stone.

SIDDHIS—Magical powers such as clairaudience, levitation, telepathy, and clairvoyance that manifest themselves as the by-products of yogic practices. They are denigrated by Hindu and Buddhist yogis but are actively sought in their own right by magicians.

SILENCE, OCCULT—An inward stilling and letting go of the emotions and mental preoccupations that prevent a ritual from working effectively. Outward silence is also necessary to prevent a similar destructive dissonance in the thoughts and feelings of others.

SKYCLAD—Naked. Gardnarian Witches are supposed to work their rituals in this state. In fact, most wear robes.

SOUL—Here the word is used to indicate the personal identity of a living being, its feelings, thoughts, impulses, memories, and sense of self.

SPIRIT, HUMAN—The vitalizing energy that burns within each individual and is one with the divine radiance.

SPIRITISM—French equivalent to the spiritualism of England and America. Thanks to the writings of the French occultist Allan Kardec (1804–69), it had an immense influence on the spirit possession cults of Brazil and other nations of South America.

SPIRITS—Self-aware beings that lack a living body. Some spirits have the power to borrow the bodies of men and women and use them as their own.

STATUES, LIVING—Greek magicians possessed the power, most probably learned from the Egyptians, to cause gods or spirits to indwell in statues, which could then be made to speak oracular utterances or answer questions through signs.

SUCCUBUS—A spirit that comes in a feminine shape to have sexual union with a mortal man, often against his will and usually while he is asleep. The plural is *succubi*.

SYMBOL—A sign or object that represents something else, especially what is obscure or hidden and cannot be expressed or manipulated directly.

SYMPATHETIC MAGIC—The term used by James G. Frazer to describe the presumed mechanism of magic. It may be divided into the Law of Contagion (objects once in contact forever remain in occult connection) and the Law of Similarity (effects can be produced through imitation).

SYNCHRONICITY—A word coined by Carl G. Jung to describe the meaningful coincidence of events that have no discernible causal connection. Luck is an example of synchronicity.

TANTRA—Literally, "that which extends knowledge," tantra is a complex system of religious philosophy that centers on the Great Mother, Shakti, as the fountain of all life. In the West, it is understood in a narrow sense to be the yogic practices and rituals that involve piercing the seven major chakras of the body with awakened kundalini energy. Tantra of the "left hand" advocates sexual practices that have been condemned by ascetic Christian and Buddhist priests, yet their ultimate goal is an exalted one—no less than the union of Shiva and Shakti in vessels of human flesh for the purpose of transcendent enlightenment.

TAOISM—Tao means "way." The teachings of the Chinese philosopher and mystic Lao-tse who, like the Buddha, lived in the 6th century BC. The Tao cannot be defined. It may be inadequately described as the undivided, unknowable spiritual source that generated and continues to vitalize all manifest things. In occultism, it may be likened to *mana*.

TAROT—A set of playing cards, most commonly 78 in number, of which 22, called the Greater Arcana, bear emblematic images that have been related in modern magic to the letters of the Hebrew alphabet. Many occult writers claim an Egyptian origin for the Tarot, but it appears to have originated in Italy around the 15th century.

TELEKINESIS—The movement of objects without obvious material agency.

TELESMATIC IMAGES—In Golden Dawn magic and its derivatives, the composite image of a spirit constructed in the astral world by the imagination through the use of visualization. Each Hebrew letter in the name of the spirit contributes part of the image through its occult associations.

TETRAGRAMMATON—Literally, the name of four letters, it is what the Greeks called the occult name of the Hebrew God, יהוה, which is supposed to possess vast potency in magic.

THELEMITES—The followers of the 93 Current revealed by Aleister Crowley through his *Book of the Law*. Their motto is "Do what thou wilt shall be the whole of the Law."

THEURGY—see HIGH MAGIC

THIRD EYE—An imaginary eye located on the forehead between the eyebrows which sees psychically.

TIMES, OBSERVANCE OF—Traditionally in magic it has been considered essential to take into account the arrangement of the stars and planets in the heavens when working a ritual. Even the hours of the day and night were assigned to the seven ancient planets. A magician who takes astrology into account when working magic is said to observe times.

TRANSMIGRATION—see REINCARNATION

TRANSMUTATION—The changing of base things into precious things, the work of alchemy. Base metal is transmuted into gold, common liquid into the elixir of life, and the ordinary soul into the soul of an enlightened being.

UMBANDA—One of the African-based cults of Brazil that is heavily influenced by Western spiritualism via the writings of Allan Kardec. It involves ecstatic possession.

UNMANIFEST—My own term for the unknowable source of existence. It is God stripped of all attributes, equivalent to the *Tao* of the Chinese philosopher Lao-tse, the *Unground* of Jacob Boehme, and the *Ain Soph* of the Kabbalah.

VEIL OF UNKNOWING—A term I use to indicate the boundary between manifest being and the unknowable source, which Kabbalists call the *Ain Soph*.

VERVER—The personal seal of a loa, or god, in Voudoun. It is drawn upon the earth around the centerpost in the peristyle, or ceremonial enclosure, with flour or ashes.

VIRTUES, OCCULT—The magical potency or efficacy of herbs, stones, beasts, and other things impressed upon them through the stars at the time of their creation by the heavenly Intelligences.

VISUALIZATION—The practice of imagining a place, person, thing, or event with unusual clarity and intensity .Often it is done in a ritual context and reinforced by repetition.

VOUDOUN—The religion created by the black slaves of Haiti. It has its roots in African tribal shamanism. The central rite is possession by spirits called loa.

VRIL—The occult energy described by the English writer Edward Bulwer-Lytton in his science-fiction novel, *The Coming Race* (1871). Much the same as Mesmer's *animal magnetism* or Baron Reichenbach's *odic force.*

WESTERN OCCULTISM—The magic of Europe and English-speaking nations around the world that has descended from the magic of Sumeria, Babylonia, Egypt, Greece, and Rome, as well as from the indigenous European magic of ancient times. Its range is roughly coequal with that of Christianity. The magic of Arabs and Jews is also in the Western tradition.

WHITE MAGIC—Magic that is worked for good purposes through benign actions and agents.

WIDDERSHINS—Counterclockwise, or against the movement of the Sun. Drawing a circle widdershins, or walking widdershins during a ritual, is generally considered to aid in malefic magic.

WILL, TRUE—True will is the impulse inherent in human nature to realize individual human potential and thereby achieve harmony between the individual and the universe. Crowley coined the term to distinguish this constant, unvarying impulse from what is *called* will but which is really no more than the vague impulse of the moment born of circumstance.

WISE WOMAN—The solitary female Witch who dispensed charms and prescribed healing herbs to the common inhabitants of rural villages in Europe.

WITCHCRAFT—A religion centered around the worship of the Goddess, a female supreme deity. Witches venerate the life force in nature and seek to be in tune with natural cycles. The modern Witchcraft, or Wicca, revival was inspired by the writings and example of Gerald B. Gardner in the 1950s.

WIZARD—Literally a skillful or clever person, a wizard is a male magician who uses *theurgy* or *goety.*

WORD OF POWER—A word or name, often unintelligible, that is supposed to carry an occult potency. Many of the barbarous names mentioned by the ancient Greeks were undoubtedly once names of gods and goddesses that became corrupted over time.

WORK, MAGICAL—The series of ritual actions conducted in order to realize a ritual desire, such as the Great Work of alchemy. A working is an extended series of rituals designed to attain a single object.

WORLD TREE—The great tree at the axis of the world that was believed in shamanism to hold up the heavens with its branches and provide the framework for the entire universe.

YEHESHUAH—יהשוה, the name given to Jesus by Christian Kabbalists during the Renaissance, who used it as the supreme word of power in their magic and worship. They intended it to replace the Tetragrammaton (יהוה) of the Jews.

YOGA—A Sanskrit word signifying "union." Hatha yoga, which involves physical postures and breathing techniques designed to promote a unity of mind and body, and a unity between man and God, is only one of many systems of yoga. Raja yoga involves mental exercises, karma yoga relies on good works, bhakti yoga uses religious devotion, mantra yoga involves chanting, laya yoga seeks to awaken kundalini, and jnana yoga concentrates on philosophical analysis.

ZEN—A Buddhist sect widespread in Japan that seeks enlightenment through spontaneous insights that are generated by a single-minded devotion to simple physical actions, or by verbal paradoxes that cannot be solved in logical terms. In Zen, the intellect is looked upon as an obstruction to truth that must be circumvented by fatigue, distraction, or trickery.

A work cited.

WORKS CITED

Adler, Margot. *Drawing Down the Moon*. New York: Viking, 1979.

Budge, E. A. Wallis. *Egyptian Magic*. New York: Dover, 1971.

Colquhoun, Ithell. *Sword of Wisdom*. New York: G. P. Putnam and Sons, 1975.

Crowley, Aleister. *Magick In Theory and Practice*. New York: Dover, 1976.

Eliade, Mircea. *Shamanism*. Princeton, NJ: Princeton University Press, 1964.

Frazer, James G. *The Golden Bough* (abridged edition). New York: The Macmillan Company, 1951.

Grant, Kenneth. *Cults of the Shadow*. New York: Samuel Weiser, 1976.

King, Francis, and Isabel Sutherland. *The Rebirth of Magic*. London: Corgi Books, 1982.

LaVey, Anton S. *The Satanic Bible*. New York: Avon Books, 1969.

Levi, Eliphas. *The History of Magic*. London: Rider, London, 1986.

Levi, Eliphas. *Transcendental Magic: Its Doctrine and Ritual*. New York: Samuel Weiser, 1979.

Mauss, Marcel. "Introduction a l'oeuvre de Marcel Mauss," in *Sociologie et anthropologie,* Marcel Mauss. Paris: Presses Universitaires de France, 1950.

————. *A General Theory Of Magic*. London and Boston: Routledge & Kegan Paul, 1972.

Murray, Margaret A. *The Witch-Cult in Western Europe.* New York: Oxford University Press, 1967.

——————. *The God of the Witches.* New York: Oxford University Press, 1970.

Regardie, Israel. *The Golden Dawn.* St. Paul, MN: Llewellyn Publications, 6th ed., 1989.

Scott, Walter. *Hermetica.* Boston, MA: Shambhala, 1985.

Weinstein, Marion. *Positive Magic.* British Columbia: Phoenix Publishing Co., 1981.

Mother Nature = Soul of the World = anima mundi
Personal Legend = Destiny = Unconscious Synchronicity

In the one there is the belief that one is all.
One is not all. One is of all, or as all —
and this as relevation is limited.

- every person has a daemon or guardian spirit
- Witch covens
- Ayami — spirit spouse/teacher
- Book of Shadows — magical workbook
- ~~Trick~~ Skill of silence

GENERAL INDEX

STAY IN TOUCH

On the following pages you will find listed, with their current prices, some of the books now available on related subjects. Your book dealer stocks most of these, and will stock new titles in the Llewellyn series as they become available. We urge your patronage.

However, to obtain our full catalog, to keep informed of new titles as they are released and to benefit from informative articles and helpful news, you are invited to write for our bi-monthly news magazine/catalog. A sample copy is free, and it will continue coming to you at no cost as long as you are an active mail customer. Or you may keep it coming for a full year with a donation of just $7.00 in U.S.A. & Canada ($20.00 overseas, first class mail). Many bookstores also have *The Llewellyn New Times* available to their customers. Ask for it.

Stay in touch! In *The Llewellyn New Times'* pages you will find news and reviews of new books, tapes and services, announcements of meetings and seminars, articles helpful to our readers, news of authors, advertising of products and services, special money-making opportunities, and much more.

The Llewellyn New Times
P.O. Box 64383, Dept. 835, St. Paul, MN 55164-0383, U.S.A.
* * *

TO ORDER BOOKS AND TAPES

If your book dealer does not have the books described on the following pages readily available, you may order them direct from the publisher by sending full price in U.S. funds, plus $3.00 for postage and handling for orders *under* $10.00; $4.00 for orders *over* $10.00. There are no postage and handling charges for orders over $50.00. Postage and handling rates are subject to change. UPS Delivery: We ship UPS whenever possible. Delivery guaranteed. Provide your street address as UPS does not deliver to P.O. Boxes. UPS to Canada requires a $50.00 minimum order. Allow 4-6 weeks for delivery. Orders outside the U.S.A. and Canada: Airmail—add retail price of book; add $5.00 for each non-book item (tapes, etc.); add $1.00 per item for surface mail.

FOR GROUP STUDY AND PURCHASE

Because there is a great deal of interest in group discussion and study of the subject matter of this book, we feel that we should encourage the adoption and use of this particular book by such groups by offering a special quantity" price to group leaders or agents."

Our Special Quantity Price for a minimum order of five copies of *Ritual Magic* is $38.85 cash-with-order. This price includes postage and handling within the United States. Minnesota residents must add 6.5% sales tax. For additional quantities, please order in multiples of five. For Canadian and foreign orders, add postage and handling charges as above. Credit card (VISA, Master Card, American Express) orders are accepted. Charge card orders only may be phoned free ($15.00 minimum order) within the U.S.A. or Canada by dialing 1-800-THE-MOON. Customer service calls dial 1-612-291-1970. Mail orders to:

LLEWELLYN PUBLICATIONS
P.O. Box 64383, Dept. 835, St. Paul, MN 55164-383, U.S.A.

Prices subject to change without notice.

THE NEW MAGUS
by Donald Tyson

The New Magus is a practical framework on which a student can base his or her personal system of magic. This book is filled with practical, usable magical techniques and rituals which anyone from any magical tradition can use. It includes instructions on how to design and perform rituals, create and use sigils, do invocations and evocations, do spiritual healings, learn rune magic, use god-forms, create telesmatic images, discover your personal guardian, create and use magical tools and much more. You will learn how YOU can be a New Magus!

The New Age is based on ancient concepts that have been put into terms, or metaphors, that are appropriate to life in our world today. That makes *The New Magus* the book on magic for today.

If you have found that magic seems illogical, overcomplicated and not appropriate to your lifestyle, *The New Magus* is the book for you. It will change your ideas of magic forever!

0-87542-825-8, 368 pgs., 6 x 9, illus., softcover   **$12.95**

HOW TO MAKE AND USE A MAGIC MIRROR
by Donald Tyson

There's a "boy mechanic" at home in every one of us. As Henry Ford put the world on wheels, Donald Tyson is now opening New Worlds with simple psychic technology.

Author Donald Tyson takes the reader step-by-step through the creation of this powerful mystical tool. You will learn about:

- Tools and supplies needed to create the mirror
- Construction techniques
- How to use the mirror for scrying (divination)
- How to communicate with spirits
- How to use the mirror for astral travel

Tyson also presents a history of mirror lore in magic and literature. For anyone wanting their personal magical tool, How to Make and Use a Magic Mirror is a must item.

0-87542-831-2, 176 pgs., mass market, illus.   **$3.95**

RUNE MAGIC
by Donald Tyson

Drawing upon historical records, poetic fragments, and the informed study of scholars, *Rune Magic* resurrects the ancient techniques of this tactile form of magic and integrates those methods with modern occultism, so that anyone can use the runes in a personal magical system. For the first time, every known and conjectured meaning of all 33 known runes, including the 24 runes known as futhark, is available in one volume. In addition, *Rune Magic* covers the use of runes in divination, astral traveling, skrying, and on amulets and talismans. A complete rune ritual is also provided, and 24 rune words are outlined. Gods and Goddesses of the runes are discussed, with illustrations from the National Museum of Sweden.

0-87542-826-6, 210 pgs., 6 x 9, illus., softcover **$9.95**

THE POWER OF THE RUNES
by Donald Tyson

This kit contains *Rune Magic,* Tyson's highly acclaimed guide to effective runework. In this book he clears away misconceptions surrounding this magical alphabet of the Northern Europeans, provides information on the Gods and Goddesses of the runes, and gives the meanings and uses of all 33 extant runes. The reader will be involved with practical runic rituals and advice on talisman, amulet and sigil use.

The Power of the Runes also includes the *Rune Magic Deck.* This set of 24 large cards illustrates each of the futhark runes in a stunning 2-color format. This is the first deck ever published, which makes it not only unique, but truly historical!

We have also included a set of wooden rune dice, with their own cloth bag, in this kit. These four dice, each square, were designed by Donald Tyson himself. The user casts them down, then interprets their meanings as they appear before him or her. With the 24 futhark runes graphically etched on their sides, these dice let the user perform an accurate reading in mere seconds.

0-87542-828-2, 224-pg. book, 24-card deck, 4 dice w/bag **$24.95**

RECLAIMING THE POWER
The How & Why of Practical Ritual Magic
by Lady Sabrina

By far one of the most usable and workable approaches to magic written in a long time, *Reclaiming the Power* is for anyone who has ever wondered about magic, ever wanted to try it, or ever had a goal to achieve. This is the first book to explain just ritual magic is without the trappings of a specific tradition. It is a simple, straightforward approach to magic, stressing the use of natural and seasonal energies to accomplish what needs to be done.

Getting results is what *Reclaiming the Power* is all about. The average person, untrained and uninitiated, will learn basic magic that can be performed anywhere and for any purpose. They will learn to develop individual power and use that power through structured rituals to get whatever it is they need or want.

Everything, from what magic is to spell-casting, is explained in simple, easy-to-understand language. All of the rituals presented are complete and can be easily adapted to solitary working.

0-87542-166-0, 224 pgs., 5-1/4 x 8, softcover, photos   **$9.95**

Z-5: SECRET TEACHINGS OF THE GOLDEN DAWN
BOOK II—THE ZELATOR RITUAL 1=10
by Pat & Chris Zalewski

Two of the Golden Dawn's highest initiates reveal the hidden mysteries of the best-known occult system in the world. Pat and Chris Zalewski show what actually happens when one is initiated into the Golden Dawn's second grade ceremony—the Zelator Ritual.

In the first book in this series, *Z-5 . . . The Neophyte Ritual 0=0*, Pat Zalewski showed the whole process of initial initiation. Now, in *Z-5 . . . The Zelator Ritual 1=10*, Pat and his wife Chris take things a step further as the candidate embraces the forces of the Earth Element and the effects it has on him. In this ceremony, the postulant has his aura magnetically earthed and his physical body revitalized.

Unlike any other book written on the Golden Dawn, *Z-5 . . . 1=10* presents in enormous detail all the higher explanations given on the Zelator Ceremony in one package. For those who wish to utilize magic in the privacy of their own homes, this book explains the shortcuts that can be applied on a solo basis.

0-87542-896-7, 224 pgs., 6 x 9, softcover, illus.   **$12.95**

THE SECRETS OF A GOLDEN DAWN TEMPLE
The Alchemy and Crafting of Magickal Implements
by Chic Cicero and Sandra Tabatha Cicero

From its inception 100 years ago, the Hermetic Order of the Golden Dawn continues to be *the* authority on high magick. Yet the books written on the Golden Dawn system have fallen far short in explaining how to construct the tools and implements necessary for ritual. Until now.

Secrets of a Golden Dawn Temple picks up where all the other books leave off. Here is a unique compilation of the various tools used, all described in full: wands, ritual clothing, elemental tools, Enochian tablets, altars, temple furniture, banners, lamens, admission badges and much more. This book provides complete step-by-step instructions for the construction of nearly 80 different implements, all displayed in photographs or drawings, along with the exact symbolism behind each and every item. Plus, it gives a ritual or meditation for every magickal instrument presented. It truly is an indispensable guide for any student of the Western Magickal Tradition.

0-87542-150-4, 592 pgs., 6 x 9, softcover, illus.   **$19.95**

THE GOLDEN DAWN
by Israel Regardie

The Original Account of the Teachings, Rites and Ceremonies of the Hermetic Order of the Golden Dawn as revealed by Israel Regardie, with further revision, expansion, and additional notes by Regardie, Cris Monnastre, and others. Expanded with an index of more than 100 pages!

Originally published in four bulky volumes of some 1200 pages, this 6th Revised and Enlarged Edition has been entirely reset in modern, less space-consuming type, in half the pages (while retaining the original pagination in marginal notation for reference) for greater ease and use.

Also included are Initiation Ceremonies, important rituals for consecration and invocation, methods of meditation and magical working based on the Enochian Tablets, studies in the Tarot, and the system of Qabalistic Correspondences that unite the World's religions and magical traditions into a comprehensive and practical whole.

This volume is designed as a study and practice curriculum suited to both group and private practice. Meditation upon, and following with the Active Imagination, the Initiation Ceremonies is fully experiential without need of participation in group or lodge. A very complete reference encyclopedia of Western Magick.

0-87542-663-8, 840 pgs., 6 x 9, illus., softcover   **$19.95**

Prices subject to change without notice.

LIGHT IN EXTENSION
Greek Magic from Homer to Modern Times
by David Godwin

Greek magic is the foundation of almost every form of ceremonial magic being practiced today. Elements of Greek philosophy summarize the bulk of modern esoteric thought and occult teachings. The systems formulated by the direct progenitors of Western culture speak to the modern soul of the Western world.

This book explains in plain, informal language the grand sweep of Greek magic and Greek philosophical and religious concepts from the archaic period of Homer's *Iliad* right down to the present. It begins with the magic and mythology of the days of classical Athens and its antecedent cultures, gives detailed considerations of Gnosticism, early Christianity and Neoplatonism—all phenomena with a Greek foundation—explains the manifestations of Greek thought in the Renaissance, and explores modern times with the Greek elements of the magic of the Golden Dawn, Aleister Crowley and others.

From the plains of Troy to the streets of Los Angeles, Greek magic is alive and well. No one who has any interest in magic, occultism, or hermetic thought and who is also a citizen of Western civilization can afford to ignore this heritage.

0-87542-285-3, 272 pgs., 6 x 9, illus., softcover **$12.95**

GODWIN'S CABALISTIC ENCYCLOPEDIA
by David Godwin

This is the most complete correlation of Hebrew and English ideas ever offered. It is a dictionary of Cabalism arranged, with definitions, alphabetically, alphabetically in Hebrew, and numerically. With this book the practicing Cabalist or student no longer needs access to a large number of books on mysticism, magic and the occult in order to trace down the basic meanings, Hebrew spellings, and enumerations of the hundreds of terms, words, and names that are included in this book.

This book includes: all of the two-letter root words found in Biblical Hebrew, the many names of God, the Planets, the Astrological Signs, Numerous Angels, the Shem ha-Mephorash, the Spirits of the *Goetia*, the correspondences of the 32 Paths, a comparison of the Tarot and the Cabala, a guide to Hebrew Pronunciation, and a complete edition of Aleister Crowley's valuable book *Sepher Sephiroth*.

Here is a book that is a must for the shelf of all Magicians, Cabalists, Astrologers, Tarot students, Thelemites, and those with any interest at all in the spiritual aspects of our universe.

0-87542-292-6, 528 pgs., 6 x 9, softcover **$15.00**